# HOW IT IS DISCARDED

# HOW IT IS

The Native American Philosophy of V. F. Cordova

Edited by Kathleen Dean Moore, Kurt Peters,
Ted Jojola, and Amber Lacy

With a Foreword by Linda Hogan

The University of Arizona Press
Tucson

The University of Arizona Press
© 2007 The Arizona Board of Regents

Library of Congress Cataloging-in-Publication Data
Cordova, V. F. (Viola Faye)
How it is : the Native American philosophy of V. F.
Cordova / edited by Kathleen Dean Moore ... [et al.] ;
with a foreword by Linda Hogan.
p. cm.
Includes bibliographical references and index.
ISBN 978-0-8165-2648-2 (hardcover : alk. paper) —
ISBN 978-0-8165-2649-9 (pbk. : alk. paper)
1. Indian philosophy—North America. 2. Indians of
North America—Religion. 3. Cordova, V. F. (Viola Faye)
I. Moore, Kathleen Dean. II. Title.
E98.P5C67 2007
191.089′97–dc22            2007020528

Publication of this book is made possible in part by
the proceeds of a permanent endowment created with
the assistance of a Challenge Grant from the National
Endowment for the Humanities, a federal agency.

Manufactured in the United States of America on acid-
free, archival-quality paper containing a minimum of
50% post-consumer waste and processed chlorine free.

12 11 10 09 08 07   6 5 4 3 2 1

# CONTENTS

Foreword: Viola Cordova—Perspectives by Linda Hogan    vii

Editors' Introduction    xiii

Author's Introduction: Why *Native American* Philosophy?    1

Biographical Essay    5

## I. BRIDGES

The Bridge over Romero Creek    11

Taos Bridge    19

The Bridge to America    30

America    40

## II. WINDOWS

Windows on Academics    49

Windows on Native American Philosophy    54

Matrix: A Context for Thought    61

Method: A Search for Fundamental Concepts    67

"They Have a Different Idea about That . . ."    69

Language as Window    76

The Philosophical Questions    80

## III. WHAT IS THE WORLD?

How It Is: A Native American Creation Story    87

What Is the World?    100

*Usen*: The Unidentifiable Is    107

Mother Earth    113

Time and the Universe    117

What Is Reality?    121

Artesian Spring: A Poem    127

## IV. WHAT IS IT TO BE HUMAN?

Who We Are: An Exploration of Identity    133

What Is It to Be Human in a Native American Worldview?    145

Credo: This I Believe    151

Critiques    154
    I. Against Individualism    154
    II. Against the Singularity of the Human *Species*    159

Becoming Human    166

Time, Culture, and Self    171

Cowboys and Indians: A Story    177

## V. WHAT IS THE ROLE OF A HUMAN IN THE WORLD?

What Is the Role of a Human Being?    183

Bounded Space    186
    I. The Four Directions    186
    II. A Sense of Place    192

Biodiversity: The Human Factor    201

A New Reverence    208

Preparing for the Seventh Generation    215

Native Americans in the New Millennium    221

The Dream    228

Coda: Living in a Sacred Universe    229

Notes    233

Works Cited    241

Sources    243

# FOREWORD: VIOLA CORDOVA

## PERSPECTIVES BY LINDA HOGAN

*I am always on my way home.*
*There is the breathing landscape, the wind.*

Ever so rarely a writer comes along and says what others have not found words to say. Usually this writer is a poet and not a philosopher. And yet, philosopher Viola Cordova writes like a poet. As an American Indian woman and thinker, I have long wished for a person who could bring to light and language the significance of indigenous knowledge and the cultural differences of our peoples so eloquently and brilliantly as Viola Cordova, an Apache philosopher. She has gone beyond Euro-Western philosophy into the heart of the indigenous knowledge system and philosophy, as far as the limits of English will allow.

Because our histories, experiences, and ethical thought systems are different from those of Western thinkers she speaks about, the inner architecture of our thought is not easily understood. Cordova does so with an amazing knowledge of the significance of diversity, language, and world knowledge systems. And, because notions of the sacred in Native communities have enough similarities, she is able to speak about these likenesses together in order to further the understanding of indigenous human beings for those who are newer arrivals to this continent.

We dwell in different matrixes in many areas. There is first the relationship with the earth that is the primary experience of tribal peoples whose theology is land-based. Christianity, upon which the Euro-American social structure has come to be based, has what Cordova calls an extraterrestrial god, and traditionally believes in the human "elevation out of nature," out of dumb matter. Much is missing in such a belief system, and she notes that it is also a belief system that requires unquestioned foundations of its own mind-set.

"I study white people," Viola writes. And she has. As a philosophy major she first learned only one kind of philosophy. It was, for a Native thinker, a closed society that heard only its own voice. Her work here is a life's work that has tried to add more to these voices.

Missing from those unquestioned regions of belief are stories of our environment, and significant knowledge of the world around us. Our indigenous lives are deeply embedded in nature and place. Our views and understandings of the world are the result of centuries of observing nature and our own place in it. These have remained, in places, for thousands of years. For Native peoples, our systems of knowledge are not about beliefs but about ways of knowing and *how* we know, through experience itself. It is not what is taught in books, not in ordinary classes, but what lies beneath all the new ideas.

As for the European Americans, she states that they are, "a people without a sense of boundaries for themselves, have a lack of attachment to the land, and do not recognize the boundaries of others." They have forgotten the niche they occupy and the stories accompanying that particular bounded place that Cordova calls a homeland. "Without a sense of bounded space, there is no sacredness accorded to one's own space of place;" one is not standing "in the center of the universe" looking out onto definite boundaries that define who and what one becomes. There are no sacred mountains, no deep knowledge of the land, the night sky and its own multiple astronomies.

Viola Cordova writes that the stories of *all* people need to be laid out on the table before one understands how to be fully human. We need to acknowledge the differences and their spectrum of human being, the significance of accepting all and not wishing for a monoculture. Diversity is a way of being, and the attempt to find an absolute is yet another part of the separate matrixes. Tribal peoples do not require a sameness of thought or belief. We come from different stories, different origins, and we respect the differences.

When the fact of human diversity takes second place to the notion of singularity, Cordova writes that this concept of singularity is a dangerous, pernicious concept that ends in misery and hunger. The idea of progress creates sacrificial hostages of the superior beings who make the acme of the end being of that progress.

Part of Cordova's interest in writing and speaking is because others are stealing our voices and telling our stories. Even when they speak with us, even when they interview, what comes out is an interpretation. It is about them, their thoughts.

*Usen*, which might be considered the word for God for the Jicarilla Apache, means *is*. According to Viola Cordova, the mystery of understanding tribal concepts of being and goodness seems beyond the comprehension of Europeans who have tried to understand systems that seem to be too complex for them.

The anthropologists and those studying tribal peoples too often write their own interpretation of what is said because they are unable to see larger, to think beyond their own thinking enough to come to what is really spoken, meant, and known about the world. For indigenous peoples, each place has its own intelligence, its own stories. "We are not only creatures of this planet but of very specific and fragile circumstances of this planet. We are herd animals. Humans are animals of the group."

The physical space we all share may be the same, but the philosophical space isn't. Native Americans have survived all attempts of eradication and assimilation, for a variety of reasons: the environment is sacred, it is storied, and we are not in a world layered with ideas.

Viola Cordova looks at Native knowledge systems and languages across the country, encompassing a history of continent-wide pain and the effects of European colonization and dominance, and bringing to words how all of our Native systems derive from the heart of place. Even when we have been sent away from that place or have not learned our own languages, we still have it; from subtle gesture and learned ways of being, it is passed down to us. This is "How It Is." The knowledge is in the manner of being, even when the words are not spoken. Our philosophies come of being from a place and a community, of knowing a place and respecting its boundaries.

In part, this is why we Native peoples persist in our identities. There is cultural mooring and values having to do with the environment, the place, and the stories of that place. Language is significant also, but even without it, English-speaking Natives see through windows of their old language because of cultural practice. From this she derives her sense of humans in their place in the world, knowing the workings of that place in the world, her notions of "bounded space," the territory that is tribal, and the human participation in that space while respecting the boundaries of others.

Language is the bonding mechanism, she writes, and empathy is the cause. There are different interpretations of the world, universe, and human thought among various tribes and we each respect that of the other, their creations, their stories of the land. The languages embody concepts that have survived the loss of the language. "You do not have to be fluent. The view of the world survived all attempts to eradicate the understanding. Behind the language is a pattern, system, a way of being." It is implicit.

After all the occupation, Viola makes clear, we are not assimilated. We live daily with an understanding of our differences, with two or even more processes taking place at the same time, mentally, emotionally, and spiritually.

In addition, we know these differences.

"We are bombarded every time we leave home." And it is true: we walk into another layer over our world and have to comprehend it, work within it as well as within our own.

She defines what it is to live in more than one world understanding. Still, she asks the important question of how to be fully human in this magnificent world. The questions she asks are ones I think of constantly: What is a human? How should a human be a whole person? What is our role here? What is the earth? Most of us think of the earth as a living being and that we must live upon it with care and love and respect. The idea of subjugating the earth is the product of another mind. Even environmentalists, she maintains, are of another mind because they are not concerned so much with the sacred as with the idea of stewardship.

In her system of knowledge, there are no Native correlates to the terms *soul* or *god*. The things we seek are balance and harmony. There is an assumption that the contemporary Indian is not "original, not real, the same form," as those people of the past, but she maintains this is not true. Even today we focus on diversity as part of Earth's creativity while Euro-Americans still search for the universal, an absolute, something that can be understood, spoken, be assimilated into their own system of knowledge.

The Native understands the world as more complex and not the static that is implicit in an absolute where all communication remains within a narrow circle of like-minded. One group emphasizes the individual as part of the whole. The Euro emphasizes the individual. There is "we" and there is "I." What defines this?

There is a given upon which everything else hinges. Viola says that troubles began when the Europeans found that the Indians did not share their sense of land. And, they had no consciousness of what other life forms they were (and are) disturbing. They were, essentially, unaware of living things.

Yet community lies beyond family within the surrounding, enfolding environment. We are co-creators in the universe, the world, within all the rest, all fluid, shifting movement, and without the emphasis on measurement. The world is there in its entirety, not in segments. And we inhabit it. This is what makes us human.

*There are juniper trees by the bank, or perhaps a horse.*

# EDITORS' INTRODUCTION

In spring 2002, Viola Cordova drove to Corvallis to speak to our Native American Philosophies class at Oregon State University. She could have flown and saved herself a lot of time—Corvallis is a long way from Pocatello, Idaho. But she wanted to make a trip of it, to see the mountains before winter closed in—the Bitterroots, the Blues, the Cascades—to move west along the course of the rivers.

This would not be her first visit to Corvallis. Some time ago, she was a professor here in the philosophy and ethnic studies departments, a challenging, chain-smoking, idea- and laughter-driven professor. Students gathered around her the way elk come to hay in the winter, half-starved for ideas that can sustain them. A Jicarilla Apache/Hispanic woman with a PhD in classical Western philosophy, Viola empowered our students to ask hard questions of the culture she called "Euroman's" and gave them a vision of a different way to see and act in the world.

We wanted her to stay. But she never stayed in a university more than three years, Viola told us, because that's when a professor begins to be slowly poisoned by the artificial accolades and driven by the arcane rules of academic life, publishing just to publish, teaching just to teach. She returned to her family in Denver and a new job in Idaho, leaving us with a renewed challenge to tell the truth and a watercolor painting of a hillside north of town.

In her lecture, Dr. Cordova, Viola, spoke to the students about the past and the future. There was a big crowd, probably two hundred people in the audience—OSU students and town folk and students from the tribal school. The past is real and present, she told us, held in our memories and in the shape of the world. It is the ground of our being, its actuality, its particular substance. The future? The future doesn't exist. We must create the future by our decisions, our actions and inactions. Together with the place we live, we are cocreators of the world, bringing it into existence moment by moment.

So there is no escaping responsibility. Whether the world is beautiful and true, or ugly and degrading, hurtful or grieving, depends on us. Viola paused, picked up a piece of chalk, and drew a picture of a pond rimmed with cattails. "Your life is a pebble thrown in a pond," she told the students, and drew concentric rings spreading from the splash a small stone raised on the water. "And not just the pebble; your life is the pebble and the water and the energy that moves the waves and the movement of the waves themselves." She drew an arrow to show how waves rock the cattails and ripple the sand. The students listened intently, leaning forward in their seats. They knew the magnitude of the gift of self-respect and wisdom she was giving them.

She answered questions, turned away from the applause, went to dinner with students but ate only dessert, laughed with them and challenged them, and then she was gone. A week later, I learned from her husband that she had passed away.

It was a terrible thing, to stand in front of those students the next class meeting and tell them she had passed. I remember gripping the lectern to keep from trembling. I remember a loud cry that went up from the students. I remember their silence as they tried to understand. But how can anyone understand this, an embolism bursting in that magnificent brain, waves rocking, rocking the reeds, carving scallops on the sand, a spreading stillness?

Viola's companion, Denny, sent boxes of books from her library—Wittgenstein and Ortega y Gasset, Orwell, Deloria—and a computer disk filled with Viola's papers. He also sent a note, saying, "Do what you can." This book is what we can do.

From the beginning, our goal was to publish Viola's words as she had written them. She herself issued the challenge:

Native Americans, today, have survived almost five hundred years of forced assimilation into the larger and dominant culture in the United States. There are apparently some deeply embedded ideas that we teach to our children in some unconscious manner that defy assimilative attempts. Our identities are tied in with those ideas and it is important that we explore them. Whether we use the awareness of the importance of those very basic ideas to change ourselves or to maintain our views may be of secondary importance. What is important is that the Native American recover his own voice in such matters.

It should be *we* who explain our beliefs rather than having them explained for us and to us.[1]

In her written work, as in her teaching, Viola explains her beliefs in a clear, informed, insightful, and eloquent voice. What she offers us is a carefully considered and beautifully expressed Native American philosophy of life, an explanation of "how it is." It is an extraordinary gift and an invaluable addition to the record of human wisdom.

Viola left many unpublished papers, talks, poems, drawings, booklets, and essays—many of them unfinished, most of them undated—and perhaps several chapters of what might have become a book. Our first effort was to assemble them. Amber Lacey, a philosophy graduate student, undertook this assignment as a labor of love for a professor who had befriended her. From archives at the Center for Southwest Research at the University of New Mexico and from the papers Denny sent to Oregon State, Amber searched out all the materials available and arranged them in the order Viola had herself indirectly suggested.

These are the questions we ought to be asking ourselves, Viola wrote:

1. What is the world?
2. What is a human being?
3. What is the role of a human being in the world?

So these became the ordering questions of this book.

Our second effort was to create from Viola's work one whole and singular thing, a book. This forced us to make guesses as to how Viola might have combined essays on the same subject, arranged essays in relation to one another, what she might have included and what she might have left out. We can't claim to have done what she would have done. But in all our decisions, we have tried to intrude as little as possible and always to be respectfully attentive to Viola's vision and intelligence.

The result is something this world has not seen before: From a person who grew up nourished by Apache wisdom and worldviews, a powerful critique of European-Christian thought. From a person trained as a scholar of European thought in the analytic and classical traditions of an American PhD program, a brilliant statement of a Native American's philosophy. From a woman writer who knows firsthand what it means to be excluded *and* embraced, a moving, life-changing account of what she most deeply believes is true.

The book is composed of five sections. In the first, "Bridges," Dr. Cordova tells stories about her family and her own life as a girl moving back and forth between cultures, between towns, between her parents' differences. Bridges can divide, her stories teach, as well as unite.

The second section, "Windows," provides background for the study of Native American philosophy that will follow. We all see through windows that shape what we see, hiding some things from view, forcing others into a distorted shape. Our language, our stories, our assumptions and cultural practices, beliefs we hold so deeply we don't even know they are there—all these determine how we understand the world. It is important to be aware of the differences in the windows through which we peer at others, and to acknowledge, honor, and celebrate a variety of outlooks.

In the third section, Dr. Cordova begins to develop a systematic philosophical view, asking the basic metaphysical question, *What is the world?* How did the world begin? Of what is it made? What is the nature of time, of space? What is real, and are there many realities, or only one?

Within this world, *What is it to be human?* This is the primary question of the fourth section, in which Dr. Cordova engages questions of personal identity and the place of the human being in a complex, interconnecting world. She is particularly concerned with the question of how people might reclaim the power to define themselves and thus regain the right to shape their own lives.

The last of her central philosophical questions, *What is the role of a human in the world?* is the subject of the fifth section. Humans are of a place, born in desert or forest, raised in city or farmland or at the edge of the sea. This is a fact of profound importance that shapes not only who we are, but how we ought to act in relation to the place and to others who live and will live and have lived in that place.

The book ends with a coda, in which Dr. Cordova addresses perhaps the hardest question of all—how, then, shall I live? Her answer is simple and complex, beautiful and burdensome: "The greatest 'duty,' if it can be so called, of a human being is to cause no disruption to the greater, and 'beautiful,' whole of what it is that is."

We hope that people will read this book in courses on Native American philosophies or worldviews; here, of all places, it is a matter of moral and intellectual integrity that students hear a Native American's own voice explaining Native American beliefs. We hope people will read the book in courses on American or European philosophy; there the book will offer a perspective that will change forever how they see Western culture. We hope people will read the book in courses on the history of ideas; here they will find important ideas too long excluded from academic discourse. We hope people will read it in environmental ethics courses; it will offer them a powerful vision of how to live in a place with respect and reciprocity.

But most important, we hope people—all people, in and out of the academy—will read this book whenever they find themselves asking the most important questions: How is it, this beautiful, mysterious, powerful and vulnerable world? Who am I in this world? And how shall I then live?

KDM
Corvallis, Oregon

# HOW IT IS

# Author's Introduction

## Why *Native American* Philosophy?

Two questions are important in introducing a book about "Native American philosophy." The first deals with "why." The second with "how."

The "why" is important because Native American thought represents a variety of human thought that has not been thoroughly explored. When we make such statements as "All humans . . . [whatever characteristic one wishes to apply here]," we fail to take into account the many possible ways that human beings might be defined. Each distinct cultural group, perhaps in an original isolation from other groups, provides three definitions around which they build all subsequent determinations about the world they live in. First, each has a definition or description of the world; second, there is a definition of what it is to be *human* in the world as it is so defined and described; and, third, there is an attempt to outline the role of a human in that world.

The distinct pattern of a culture may be seen to derive from these three definitions and may account for the distinctions between cultural groups. I refer to these definitions and descriptions as a worldview or *matrix*, because they are not singular and disconnected definitions, but compose a whole picture of interrelated concepts and ideas.

An exploration of Native American thought is an experiment in discovering the differences between Native American thought and what is most familiar: European thought. The term "European" encompasses and goes beyond all those people who have an intellectual and biological background that derives from Europe, people of Canadian, Australian, American, or South African European ancestry. While it acknowledges the diversity of the experiences and beliefs of Europeans, the term represents that mixture of European, Christian, and scientific or "modernist" thought that has come to dominate the world. It is what Ortega y Gasset called "the doctrine of human existence which, like a leitmotiv, is interwoven, insinuated, whispered in" Europeans, the "psychological architecture" of "the common European stock."[1] In music, a leitmotiv is a melodic theme associated with an idea or a person. In philosophy, it is the unquestioned truth that served, and still serves, as the foundation for all that the West stood for and did.[2]

Explaining the "why" is merely a matter of stating that one wishes to explore the varieties of thought of which human beings appear to be capable—Native American as well as European. By understanding the leitmotiv of Euro-Christian thought and all the ways it has distorted or created a parody of Native American thought, we can discover what our beliefs are not. And that, in turn, can open a window to an understanding of what a Native American philosophy is, a complex context of beliefs and stories—a worldview—that has sustained life in North America since times beyond memory, even against extraordinary efforts to exterminate it, a philosophy that has ideas that might sustain all of us into the future despite Euroman's apparent efforts to exterminate the entire species. The challenge to find a way to live on the earth without wrecking it is so great, that we cannot afford to limit ourselves to only one way of thinking. That's why.[3]

The "how" proves a greater difficulty. Study of the variety of European thought is accessible because the cultures involved have participated in a written tradition for a very long time. We may not have more than a few writings made by early northern European Vikings, but there is access through the writings of literate peoples of the Mediterranean who recorded their observations of such people. The tracing of Western civilization to the ancient and literate Greeks also provides a means to explore the early beginnings and the subsequent changes that the European people experienced. This is not what one finds in exploring Native American thought.

There were some literate societies in North America when the Europeans first arrived in Central America. Many of their written materials were destroyed as containing only "heathen" ideas. Nevertheless some have survived. There are also accounts of the lives and forms of cultural organization that the Europeans encountered in the "new" world. Most of these early ethnographic studies were undertaken by missionaries whose role was not so much to understand the concepts and ideas of the American as to garner enough information about the American matrices so that the Natives might be converted to Christianity. There are accessible written accounts of early "contact" that cover the areas of the Americas from north to south. These written accounts produce one problem that must be considered: the writers were viewing a very alien group of people from a matrix equally alien to the Native peoples.

One of the most common approaches in the early contact literature is an attempt to find equivalent terms in Native languages concerning concepts of importance to *Europeans*. The terms here are those relating to religious ideas: *soul*, *good and evil*, *God*, *sin*, and the *afterlife*. Whether the European religious terms actually have equivalents in Native languages is a topic that is of much interest to Native Americans who are only now beginning to explore the discipline of philosophy. One of the explorations we will conduct is the comparison and contrast between the terms used to denote what each group deems 'sacred.'

One of the objections to studying "Native American philosophy" is that the groups called "Native American" represent too diverse a group to subsume under one label. The ideas of each group, it is argued, might be so different as to require an exploration of each group. In other words, one cannot generalize about the Native American peoples. The same is also argued in defending the diversity of European peoples and their thought: "A Descartes and Kant are not the same," one might hear. Nevertheless, there are enough similarities in the thought patterns of Descartes and Kant that no one would doubt that both are "Western" thinkers. We will see that there are, spread throughout the Americas, some similar concepts that allow one to speak of Native American thought *in general*.

Other sources for exploring Native American thought, besides the early contact accounts, are the stories about how the groups came into existence and how the groups that survive today should conduct themselves in this world. Many of these stories involve the demonstration of value systems that have survived five hundred years of attempted and systematic dissolution. An examination of the differences perceived by Native Americans between themselves and the 'mainstream' will also serve as a means of exploring the differences in ethical and political systems.

One word of caution is necessary in preparing a reader for involvement in something called "Native American philosophy." "Philosophy" does not mean that we will be discussing the specific systems of Native Americans, though that will be a part of the discussions. Philosophy is a methodological endeavor. It is what philosophers "do." The methods of analyzing Native American thought will be no different than those used to analyze other forms of human thought. Philosophy is not theology; there will be no attempt to promote the validity or nonvalidity of various concepts in contrast to others. Differences will be presented as examples of the diversity of human thought patterns. We will explore what having certain concepts about the world and human beings commits us to, as well as the possible origins of specific concepts in both Western and non-Western thought.

Something else must be noted. Native Americans do not see themselves as examples of "primitive" thought, ways of thinking that other cultures have experienced and outgrown. We see our ideas and concepts as rational, viable, and alternative means of interpreting the world. This fact is one of the reasons that Native Americans have managed to maintain a unique identity despite attempts to eradicate that identity. Compare this strong sense of identity to those who have "roots" in a European country. They have given up one identity in order to take on another identity, an *American* identity. Not all Americans have taken this step and many groups find it important to maintain ties with their original languages, cultures, and even countries, but still identify themselves, first and foremost, as Americans. Many Native Americans will be found in this category. Others will not.

V. F. Cordova
Pocatello, Idaho

# Biographical Essay

In a small, adobe stucco home on a dusty road in Belen, New Mexico, memories of Dr. Viola Cordova linger among a collection of art and academic notebooks scattered through three or four rooms. Her once numerous paintings, papers, and mementos are few now, most given away to her family and closest friends by Denny Wilmore, Viola's companion and confidant of twenty-five years. Among the remnants is a gentle, medium-sized parrot named MASH, after the famous TV sitcom. Sleek and green and flecked with blues, MASH is the last possession Viola acquired, at her sixty-fifth birthday, just before she died. The parrot stays close to the back door, always on the alert to make a quick getaway. It is Denny's constant, and now only, companion.

After Viola succumbed to an aneurysm, Denny sold their house in Idaho Falls, Idaho, and gave away all their collected household and personal goods. He packed a battered camper-truck with the most precious remnants of her academic and artistic life, and drove with MASH to Taos, New Mexico, Viola's childhood home. From there, he decided to travel around the entire spring and summer of 2004, exploring the mysterious Southwest landscapes that Viola so cherished. Eventually, he and MASH resettled in Belen.

However, it is Idaho Falls, rather than her birthplace in New Mexico, that marks the completed circle of Viola Cordova's life. Viola's father had years before chosen Idaho as a place for the family to live, rather than their native New Mexico. Viola and Denny met in an Idaho Falls tavern. A tavern "of all places," he laughs, "since that was out of character for both of us." Viola was reading *The Tao of Physics*, and Denny was instantly attracted to the twice-married undergrad from Idaho State University.

"When she began her university studies," he says, "Viola already was well educated and had read all the major works," as her earliest education in classical philosophical literature was self-taught. Never conflicted about her Jicarilla Apache/Hispanic heritage, Cordova drew on a core of Native American beliefs, but felt she needed to study Western philosophy to complete her knowledge. An inveterate researcher, Cordova was drawn to observe disparate belief systems. For example, the decidedly anti-Christian Cordova once joined the Jehovah's Witnesses to learn more about them. She was soon expelled when she openly questioned some of the foundations of church belief. Deeply anti-authoritarian and steeped in concerns about social justice, Cordova's participation in Vietnam War protests during the early 1970s earned her a dossier with the FBI.

Cordova earned a BA in philosophy from Idaho State University and an MA in philosophy from the University of New Mexico. She went on to earn her doctorate from the University of New Mexico in 1992. She was one of the first, if not the first, American Indians to receive a PhD in philosophy in the United States. "If [the late] Dr. Fred Sturm had not come to her rescue and mentored her, she never would have been allowed to graduate by the faculty [at UNM]," says Wilmore.

She then went on to teach Native American and comparative philosophies at many universities—the University of Alaska at Fairbanks, Colorado State University, Oregon State University, Lakehead University, and Idaho State University—choosing never to stay long enough to fall into academic patterns she did not respect. At Lakehead University in Thunder Bay, Ontario, in 1996–97, Dr. Cordova worked under a Rockefeller grant to establish the first university graduate program in Native American philosophies. There, she founded *Ayaangwaamizin*, an international journal of indigenous philosophy. She was founding coeditor of the *Newsletter on American Indian Philosophy* for the American Philosophical Association.

Dr. Cordova traveled extensively to lecture from a position defined by her carefully considered and passionately held philosophy. She spoke at Fairbanks, Alaska, each year on the philosophy of science, elsewhere comparing the Israeli-Palestinian conflict to the Native American experience with the United States, but "always Indian, first," as Wilmore says. In her travels, she mentored countless others.

Cordova was a talented painter, as well as philosopher. Wilmore likes to take a tour through the few paintings by Cordova still on hand. One is a self-portrait done during her war protest years. Another is a watercolor of an Idaho landscape, near the university. He points to a very small, nearly indistinguishable feature in the bottom-right corner. It is a gazebo where they liked to sit and have long discussions on matters of importance, finding peace in a distressed world. His eyes are distracted by something unseen, then they quicken and the conversation returns. Much of her art was done while Cordova served as the Fine Arts superintendent at the Idaho State Fair. Over a thirteen-year period, the fair exhibited the best of the Idaho artists, including her own.

Perhaps driven by a lifelong belief that she had a "weak" heart, the fiercely independent Cordova was never intimidated. Even as she earned her place in academics, Dr. Cordova mothered five children to adulthood. Cordova's diverse interests also led her willingly into the newest technology, and she was adept at all the latest computer fads—a "thoroughly modern Millie," says Wilmore, laughing again. But, he cautions, she took no vows of poverty, even moving through a "clothes horse" stage, loving shoes in abundance, and copying the latest styles on her sewing machine. However, the importance of knowing herself, living her philosophies, and maintaining her strong-willed independence remained of utmost importance.

One morning, Wilmore explains, Viola felt the effects of the ruptured blood vessel in her brain. Thinking that she was only feeling the occasional pangs of her self-diagnosed weak heart, Viola dressed, called someone to pick up her grandson from school, and only then drove herself to the hospital. When doctors notified the immediate family that Viola was dying of a brain aneurysm, her far-away children were summoned to keep vigil during the few, waning days that remained.

Dr. Viola Cordova passed this way forever on November 2, 2002. She left behind a legacy of scholarly pieces as well as personal musings on "how it is" in this world. The bulk of these now reside at Oregon State University and the University of New Mexico. The papers represent a unique and important voice in indigenous thought and philosophy.

The rooms Denny and the parrot occupy are filled now with twenty-five years of transplanted memories. Denny is still quick to recall the indescribable care, deep respect, and admiration he felt for Viola, and his good luck at metaphorically "winning the lottery" when he met her. The back door is opened. MASH eyes it cautiously. The parrot flies to Wilmore's hand, nudging ever closer for his undivided attention.

Kurt Peters
Corvallis, Oregon

# I  BRIDGES

# The Bridge over Romero Creek

My father's earliest image of his mother is of a tall girl running back and forth over a bridge that spans a small creek.

On one side of the creek is an indigenous settlement. The girl lives there in her father's house; her grown brothers live in additions built on to the main house. This in itself is unusual, because her people are matrilineal. That is, the males go to the homes of their wives when they marry. The women bring their mates to the house of their mothers. Property, such as it is, passes through the hands of the maternal line. But not here.

Nasaria Romero is the last child of an old man. She has no sisters. Her mother died shortly after giving birth to Nasaria. The only women she sees are the wives of her brothers. When my father dies, she wonders, will my brothers go to live with the families of their wives? Even now, she, at the age of twelve, is her father's keeper.

She has also a grandfather, and he is in better physical shape than her father. He goes every other day into the hills to pick firewood. He never rides his old horse, but when he returns in the late afternoon the horse is laden with sacks of firewood that he has picked from the forest floor. Some say that the grandfather is close to a hundred years old. Nasaria does not know. When he comes home from gathering wood she offers him warm stew and a tortilla. Sometimes she sits with him on the bench against the wall that faces the sun in the afternoon. He tells her about the things he encountered in the woods. Turkeys, sage hens, ravens. They are, themselves, Grandfather says, a family of Ravens. He tells her a story.

> Once, a long time ago, the People were hungry. The food they had stored for the winter barely lasted and the spring was long in coming. Game was hard to find.
>
> In the midst of this despair, Ravens began to appear among the People. They would come with their raucous calls and playful ways and cavort among the People. Having gathered the People together as audience, the Ravens would take a low flight and move on to other places.

The People did not fail to notice that the Ravens always looked healthy and well fed. Their eyes would shine and the feathers, which they groomed so carefully, glistened like raindrops in the Sun.

"These Ravens know where to find food," said the People. And each day they watched as the Ravens came to play and groom and taunt the People.

One day the People hatched a plan. They would trap one of the Ravens and coerce him into telling them where they were finding food. They succeeded in trapping a young Raven and tied a string to his foot to keep him from escaping.

"Where do you go, Raven, when you fly away from here?" asked the People. (In those days, of course, the birds and humans could understand one another.)

"What do you eat, Raven, when you are not here with us?" Raven said nothing. He struggled and cried but he said nothing.

Eventually, Raven's feathers began to dull and he blinked his eyes slowly and carefully, as he cast accusatory glances at his captors.

Finally, he spoke.

"Untie me," he said, "and I will show you where to find food."

The People did not believe him. "If he was willing to show us," asked some of the People, "why didn't he do it before?" They would not untie him.

Raven grew more and more silent. There were no chirps, no cries, and then even the other Ravens seemed to have stopped watching for him.

"It is useless," the People decided. "There is no use in keeping him here. He will only starve along with the rest of us."

The People began to untie Raven.

"Now," said Raven in a weakened voice, "follow me."

Raven flapped his wings and strutted a little here and there in front of the People. He waited for them to gather their children and their hunting weapons. And then he began his low flight through the gathered crowd. "Follow me," he crowed. And they did.

Suddenly the Raven's brothers joined the group and greeted their missing brother with great glee. They dived and circled and played in the skies. The People watched the antics with patience. No one asked, "Should we trust these playing beings?" They simply watched and slowly followed the proceeding flock of Ravens.

Eventually, after climbing many hills and wandering through valleys, the People came upon a herd of Buffalo. Many Ravens rose to greet the People. "Welcome," they cawed. "Welcome!" Many days later, the People had gathered enough food to last them until Springtime arrived. They had called together all of their children and old ones and made ready to go home. Before they left they stood in silence for a few moments and then gave a prayer of thanksgiving to the Ravens. They had already thanked the Buffalo People.

On their way into their own homeland they encountered a large Raven, larger than they had ever seen. Raven spoke to them: "It is our way to share what we have with others. Many times, we invited you to come with us and you ignored our invitation. Our children played among you and you did not pay them any attention. It was not necessary to trap one of our children. They had come to invite you and they wanted only that you should follow them. You would not do that. There will come a time, said the Old Raven, when our peoples will not speak directly to one another. We will have different languages, different homes, but we will always experience hunger. That is the way of beings on this Earth. The next time our children come among you," he said, "do not ignore them. They come to invite you to a feast."

"That is why," Grandfather said to Nasaria, "the sight of Raven lifts our spirits so. He is a true brother and spirit of the People. In his honor we call ourselves Ravens, that we might remember and share his spirit."

In the Springtime, it was an old custom that the People of the Raven hunted the Buffalo and took the hides and food to the People of the South (the Pueblos). In return they brought home beans and corn, fabrics and pottery, and, sometimes, beautiful young men and women as brides and grooms. As Grandfather said the latter, he winked and nodded his playful head at his granddaughter.

Across the creek from the indigenous village there was another village. These were the Spaniards that had come from across the seas to settle among the People. The People taught them to grow corn and beans and squash and taught them to hunt deer and buffalo and the wild ground fowl. The Spaniards taught the People to raise sheep and goats and pigs. The bridge across the creek joined the two peoples. The creek served to separate them.

On one side of the creek the People offered thanks to the Raven, the Sun, the Earth, the Rain, and the Lightning. On the other side the Spaniards hid in the buildings they called "church" and offered prayers to their invisible gods. In the Springtime, when the People were most happy, the Spaniards engaged in a strange ritual. They fashioned crosses of wood and marched their sacred statues around the village. Some of the men whipped their backs as they asked for the forgiveness of the sins of their families. And when they were done with their strange ritual they dropped their mournful faces and laughed and invited their neighbors from across the creek to join them in the festive foods set out for all.

One of Nasaria's chores was to go to the creek every day to bring home drinking water. One day a man from the Spanish village, who happened to be at the creek, walked over the bridge and gave her a loaf of Spanish bread. The bread was wrapped in a soft white cloth embroidered with small flowers. Shyly, Nasaria accepted the bread.

Another time the man brought her some cheese wrapped in wax and tied with twine. Her brothers began to tease her about having an admirer. Her grandfather winked.

The man across the river was small and had curly red hair. He was not a young man, but not so old as her father. Nasaria was thirteen years old. She was the tallest girl in her village and probably the most responsible. She did look older than other girls her age; perhaps the man across the river thought she was. She began to refuse to go after the drinking water. Then the man came to visit her father and grandfather.

He said his name was Faustin. He was a widower and had teenaged sons and a daughter who was only ten. He wanted Nasaria to help him in his home. Her father and grandfather called in Nasaria. The proposal was put to her and she agreed to work for a few hours a day.

Several months later Nasaria married the man from across the river. He was in his midforties. She spent the next few years running across the bridge, back and forth. "Taking care," her brothers said, "of her old men."

. . .

Bridges can serve to unite, but they can also signify separations.[1] The People who lived on one side of the bridge were indigenous to the area. Those on the other side were newcomers. Each group lived on opposite sides of the creek and seemingly had opposite ways of looking at the world.

The People were called "Apache." More specifically, and to distinguish them from the many others the Spaniards called "Apache," they were called "Jicarilla." Those of whom we speak here were called another name besides the two: they were called "Romero."

In the Mediterranean areas there is an aromatic shrub that covers the hillsides; in English the shrub is called "rosemary," in Spanish "romero." There was no rosemary in the Nuevo España where the People who came to be called Romero lived. There was sagebrush that, like rosemary, is aromatic. There was also a spring that fed a small creek that was, on the maps of Spaniards, named Romero Springs, and, hence, Romero Creek. The People called themselves simply, "the People," or *seiji*.

On the opposite side of the creek, where the Spaniards lived, there were different customs. They revolved around strict authoritarian figures: majordomos and the long-robed men they called "padres." The Spaniards prayed in a kneeling position as supplicants and were ministered to by the padres. In their hands, they wound chains of glass or wooden beads. On each chain was a cross.

The People prayed thanksgivings on the hilltops with their heads held high, with pride rather than supplication. They were, after all, the People. They had a special relationship to the land, which required a certain responsibility on their part. They did not chop down all the surrounding trees but only enough to grow their vegetables. They hunted only at certain times in the life cycle of the animals. And they did not breed themselves to excess as did the Spaniards. The fact that the Romeros, through accident and chance, seemed to be largely a society of males did not detract from the fact that the Spanish women, in comparison to the People's women, were weak and therefore spiteful. Nasaria, in her early teens, had a grace and confidence that was missing from the tiny women across the river. With her strength and self-confidence, she made up for the daintiness that was prized on the other side of the creek.

Had her father and grandfather allowed her marriage, perhaps encouraged her marriage, to the small man across the creek because they worried about what would become of her when they were no longer part of her family? Should they instead have let her attach herself to one of her brother's families?[2]

Nasaria's husband, Faustin, called himself a *nuevo espanol*, a *criollo*, a Spanish Creole. His family took pride in their white skins and various shades of reddish hair and hazel eyes. But somewhere along the way and during their nearly two centuries in Nuevo España there had been indigenous grandmothers brought into the fold. This was a matter, as far as Faustin's extended family was concerned, best left forgotten and unmentioned. Faustin had shamed the family by bringing in this *india*, this child bride of his. She was not only tall and homely but so obviously an Indian.

Nasaria's first son was as white as her husband. He had her father's gentle red curly hair and the hazel eyes. The Spanish relatives found this a cause for agony. "How could she raise such a child as one of us?" they asked and tittered among themselves. With feigned kindness and insincere concern over Nasaria's second pregnancy, they offered to "help" with the eldest child. As the pregnancy progressed Nasaria saw less and less of her child. When the new son was born she swore, "Not this one."

She named him Solis, which she knew meant "child of the Sun."[3]

The People are the Children of the Sun. As such they pay homage to him and give thanks not only to the Mother who nurtures them with her plants and animals but to the Sun who fathered them. Coyote, that wily symbol of everything it means to be not fully human, is a Child of the Moon. He, too, pays homage to his "father"—he bays at the Moon when it is full. The nonindigenous people who came into the land of the People were "coyotes," Children of the Moon. They did not pay homage to the Moon at full but they bore its mark in the pallor of their skin.

The half-breed child of the union of indigenous and nonindigenous would also be "coyote," though the term would be given a diminutive form so as not to be terribly insulting, "little coyote."

Nasaria kept the infant Solis at her side at all times. She spoke to him in her own language, "loaned" him to her brothers for training in the art of becoming one of the People. She refused to cut his hair. He was younger than his cousins, the sons of his mother's brothers, but he ran full flight in their groups, red braids flying in the wind behind him. The People thought nothing of his red hair. His father did not object.

Faustin had two teenaged sons from his former wife. His daughter, younger by only a couple of years than Nasaria, lived with Faustin's relatives. His sons made Nasaria's life especially trying at times. One especially took pleasure in ordering her about and criticizing her; he was not above giving her a clout to the head when the coffee was cold or a shirt unwashed. He never engaged in such behavior in the presence of his father. And Nasaria, who held her own husband's small stature as insignificant, felt contempt for the "little rooster" who pushed her around. She felt not only contempt for his bullying but prided herself on not having risen to his taunts. One day, in the presence of her two sons, then aged four and six, the bully slapped her on the side of head. Nasaria ignored him. He slapped her again. She walked away and the bully left.

The two young brothers followed the bully as he swaggered to his chores. Silently, the elder boy motioned to Solis to follow him. The elder picked up a pitchfork propped against the side of the barn. "That is the last time," the boy said, "that he touches our mother."

The boys crept silently into the barn and spotted the bully as he hung tools on the barn wall. The elder boy, pitchfork in hands, ran to the bully and slammed him against the wall with the pitchfork. The bully gasped once and turned to see his attacker. He attempted a laugh of derision. The pitchfork was pressed tighter against his back.

"This time," said the boy, "I will not kill you. The next time you touch or mistreat my mother, we will run you through when you least expect it!"

The boy gave the pitchfork a harsh jab and the bully gasped again. Then slowly the boy withdrew the pitchfork but kept it aimed at the bully.

"Get out of here," said the boy. "I will wait for you in another place, at another time."

Solis would recount this story to his children with the same sort of awe that he must have felt when he saw his brother raise the pitchfork to the bully. They were only small boys and Solis's brother was seldom at home; he spent most of his time in the home of his father's relatives. It surprised Solis to know that his brother held his mother in such high regard despite the ministrations of the relatives. "He was only a small boy," said Solis, "and he had absolutely no fear. None at all." The bully saw the fearlessness of the boy with the pitchfork. He never bothered Nasaria again and he kept his distance from "the sons of *la india*."

The times were changing as Solis grew up in the late nineteenth century. Most of the indigenous Apache peoples had been killed or captured and locked away in concentration camps from which they could not flee. The Romeros had survived by fleeing to the nearby pueblos of Picuris and Taos. The Romeros that remained at Romero Creek did so only because their land was "allotted" to them by the new American government. The Catholic Church, having declared the Romeros harmless and even suitable as marriage partners for the Spaniards, had baptized the Romeros and "put in a good word" for them to the new government.

But the Americans, who came at first in a trickle, began to come in hordes. Mines and railroads began to appear in the area. Small settlements became villages. Ranchers moved in with their enormous cattle droves. The People had a choice: they could go to Dulce in western New Mexico with the other Jicarillas or to southern New Mexico with the "Mescaleros." Some did. Nasaria's family stayed on. Her father and grandfather wanted to die in their own homes.

The water in the creek began to dry up as American ranchers diverted waters in other directions. The Spanish settlement, too, was affected. What had at first seemed a boom of business to them eventually died down. The Spaniards had provided meat and cheese to the Americans. But as the new immigrants arrived, there were new purveyors of meat and cheese, and the growth of the nearby towns made the trek to the creek unnecessary. Over the years, the Spaniards moved into the new towns or to the towns from which they had originally dispersed into the area—all of the small towns along the upper Rio Grande Valley. Still Nasaria's family stayed on.

One day Nasaria's grandfather came down out of the hills with his old horse laden with firewood. He carefully unloaded and stacked the wood, watered the horse and wiped him down, and then sat on his bench to sleep against the wall in the late afternoon sunlight.

"Go," said Nasaria, to her two young sons. "Go, wake your grandfather to come into supper." But Grandfather did not wake up. "He's asleep," said one of the boys, "and he won't wake up." Nasaria dropped what she was doing and ran to her grandfather. She dropped to her knees and laid her head in his lap. Not only had her grandfather died, but a way of life was to come to a close.

In the spring of 1915, Nasaria's husband gathered his family, his flocks of sheep and goats, all of their transportable belongings, and set out for Taos.

"New bridges," thought Nasaria, "there will be new bridges that I must cross."

# Taos Bridge

## I.

With their two young sons, Nasaria and Faustin walk from their Colorado home to Taos. They arrive with their sheep and their goats in late summer. They settle in a small village called Arroyo Seco, ten miles north of Taos.[1] The year is 1915.[2] Here also, a small river divides two communities, connected by the Taos Bridge. On one side is a Hispanic community and on the other a community of mixed breeds, the result of marriages between Hispanics and Indians and of one tribe with another. There are connections between the two communities through marriage and another connection between the mixed-breed community and the indigenous community of "pueblo" Indians who officially own the land where the mixed breeds have settled.

My grandmother, Nasaria Romero Cordova, an Apache Indian of the Romero Clan, has relatives that have intermarried with the Tiwas of the pueblo. She is married to a Hispanic who has relatives on the other side of the river. But Faustin prefers not to live among his relatives. His relatives in Colorado have not been kind to his young Apache wife; he sees no need to subject her to more of the same treatment in New Mexico. So through Nasaria's brothers who have married into the tribe, they negotiate with the Tiwas for a bit of ground on the "Indian side" of the river. Faustin and his sons will herd their sheep and goats up into the surrounding mountains for forage.

"A loaf of bread," my father says, "some cheese and onions—that's our lunch while we tend to the sheep and goats." In 1915 he is nine years old, sports a head of unruly curly dark red hair, and, despite the hair color, is "*puro indio*," to his mother's delight. Her elder son, nicknamed "Willie," has often been abducted by Faustin's relatives under the guise of civilizing this son of an Indian into the Hispanic community—Faustin's rightful community, as far as the relatives are concerned. Solis, the second son, is granted to Nasaria. No one makes an attempt to abduct him to the other side of the river.

In the autumn season the sheep and goats have been brought down from the mountains in order to secure them for the winter. Solis and Willie are put to work cutting cottonwood trees for fences. They attend school across the river in the Hispanic village named Arroyo Seco.

Early on a Saturday morning a wagon crosses the river from Arroyo Seco. The wagon, harnessed to two horses, is driven by an old Hispanic woman. "The witch," Willie calls her, and runs and hides when he sees her coming.

"¿Donde esta el Willie?" inquires the old woman of Faustin. Willie is nowhere to be found. Solis hangs about watching the old woman. He's curious about this woman his brother brands a witch. Suddenly he finds that he has been recruited to help the old woman deliver her trade goods to the Indian village. He will help her unload her wares and then reload what she receives in trade. She makes room for him on the driver's seat. He jumps, instead, into the back of the wagon. With a quick sharp look at Solis, she gives the horses a signal to move on.

Solis has not been into the village proper. He has gone only so far as to visit his uncles. The trip is not a total loss, as he gets to see what he has seen from only a distance. The old woman barters and cajoles and examines the Indian trade goods. Solis stands at a safe distance as though to create the impression that though he is accompanying the old woman, he has, in reality, nothing to do with her.

Her trade mission accomplished and the wagon reloaded, they head back toward Arroyo Seco. Except that they make a slight diversion. Solis is not familiar with the area they now traverse, but when the wagon stops, a chill runs through him. They are in a Tiwa burial ground. He sits frozen on the back of the wagon. The old woman motions to him to get down off the wagon. He sits.

"¡Abajete!" the old woman shouts. And when she receives no response from Solis, she shouts in English, "Get down!" She shakes her head as if in disgust. "This stupid Indian," she thinks, "probably doesn't even understand Spanish." And, "That Faustin, what a fool!" Solis slowly descends from the wagon and follows the old woman.

"Look around," she says to Solis. "The Indians bring good things to the graves. They bring gifts to their dead. As if it mattered," she snorts to herself. She has the greatest contempt for the pagan. Nevertheless, before retrieving the "gifts" scattered about, she makes the sign of the cross. She is, after all, a good Christian.

Solis purposely looks in all of the wrong places and finds no "gifts." She chastises him while picking up pottery and feathered sticks. She wraps the artifacts in a large blanket and proceeds on her way home. "Fool," she thinks. "The Americans in Taos will pay good money for these things!" When they arrive at Faustin's home, Faustin comes out to greet her. Solis jumps out of the wagon and runs away. "Hey!" she hollers to Solis, but he keeps running. She motions for Faustin to come near and deposits a few coins in his hand. "For the boy," she says, and drives off.

Solis's running is not haphazard. He is looking for Willie. He spots him off in the distance hitting at weeds with a walking stick. "Willie!" he calls. Willie stops and turns to look at Solis, waits for him to catch up.

"The Witch," says Solis, panting and slightly winded from his run.

Willie smiles and then turns serious, "The Witch," he repeats, and is silent.

## II.

Solis walks across the river from his home to Arroyo Seco to go to school.[3] On his way home after school he dawdles, takes a stroll through the street where the stores are located, looks into the windows.

In one window there is a shiny pair of black shoes. Solis has not seen anything as beautiful. Not only are they beautiful, they look as though they would fit. Solis mentally measures the size of his feet and the size of the shoes. The next day he again stops to look at the shoes. He walks back and forth in front of the window. On impulse, he steps into the store, walks up to the storekeeper.

"I want that pair of shoes," he says to the storekeeper. "I will sweep your floors every day and clean your windows and dust your shelves. I will bring in firewood and clean out the ashes." All of this comes out as if it were planned. Solis had no such plan. "It just came out," he said, "as if the storekeeper drew it out of me, or maybe it was the shoes."

The storekeeper listens to this animated young boy and smiles. "Oh, you will, will you?" He turns around. My father is dismayed. "I thought I was being ignored," he said. The storekeeper hands my father a broom. "In the back room," says the storekeeper, "there are boxes that must be stacked neatly." My father breaks into a smile, takes the broom, and heads off in the direction the storekeeper has pointed. "Take a bucket," the storekeeper says, "and sprinkle a little water on the floor with your hand before you sweep so as not to raise too much dust."

Solis works for the storekeeper for a week. He takes pride in how neat the store is looking. The storekeeper has taken to wiping down the counter every now and then, in response to his new helper's enthusiasm for a tidy shop. At the end of the week the storekeeper calls Solis to him. In one hand he has the pair of shoes; in the other he has a new pair of socks. He motions for Solis to sit at a chair and helps him put the new shoes on. Solis walks around the store. They fit. They fit just as he knew they would!

"And with the shoes," says the shopkeeper, "you will need a nice pair of pants, and then a shirt, and a jacket. Maybe even a hat."

By the time the winter is over Solis has all of that and a few coins in his pocket. He is ten years old, the sharpest dresser in his schoolhouse. He carried a special cloth in his pocket to keep the shine on his shoes.

## III.

After supper, when my mother and grandmother have completed cleaning up the evening meal, my father Solis wipes down the oilcloth on the kitchen table with a dry cloth.[4] He then lays out his books and pamphlets, sharpens his pencils with his pocket knife, and trims the wick on the kerosene lamp. I sit on his lap.

Together, my father and I do "our lessons." My father subscribes to the many offerings that appear on the back of popular magazines. They offer to teach him "to speak and write like a high school graduate." We do the lessons, practice our "penmanship," and, as a treat, we read the newspaper, the *Denver Post*.

The headlines are full of pejorative comments on Hitler and Tojo, the Huns and the Japs. We live in a small town, one of those referred to as "section towns" and that are strung across southern Wyoming; its sole reason for existence is as a fueling stop for the railroad train. It represents a "section" of the railroad. My father works on the railroad. My mother's only sibling, her younger brother, is "in the War," stationed, he reminds us, in the safe haven of Hawaii, assigned as a "pencil pusher" to "general headquarters." His letters, nonetheless, come to us with the marks of the censor, so that the portions of his letters that address his duties are blacked out. We know only that he loves and misses us. The imagination of my family runs rampant with worry over the blackened portions.

So successful are the advertised courses over which my father and I labor that I know how to read at the age of four. I enter school shortly

before my fifth birthday. My father had only three years of formal school-
ing. He attended school in Taos, New Mexico, from the time he was nine
until he was twelve. At the age of twelve he left with his older brother to
become a cowboy in Montana. His father, who had been in his forties
when he married my grandmother, had suffered a stroke. My father and
his brother left home to supplement the family's income.

My father's previous experience with schools had happened much
earlier, in an Indian community in southeastern Colorado. The government established a school, and the children were duly rounded up and
deposited in the schoolhouse. The schoolmaster locked the door after the
children were seated. He cut their hair, threw their braids into the pot-
bellied stove, and paraded in front of the classroom, slapping his palm
with a steel-edged yardstick. Once, my father said, an official came to
inspect the school. He was surprised that the "children," some of whom
were young adults, could neither read nor write.

"First," said the schoolmaster, "I must teach them how to sit in a
classroom."

Not too long after the inspector left, the schoolmaster—as was his
manner—headed down the aisle between desks to punish a squirming
student with the yardstick brandished before him. The student stood and
rushed to meet the teacher, grabbed the ruler from the teacher's hand and
broke it over his own knee. As the teacher stood stunned, the student
threw the pieces of the ruler into the stove and proceeded to exit the
schoolhouse through an open window. The rest of the students sat in awe.
The teacher wandered back to his desk, sat down, and said not a word. The
students, one by one, climbed out the window. The next day someone
reported that the teacher had left town. This is why my father did not
begin a formal education until he was nine years old.

My sister and I found it incredible that my father would have left home
at the age of twelve to "be a cowboy." People who are twelve, we argued, are
only *children*. As an adult, however, I had the good fortune to see a class
picture of the New Mexico school my father attended. The year is 1918,
my father is twelve years old. He stands in the back row, lined up with the
school's teachers. He stands apart from them and is immediately recogniz-
able to those who knew him. His hair, which at that time in his life was
bright red, stands straight up from his head in kinked curls and frames a
countenance that is most similar to one's idea of the Viking berserker. I

had no doubt then that my father, at the age of twelve, could decide to go to Montana to be a cowboy. He sent home money every month to his parents. He did not go home for his father's funeral, only returning to his mother's home when he was thirty years old.

He arrived in 1936 in fine gabardine clothes, with rings on his fingers. He was driving a bright yellow convertible Cord automobile. His once unruly hair had turned jet black and clung in soft curls to his friendly and, many would say, handsome face. He came to visit with his mother. While he was there, he met and fell in love with my mother. The local priest refused to marry them—objecting that my father was not a "true" Catholic—until my father slipped the priest fifty dollars. I was born in the fall of 1937.

## IV.

What is it that initiates the search for one's own history?[5] Is it a search for explanation? For justification? Where do those actions come from that seem so natural and yet seem so out of step with the people around us? Or, why is it that I look different from the others? Do I feel different because people ask about "where I came from" or want to know my "background"? They do not seem so ready to ask such questions of themselves. Are you "oriental"? they ask. Am I?

Once, when my second daughter was around six or seven years old, she came running into the house in what seemed like an interruption to her play. "Mom! Mom!" she calls, when she doesn't immediately see me. When she catches sight of me she asks quickly, "Am I Chinese!?" I respond that she is not. Without waiting for an explanation she quickly runs out the door only to return a few minutes later. Again, without explanation, she bursts into the door and asks, "Am I Hawaiian?" She gets from me a very quizzical shake of "no." She comes back a third time. This time she seems not so much in a hurry. "What am I?" she asks and pauses for my answer.

"Who wants to know?" I ask.

She tells me that she is playing in the school yard a few minutes away and there is a crew of young men installing a sprinkler system. One of them, she says, is a Samoan, "and he wants to know if I am one of them!"

She has been alerted to her difference. She stares long and with interest at her image in the hall mirror. "We're Indians," I tell her. She turns around quickly. "In-dee-un?!!" She stretches out the term with shock and amazement. She wants to know if her stepfather is an "Indian." "No," I say, "he isn't." I also am amazed—that she has so readily signaled out a difference.

"Well . . . ," she drawls, with a bit of impatience, "what is he?" "Oh . . . ," I try to slow her impatience, "Welsh, Irish, maybe a little bit of German." She comments that "that's a lot of things!" I inform her that we also have some Spanish blood in us. She looks at me with exasperation: "I thought I was just a plain old American!"

She approaches her inquiry about history through having confronted her difference from her playmates. I, as an adult, confront my difference through a clash of value systems and ways of acting in the world.

For example, I cannot ask for anything. I cannot command others to do my bidding. "Your room is messy!" I announce to my children. "The garbage can is full!" Shortly after my announcements someone begins to clean a room or to rush out the door with the garbage can. That is the way it is supposed to happen. One day my husband says to me, with much annoyance, "Do you want me to take out the garbage? If you do, then say so." I am shocked. I've been found out. I actually did want someone to take the garbage can out for me. I should not have said anything. "No," I mutter, somewhat confused—"I'll take it out." But he knows that I don't want to take out the garbage. I am busy, I am cooking. "Why can't you just ask?" he says. Why can't I?

No one in my family gives orders. That is one of the differences between "us" and "them." "They" are always commanding others to do something, demanding that someone specific do some specific thing. It takes me years to find out why I do the things that I do and in the way that I do them.

My value system is built around the concept of a human being that says that all humans are equal and therefore deserving of respect. Who am I to command another to do my bidding? I remember that my father would announce his needs: "A cold glass of water is a good thing on a hot day." "I sure am thirsty." Someone would get him a glass of water or offer an excuse as to why they could not do so. An excuse would mean that he would have to drop everything he was doing to come indoors for a glass of water. And he would do so—without complaint. Just as one cannot tell another person what to do, one can also not ask for anything. To ask for something is to imply an inability to be independent. To ask for anything is to imply to the person asked that he or she has failed to be perceptive to the other's existence or needs. Telling another what to do implies a position of command that no human being, or *no real human being*, would presume to take upon him- or herself.

There are no rules that say, "Thou shalt not tell another person what to do." There is a gradual understanding that that is the way things stand.

When I was a child my sister and I slept in a large bed with a tall brass headboard. We entertained ourselves by using the bed as a trampoline. Once my father heard our jumping and shouts of joy. When he appeared at the door, we stopped our jumping. He proceeded to show us how the bed was constructed. He told us that many of the parts were irreplaceable. He showed us how the parts could break. He told us of the potential hazards to our health of falling as the bed broke under our jumps. After he had finished his instructional discourse he smoothed the bed over. My younger brother sat on it and gave a few bounces. My father left the room. We inspected the bed, saw again how it was put together, imagined ourselves with various broken parts—arms, ankles, wrists, elbows and "even heads," said my little brother. And never used the bed as a trampoline again.

Another time, my father had bought us a rather tricky toy. It was a wagon that could be ridden like a sled. It had metal wheels with rubber treads. We quickly discovered that the treads could be removed and that the metal wheels made sparks on the sidewalk and also created a wonderful noise. Again my father showed us why the wagon sled was constructed the way it was—why the rubber coatings were placed over the steering mechanism and the tires. My sister, brother, and I continued to remove the rubber coverings. One of us was stabbed by the steering mechanism. We tried to hide the injury that could not be hidden. I was ashamed to tell my father of how I had been injured. I had undertaken my actions on the wagon sled with full knowledge of what could happen if the rubber coatings were removed. I was responsible for my own accident. I had, in effect, caused it.

My father cleansed and wrapped my mangled finger. My sister and brother stood by filled with shame. We were, all three, ashamed. We had acted out of willful disregard of rational information given us by our father. My father had not one word of recrimination. I was bandaged and comforted. My father, however, had another task to perform before the episode could be called done. He went outside and chopped the wagon sled to pieces with an axe. He did not do this in anger, but rather went about the task carefully and methodically. We watched and we also helped pick up the pieces for deposit into the garbage can. We knew exactly what he was doing and why. No discussion was necessary.

At the age of fifteen, and after passing the driving course at school, I qualified for my driver's license. My father and I rode the bus into town with the rest of the driving graduates and their parents and we all received our driver's licenses. The bus driver allowed us to have a couple of hours in town before we had to go home. My father and I agreed to meet at the bus stop in two hours. When I arrived, the bus was already loading up. I saw my father and ran to him to get on the bus. "We're not going on the bus," he said. He had a mischievous look about him. I could tell he was up to something. Whatever he was up to, I was game. Nevertheless, I wanted to know how we would get home. "With this," he said, and he held out to me a set of car keys. He had bought me a car. It wasn't just a car—it was a car that most kids in the fifties would have lusted after: chrome fittings, sunshade, steering knob, the whole thing. There was only one catch: I would be the family chauffeur—and—I had to teach my mother how to drive. I had no problem with those duties. I had a car!

But of course there are hidden trappings to possessing a mighty machine. I was not prepared for the sense of power that such a machine could give. One night I drove my car to a basketball game. After the game, and with the car full of my friends, we happened to pass another car that contained in it the cheerleaders for the opposing team. The adult woman driving the opposition's car gave us a dour look as we passed her. I slowed down in front of her so that the girls in the back seat could get a look at "the sourpuss." She tried to pass us. "Don't let her pass!" someone shouted. And I didn't.

When we got to our small downtown area I pulled into a parking spot right in front of the local teen hangout. When we got out I was approached by the town marshal. I wasn't sure what I'd done. The others began giggling. Henry, the night marshal, was a joke to the teenagers around town. He kept an eye on all teenagers as though we were perpetually sitting around plotting mischief. We called him "Henry the Hawk." And then Henry the Hawk proceeded to tell me what I had done. I had misused my car. I had obstructed passage of another car. I had done something not only dangerous but quite stupid. "Now," said Henry the Hawk, "go home and tell your father that I will be right there." My friends stood around watching as I got into my car and drove home. Now I had to face my father.

My father was sitting in the kitchen reading a newspaper when I walked in. I handed him my car keys. He wondered what had happened. I told him the whole story. I told him that I did not deserve to drive. Then Henry the Hawk knocked on the door. He told my father the whole story exactly as I had told it. There were a few moments of silence when both men stood staring at me. Then my father reached out and handed me the car keys. "She will never do that again," he said to Henry the Hawk. And I never did.

Many years later my own daughter confronted me with a similar situation. She came home early one afternoon from what was to be an afternoon at the park with friends. "Here," she said to me and handed me the car keys. "I cannot drive for two weeks." "Did you wreck the car?" I asked. "No," she said, "everything is fine. I just can't drive for two weeks." She offered no explanation and I asked for none. If she had wanted to give an explanation, she would have done so. A few days later I overheard a friend of my daughter's whispering to my daughter about the car. The friend assumed that I had "grounded" my daughter from use of the car. "Couldn't you just tell her that we'd be right back?" begged the friend. My daughter responded, "My mother has nothing to do with it." As I walked into the room I saw on the friend a look of stunned silence. She couldn't imagine anyone "grounding" herself.

How had I passed on to my daughter a way of acting that I had not specifically taught? How is it that I could now identify my own behavior in my children?

There are many treatises on "human" behavior and there are many on "Indians." Nowhere did I see a "recipe" on how to end up as an autonomous adult. Who was I? How did I come to be what I was? What exactly did it mean to "be Indian"?

Today there are few Native Americans who can speak their own languages. It is often stated by scholars that unless one knows the language of a specific culture one cannot know the culture. I grew up, as do so many Native Americans, without "my own" language. I also knew many "Indians" who did not "act" like Indians. What were the identifying factors? How is it that an identity could persist despite the concerted efforts to eradicate it? For five hundred years the European-American population has tried to assimilate the Native American through secular education and through the many missionary efforts. The Native American has endured attempts of not only assimilation but outright eradication of an entire culture. How and why did these attempts fail?

# The Bridge to America

## Coming to America

An ancestor of mine crossed the land bridge that spanned the Bering Strait. Ten thousand, thirty thousand years ago. The dates are disputed.

When the Athabascan peoples made their crossing, there were already people on the American continent. We were the late arrivals. There are Athabascan peoples scattered from Alaska, through Canada, to the southwestern United States.

My father's mother was born near Folsom, New Mexico. So were her father and her grandfather. My father claims to be a descendant of Folsom man. The Folsom culture represents some of the oldest remains of early man on the continent. Who knows when my people arrived? When my great-grandfather confronted his first white man in the flesh, it was after the "Americans" had taken control of the Southwest from Mexico. This grandfather was mistaken for a "Mexican."

"Who are you, old man? And where do you come from?" asked the white man.

"I am from here," said the grandfather, "and I have *always* been here."

Maybe not always. But being as how his memory had no thought of any other place, "always" was good enough.

The Taos people, living to the grandfather's southwest, had an interesting story of origin: they evolved out of a lake on top of Taos Mountain. The story was adopted by the Apache groups that came to be called the "Jicarilla." The Taos people came out of the lake and wandered to the southwestern foot of the mountain. The Jicarilla came out of the lake and headed northeast.

My father was born near what is now Trinchera, Colorado. Their home was on Romero Creek. Was the creek named after your family? I naively asked, since that was his family name. My father laughed. "We're Indians! Most likely we were named after the creek!" Some of his relatives had French names.

"Are you part French?" I knew of his Spanish blood.

Another laugh. "The names are nothing," he smiled. "We got names from whoever caught us and baptized us: some were French priests, some were Spanish, and some were even Irish." Another chuckle.

The names held. The religion was held in mild contempt. My father remained a pagan. He believed that the Earth had created us through the fertilization of the Sun. "Prove to me," he would say as he pointed to my science textbook from grade school, "that there could be life without the Sun—or without the Earth." He would sit back and smirk. Of course. He was right. I thought him the smartest person in the whole world.

Many of my father's relatives married my mother's relatives. Not all of his relatives were Indians, and those who were "made up for their color" with industriousness and charm. Although my father's features were those of "la India," his coloring was that of his father. He was light enough to please the color and racial consciousness of his new in-laws. I grew up in extended family situations where cousins resembled each other and our parents had complicated titles. My cousin Lena's father was my mother's cousin, but her mother was my father's cousin. She and I, on the other hand, resembled each other more than we resembled our respective siblings.

Some of my father's relatives "forgot" about their being Indians.

My father couldn't forget.

In 1914 his family left Colorado. They went to Arroyo Seco, near Taos, New Mexico, his father's home. They could have gone to the Apache reservation in Dulce, New Mexico, but the reservations were viewed at that time as concentration camps. In Colorado, the Indian and Spanish communities had learned to get along in order to serve as a unified force against marauding Comanches, encroaching Frenchmen, and American intrusion. There was no such easy alliance in Arroyo Seco. My father was a half-breed. He was a foreign "other." He could, as did so many of his cousins, give up his Indian identity, speak Spanish, go to church, and spend his time on the other side of the river. He refused. He was his mother's son. He did, however, speak Spanish. He did not mind leaving Taos at the age of twelve.

Years later, as an adult, I moved to Taos. I had grown up with the myth of Taos as "home." It was the home of my mother's family for several generations. Old people told me stories about having bought their land from my mother's grandfather. My mother *was* Taos. Specifically Arroyo Seco. I wanted to be there.

And then one day I called my father, then living in happy retirement in northern California near other Folsom people. "Taos is racist," I moaned at my father.

"I knew that," he said. "Why do you think I left?" No sympathy there.

I grew up in Wyoming and Idaho. Taos was where we went in summer to visit with relatives. But I learned to know Taos like I knew my own face. Taos was where people looked like me. How could racism exist in Taos?

Taos prides itself, or rather the Chamber of Commerce of Taos does, on its cultural diversity. Three cultures living side by side, they say. We think that means they exist in some sort of communion. They don't. Indians stay with Indians. The Hispanics deal with Hispanics; and the Anglos are Anglos. And seldom do the two meet except on polite and superficial levels. Intermarriages occur, but the couple chooses which side to be on. The reason that three cultures exist side by side is that they don't really mix.

Example: One of my deceased mother's favorite cousins lives in Arroyo Seco. Occasionally I would stop in to visit her, for my mother's sake. One day after spending a particularly harrowing morning in the local Laundromat in Taos, I decided to drop in on this cousin. I told her about my morning. I said I hated Laundromats; I hated dealing with the people who frequented such places. The people I referred to were the leftover hippies. They arrived in Taos in the early seventies. They were dirty and they smelled; their children were undisciplined and aggressive and they hit the Laundromats about once every two months with barrels of laundry.

When I was a child, gypsies would come through Taos in the summer. People locked their doors and swore that the chickens the gypsies sold door-to-door had been stolen from the local residents' own coops. The arrival of gypsies in town meant that children were cautioned—be careful, a gypsy will steal you. Absolute Fear.

The hippies struck the same sort of fear in the local residents.

Or so I thought. The people are so weird, I say to my cousin, it gives me the creeps. She nods in agreement and then she lets loose the zinger: "Lots of Indians, too, I bet." Her nose turns up in disgust. I sit stunned. At the Laundromat, I sat—for safety—with "the Indians." We sat huddled in a corner, afraid perhaps that some sort of contamination—a contamination of license, immorality, self-centeredness, dirt, disease—would waft through the used washing machines from the hippie effluvia to ourselves. And now here was the beloved cousin—herself contaminated as far as my mother's snobbish family was concerned because she'd married a MEXICAN— turning up her nose at INDIANS. I was speechless. Had she forgotten, I wondered, that I was an Indian? That my father was an Indian? That his own mother was denied a name by my mother's relatives because they referred to her only as "la India"?

"And did you visit 'la India'?" my mother's relatives would ask when we visited Taos in the summertime. They didn't ask my father, "How is your mother-in-law?" They asked about "the Indian."

I should have known. My father knew. I didn't say a word. I simply stopped dropping in. I was ashamed. Ashamed of what? I don't know. That I was a part of such a family? That this otherwise beloved cousin who prided herself on her devotion to the church was a racist? That she was a hypocrite? That I thought she would accept me—for my mother's sake?

Being an Indian wasn't an easy task. I thought it was just a fact of life— like the fact that I was so many feet tall and so forth.

I was an adult when I realized that my father was no longer afraid of being captured (found out) as an Indian and sent to the appropriate concentration camp. What could it have been like to live with this fear at the back of your mind all of the time?

My father voted; he gladly paid his taxes. Every house we ever lived in looked better when we left it than when we'd moved in. He was a good neighbor; aloof, said many people, but honest, hard-working, helpful, and never a problem. He was a good citizen.

But my father was born before Indians were allowed to be citizens. He was voting before Indians were allowed to vote. He was never quite sure about the year he was born. He was afraid to look for a birth certificate because it might give him away as an Indian. He had never seen a birth certificate until the Social Security Administration found one for him when he applied for his pension. His birth had been recorded from church records. My father, his worse fears confirmed, discovered he *really* had been baptized. Officially he was a Catholic. My mother, had she still been living, would have derived a perverse pleasure from that fact.

My mother was Spanish. Not MEXICAN—her mother claimed. "Twenty-two years under the Mexican flag" did not make her Mexican. Being Mexican was a fact involved with history, I was told. They had lived in northern New Spain. Their folk stories were filled with scenes and stories about kings and queens and lovely princesses. Don Quixote was woven into all the storytelling, whether for adults or children. And we hear about the village dunce, Juan Bobo, whose escapades rivaled those of Coyote in Indian tales. Both served as examples of how a *human* being should *not* act. When I grew up and read the novel written by Cervantes, I discovered that many of the stories I'd heard from my grandmother were apocryphal—sort of sequels to the actual novel. She did, however, carry with her on her travels back and forth between New Mexico and Wyoming a hefty volume of *Don Quixote*—in Spanish and with illustrations.

My maternal grandmother lived with us until she died. She was actually more of a mother than a grandmother, because my mother was in ill health. My mother was beautiful, demanding, and likely to die at any moment. My grandmother was nurturing, undemanding, accepting, and almost always on my father's side in intellectual conversations. The conversations were usually about Christianity and America.

My mother was a devout Catholic. My grandmother was also a Catholic but of a different variety. She loved the church and hated priests and nuns. She chose to deny it, but there was a strong streak of the Penitente cult in her belief system. The Penitentes consisted of Catholics who chose to bypass the official administration of the Catholic Church. They held their own services, their own pageants, and worked for the salvation of themselves and the world outside the pale of the church. She also approved of my father's paganism.

I attended church services with my mother until I was about seven or eight years old. The attendance involved not so much Catholic ritual as the ritual involved in that attendance. It meant that on Saturday night my sister, brother, and I had to endure the most intense cleaning we'd undergo through the whole week. Our ears were pulled and scrubbed; our hair was untangled and, for my sister and me, put in unbearable curling contraptions that made sleep nearly impossible. On Sunday morning we suffered part two of the torture. We were again polished and dressed in stiff clothes. My father dished out oatmeal, bacon, and pancakes and commiserated with us—in silence, so as not to disrupt my mother's fanaticism. We looked to him through the corner of an eye from under an attack with razor-sharp combs and hairpins. As long as he was willing to emit the slightest of smiles, we could keep ourselves from breaking out into revolution or, at least, cries of pain.

One Saturday night, I refused the ritual. I wasn't going to church. "Daddy doesn't go!" My mother, I swear, with *scrub brush* in her hand, leaned back from the communal bath in which my sister, brother, and I sat, and said to my father in a most exasperated wail: "It's all your fault!"

I walked out of the tub, my grandmother toweled me, and my father let me sit on his lap. My brother and sister looked from me to my mother and seemed to decide that though they admired my stance they'd stick with it for a bit longer. My mother scrubbed them twice as hard to make up for my loss to the ritual.

My father, however, decided to dispute my claim about his not going to church. "I go every day," he claimed. It was just like something he'd say simply to get an argument going.

"Huh-uh," I said, "you don't either."

"Yes I do," he insisted and even offered to take me the very next morning. I called his bluff. "It will be very early tomorrow morning," he said, as though to warn me off.

"Well then," I said, "I'm going to bed right now! So I'll be ready." I heard him laughing as I marched off to bed.

The next morning he was in my room before it was fully light. "Get up," he whispered. I literally jumped out of bed. Frantically I asked, "What shall I wear?! What shall I wear?!" He grabbed my hand and a blanket off the bed at the same time. We walked quietly out of the house with the blanket wrapped around me. My father wasn't in his usual joking mood and I asked no questions. We simply walked around to the back of the house. I looked to him to ask what this was all about and he put his finger to his mouth and said, "Shhh." He pointed to the hills beyond the house. A few seconds later the Sun appeared.

My father pointed again. "See that," he said, hushed but excited. "See that?" If I had ever seen sunbreak before, I was not aware of it and now there it was and the sky was turning golden. I had seen it. I had seen the sunrise! "See that?" he asked again. "That is all you ever have to know!" And I did know. I knew why my father was always up and about before anyone else and why he was always so cheerful in the morning. I knew what he knew. From then on I didn't participate in the Saturday night ritual torture and on Sunday mornings I helped with the oatmeal, the bacon, and the pancakes.

My mother accepted this paganism just as her own mother had

accepted it. But occasionally we would drive her to a point of exasperation and she would throw up her hands: "INDIANS," she would lament. "I'm stuck in a house full of Indians!"

Catholicism was something that existed in our household, but it wasn't an important thing. It was something that my mother and grandmother indulged in—sort of in the same realm as my grandmother's apocryphal Don Quixote and the romance magazines my mother read in the afternoons.

What were important were the discussions that took place at our dinner table. We didn't know it at the time, but we practiced philosophy. My father would begin the conversations innocently enough: "Eat your cows' feet." "Cows' feet?!" We would recoil from the table and at the same time look frantically about for the dish that could possibly hold such a horrid thing as a dismembered cow's hoof. Laughing at our reaction, my father would explain that Jello—that beautiful shimmery green stuff studded with fruit and nuts and marshmallows, waiting to reward us at the end of the meal—was made of cows' hooves. We demanded explanations. What we got were arguments over whether there was an advantage or disadvantage to the euphemistic uses of language. Disputes about whether language did or didn't conceal as much as it revealed. Whether language and its use didn't actually display and perpetuate a particular view of the world. Whether there were other possible views and what those other views meant to the way we acted in the world.

"Eat your spinach," my father would say. "It gave its life so that yours might continue." Wasting the spinach was an act of sacrilege to my father. I tried to chew as reverently as possible before getting out my query: "What do you mean?" Another provocative statement would proceed from my father. My mother and grandmother would either join in or quietly, so as not to disturb the discussion or make it hard to hear, clear the table and clean up the kitchen. The discussions seldom went beyond the dinner hour. My father, having stirred up a hornets' nest, would announce that he was going off to read the newspaper or do some chore. My sister, my brother, and I were left behind to mull over whatever had taken place. My father only posed the issues; it was up to us to wrestle with them.

I grew up in a world where questions were viewed not only as inevitable but as fun. I grew *into* a world where questions were threats and answers were something to cling to for dear life. I didn't so much leave my father's world as the other world intruded into our space. But that other world, I was told and later found to be so, was the REAL world. I didn't *come* to America; I grew into it.

I knew that that other world existed. It was the world that made my mother's belief system something more than the indulgence I thought it to be. God, Jesus Christ, and all the beliefs accompanying and dependent on those two were serious stuff and certainly nothing to be messed with or taken lightly. Everybody, it seemed—except for my father and some relatives—*believed* that there really was an extraterrestrial being called "God." Jesus Christ wasn't just a Don Quixote character in someone's store of entertaining pastimes. As small children we had mocked the Catholic prayers with a prayer of our own, recited in a Spanish pronunciation: "Queren Gwen Gwen / Queren Gwen Cruz / Hakara Makara / Amen / Jesus." My grandmother and her sisters laughed when we mocked them with this prayer and called us "little devils."

Outside of the family that recitation was an illustration of absolute blasphemy. It brought to our listeners reactions of shock and disgust. We were expected to apologize for our insensitivity. Yet these same shocked people thought nothing of dismissing "Indian" views of what was sacred: not only was the Holy Sun insignificant, it was NOTHING AT ALL. I found it difficult to believe that *they* believed the stuff that they did.

There was one more episode that clinched it for me, that made me realize how deadly serious Christianity was in the world that I had to live in.

During the summer before my ninth birthday, a flock of nuns descended on the town and set up a summer school. The classes were set up according to whether one had made their First Communion or not. Most of those who had not were first and second graders in the public schools. At the age of eight and a half I was going into the fifth grade in the fall. That meant that I had to sit in a class with my sister who was a full three years younger than I. My mother used the magic words to bribe me into attending: "Just think of all the new things that you'll learn!" I went.

Two or three days later: "It's just all that god stuff. I'm not going."

Now my mother pulls out all the stops: it would make her so happy if I would just make my First Communion.

"No."

"It's all your fault," says my mother to my father.

"Go," says my father. "It will make your mother happy."

Feeling somewhat betrayed but fully understanding why my father has done what he has done, I go.

Two or three days later, I come home ecstatic. A great weight has been lifted off my chest. The shackles have been torn from my hands and feet, not to mention my thought processes—which might add fuel to the coming fires. I am home unexpectedly in the middle of the afternoon. My sister is not with me.

"Guess what?!" I shout in glee. My parents register surprise. "I never have to go back again!" Still my parents are surprised, maybe even befuddled. I offer an explanation: "The Sister says I never have to go to their school again because I am going to Hell!"

Now I get a more definite reaction. My mother bursts into sobs. My father is laughing so hard, tears come to his eyes. Through their tears and laughter I try to give a little background to the episode: The sister was talking about Adam and Eve. I asked about the cavemen. She talked about God; I asked whether it wasn't true that the Sun was necessary for life on Earth. The sister got angry. She pointed. Pointing a shaking finger in my direction and taking a few steps, she blusters at me: "YOU! YOU! YOU! You *never* come back here again! *You* will go to hell! *You* will *burn* in hell!" I was far out of the school building before she even got close to where I had been sitting. I ran home jumping over sagebrush, over gullies, feeling the wind in my hair and through my shirt, feeling life all around me and knowing that the Sun's warmth is not so critical as the nun. And then I was home free.

There were apologies. The priest came to the house. My mother apologized; the sister apologized. I maintained silence throughout the entire ordeal. I took refuge in being my father's daughter. Aloofness is our middle name. Later on, I would drive my mother to her church activities; I would even attend special ceremonies if she insisted. She appealed to my aesthetic sensibilities—"It will be so beautiful." I watched the ceremonies as I would watch a play, a pageant—they were interesting. I remained uninvolved. Aloof.

But there was no way one could avoid involvement in an entire country that was built on variations of Christian dogma.

I became fascinated—not only with the content of belief, but with the act of believing.

I began to explore all of the belief systems I could think of. Beliefs, however, were just a starting point. They were the foundations upon which numerous contingent beliefs were based, and all of those beliefs together, through some sort of "cement" of logical consistency, created worldviews. Worldviews were not only beliefs; they actually constituted the sense of reality that people bore toward the world and other people.

Having learned that as a teenager, I learned another thing: That stuff about the Bering Strait? My father's story about evolving out of Taos Mountain? About Folsom Man? Parallel universes. The reality of my father was not the reality that I had to contend with. I had discovered America.

# America

How do you survive in a world that is different from the one you have been prepared for?

It was not just a matter of my father having initiated me into the epiphany of the Sun. The Sun was one of those foundational beliefs upon which a whole set of beliefs, each consistent with the other and the foundation, are built. We call the nonfoundational beliefs "value systems." We bandy about the term "value systems" as though they were mere matters of choice. They are deadly serious things. Scratch one and you elicit the same sort of response that I received from the wounded nun. Unless, of course, you happen to be an Indian. Or any other non-Western person in the United States of America.

Our beliefs are said to be "primitive"—remnants of modern man's own route to his present and exalted state. "As you are now, we once were," claim the representatives of "modern" man. They who say this do not recognize in their tones the whiff of condescension.[1]

For example, a New Age prophetess, discoursing on how "charming" Indian "stories" are, tells me how much she "loves" reading them to her children. She "loves" Indian *myths*.

My response? My "stories" are not "myths." *Myth* is a term used to connote something that is untrue, unreal, unfounded, and having no utilitarian value beyond entertainment either intellectual or spiritual. We give the term *myth* to those ideas that we do not happen to believe. In this sense of the term, the ancient Greeks did not have myths. Zeus and Athena were as real to the Greeks as are God, Jesus Christ, and the Virgin Mary to Christians.

I say to the prophetess, "I would never read your myths to my children. The Old Testament is full of violence; its God is a vindictive and petulant god. The New Testament is not a testament of tolerance but one of intolerance for that which is outside its own realm. I could not impose on my children such bad examples."

She is angry. Frustrated. Exposed. "But you don't understand," she moans. She rises and leans forward on her dais. She who is decorated with the turquoise jewelry made by Indian artisans, who wears the garb crafted by a *real* Indian from India, who lights the incense made for Buddhist temples, who consults the charts of Babylonian astrologers, she rises to appeal to her rapt audience: "They don't understand." "They"—how odd that a people who so take pride in their own uniqueness so willingly deprive others of the same. I am no longer "I" offering her a challenge, but a representative of the "they" who persist in showing up at her Earth Rituals convocations to challenge the misuse of their own belief systems.

Dissolved into defending the "they," *I* leave.

But it is not only the New Agers who misuse the literature, the religion, the philosophy, the rituals of Indians. There is an industry of Indian Experts—academics who would interpret Indians to the rest of the world. They make a name for themselves. We gain little. Do you want to know what a Navajo thinks? Or a Lakota? Ask a non-Indian expert. We cannot speak for ourselves. We make the mistake of taking ourselves seriously. We need to be *interpreted*.

Another example: A budding folklorist follows me after a lecture during which I have said that it's the Indians themselves who are authoritative about their own cultures.

"Don't you think," she asks, "that it is important to take down the stories that the old people know how to tell?"

"Sure," I answer. "Why don't you record the stories of your own old people?"

"Someone is already doing that," she replies.

"What do you know of the context of stories outside your own culture?" I asked her. "How many 'native' people do you actually know? Have you any native friends? Do you sit and have coffee with them after class?"

She is *acquainted* with many natives. None are her friends and she would feel "awkward" sitting with them for coffee.

She is not unusual in this. Notice how necessary it becomes for the acknowledged folklorist or other interpreter of Indian views to stress that they have been "adopted" by a particular tribe, by a family in that tribe, so that they can speak of their "Indian brother" or "sister." This happens so often one would think there must be a manual of proper procedure: *Adopting a White Person: An Intertribal Ritual*. It might even have sections dealing with special cases: Anthropologists (Cultural, Linguistic, and

Physical); Folklorists; Missionaries (Orthodox, Reformed). The manual should exist—and it should have an explanation as to what it is that this adoption does.

The budding folklorist follows me for days. She wants me to *understand* what she is doing. "If you think it so important that these old stories survive, then why don't you teach 'natives' how to do such transcriptions?" She apparently hadn't thought of it.

Each time she finds me she has a new approach. "Don't you think it is important for those voices to be heard?"

I respond: "If you write them down it isn't their voice that is speaking. It is yours." Shock. "If you speak for me, you rob me of my voice."

A coworker says, "She is seeking absolution. Don't give it to her."

The comment about stealing our voices must have done it. She now merely looks at me from afar. Guiltily.

André Brink quotes a black South African as saying of such circumstances, "Carrying whitey on your back." Whitey rides into fame and fortune. No notice is given to the mount. If we're lucky we get to be "informants" and we're assigned a number, sometimes even initials.

An Indian working on a PhD told me, "I'm tired of people getting PhD's on the information I give them. I'm getting my own degree."

I, on the other hand, decided to study White People. I wanted to be a "White Expert."

Survival required that I know "the enemy."

By the time I'd finished high school I had learned the following "facts" about Indians:

1. Indians were not like other ("normal") people.
   a. Indians represented a cul-de-sac in the evolutionary process. They were a form of living fossil that had failed to develop. As such, they served as an example—not of themselves, per se—but of "modern" man's own past. Normal people studied Indians not so much to learn about Indians but to learn about themselves.
   b. This view, though not explicitly stated, made all Indians feel like specimens on a classroom shelf, bottled and preserved in formaldehyde.
2. Indians were in the process of disintegrating.
   a. In the process of teleological evolutionary progress, some forms

of life "proved" to be unfit ("wrong turns"). Such forms *inevitably* died out.

b. Some individual Indians would survive but only if they gave up their belief systems, cultural practices, and took up the systems, cultural practices, of superior species.

3. In the "winning of the West," Indians figured only slightly higher than grizzly bears, wolves, and other potential competitors for the land and its resources. Indians were more of a menace. (My father discouraged us from attending "Western" movies. If Indians had devils in their religious systems, they would all resemble John Wayne.)

4. All Indians were essentially vicious, unreliable, traitorous, drunken, immoral, and dirty. They all lived on reservations.

About the enemy, I learned that there was not one singular view, but two intermingled and sometimes competing views: the Christian view and the "real" view.

| A. Christian | B. "Real" |
|---|---|
| An extraterrestrial and invisible "being" had made the Earth and Man. | An "invisible hand" guides the Earth toward creating higher and more complex things. Man is the acme of this process. European Man is the most highly evolved. |
| First he made the Jews, but they flubbed things up so God sent down Jesus Christ to make things right. *Real* people are Christians. | |
| | In the process of making this most recent manifestation of the coming "perfect" creature, the Earth coughed up Sumerians, Babylonians, Egyptians, Greeks, Romans, and finally Euroman. |
| | The immediate forefathers of "real" modern man are the Greeks and the Romans. |

| A. Christian | B. "Real" |
|---|---|
| The Earth is a thing to which humans are condemned for being disobedient to their owner. | The Earth is a thing out of which humans have evolved and now transcend. |
| Human beings are essentially sinful and in need of control. | Human beings, though the greatest of species, are still a transition phase on the way to becoming something even greater. Because they are a transitory species, they are riddled with leftover instincts that must be controlled. |
| In the future, God will make all things perfect again, but only if humans behave. | In the future everything will be even better than the present but only if human beings keep the evolutionary ball rolling. |

I came to the conclusion that if the definition of the Indian that I learned in school was wrong, then it was also possible that the definition of the European species was wrong. How would I know?

I could pretend to be an anthropologist. I could live among the people that I was going to study. I could then examine their leadership systems, mores, values, religious beliefs, marriage and kinship systems. I could also study their "sacred" books, which in this case would consist of not only those containing religious content but also what was called history, psychology, and science. I could also become absolutely fluent in their major language. (Actually my father had already encouraged the language proficiency: "You already look different; if you also sound different no one will listen to you.")

The flaw here, of course, was that anthropological studies don't quite make it. People who are accustomed to seeing themselves as superior beings don't relish being prodded and questioned. As long as my questions were perceived as a means of learning to become one of them, I was well received. Persisting beyond that brought about charges of aggressiveness, arrogance, impertinence, and, most of all, a charge that I had failed to *understand* what was being said. It seemed obvious to my "artifacts" that if

I had truly understood, the questions would not have persisted—understanding, in their view, being synonymous with acceptance.

"That's not true! That's not true!" I can hear the clamoring cry. After all, there are numerous Indian writers who turn out volume after volume of "their view." No one objects to hearing a different view of themselves. But, the majority of "native" writings consist of poetry and short stories. There are also elegant retellings of tribal lore. Native poetry is often only eloquent screaming. Such poetry usually consists of recording the agony of being an Indian—about drunken nights and failed lives and White folks looming over them like evil spirits. The real thinkers are co-opted by the White establishment. Native women thinkers become feminists or lesbians and turn to "greater" causes. Native men who go beyond the eloquent screaming are termed "angry" or seen as having gone "off the deep end." John Trudell, an "angry" Indian, says: "I don't trust anyone who *isn't* angry." Vine Deloria Jr. "picks on" Christianity. He must be "hostile."

It is as though there is a written rule that says, "One must not look at oneself through the eyes of others."

Many years ago, before I had joined the academic establishment, I used to record sayings that I found particularly profound and illuminating. One of my favorites is from the *New York Times*: "A closed society, where only the highest circles are permitted to debate, hears only its own voice."

I wish I knew who said that. It was said in reference to South Africa, but it is relevant just as well in the USA. In America, we ban hostile voices: Carlos Fuentes, Farley Mowat. Occasionally, a professor who undertakes a study of Marxism is accused of "preaching" communism. The reason that it is so difficult to find "qualified" minorities for positions in the U.S. institutions is that "qualified" too often means "sanitized." "Other" faces aren't so hard to take; it's those "other" voices that are uncomfortable. Had I undertaken the task of translating *The Critique of Pure Reason* into an Athabascan language, I might have received more assistance in my intellectual journey.

There is no advantage to allowing more and more people into the "higher circles" if they must all speak with the same voice. The value of survival is being able to recognize yourself *after* you've managed to survive.

## II WINDOWS

How do we see the world, through what
windows of language, story, and cultural
practice? When Native Americans and
European Americans peer out through the
matrices of their beliefs and assumptions,
do we all see the same world? If, despite our
different practices, our worlds are really the
same, how can that world be described without
distorting or diminishing it? And if our worlds
are different worlds, what are those differences,
what do we make of them, how can we
celebrate and honor them, what can we learn
from them about how we ought to live?

# Windows on Academics

My family stories provide a window to see what I have to say. I exist only in and as a context. I am what that context has created. I did not burst full bloom into the world I confront. I do not have a "hidden," "inner," or "true" self that lies waiting for my discovery. I have been created by my experiences, and I am recreated—over and over again—by each new experience.

The excursion into the mental phenomenon that I call America is for the purpose of providing a glimpse into *where* I am. Each of us occupies a world that is made by our predecessors. We are given "reality"; we do not *discover* it. We train our infants to see the world as we have been trained to see it. We, in turn, are trained to see the world by the greater conglomeration of the WE. There are no individual *realities*, only communal ones. The only true individual reality is that of the madman. Because his view is truly unique, we *know* that he must be insane.

I was trained to see my father's world, and to act in that world. As long as I could return to the safety of that world I could explore all the others. But we grow up, and, in the case of American native peoples, we do not grow up into our own world. On becoming adults we confront not the world of our fathers but the world of the OTHERS.

Had I not noticed before that their voices were too loud? Their actions too abrupt? Their manner too domineering?

My father was a gentle man and so we learned to be gentle. The touch of the alien other bore more resemblance to the bear than to a human being. My father was a private man with a relentless respect for the privacy of others. This, too, we learned. "Who are you!?" someone would demand, because I did not look "like everybody else." How *old* are you? Where do you come from? What do you do? How did you make that?

I thought I'd been released into a world of madmen. They treated each other as though they were *normal*. Was I *ab*normal?

In a cultural context we reinforce our communal sense of reality. We need not speak of this sense—we act on it. In it.

I thought that THEY were robots. I wanted to pinch them to see if they would react as I would react. What would the world look like through blue eyes? What would it feel like to think that you were a bodiless thing trapped in a mechanical body? And that is what they were. They were MINDS or SOULS inhabiting BODIES.

Question: If "I" have a mind or soul and a body, what is the "I"—a third thing?

Suicide is one of the leading causes of death among Native Americans. People get free "research" money to study the causes. No one, of course, asks us what it is like to grow into a sense of reality that seems unreal. Or what it feels like to suddenly be perceived as something OTHER, deficient, archaic, mythological. Mystical or drunken and not much in between.

Being an Indian was an IDEA. Being an American (or European) was an IDEA. Where do those ideas come from? How are they perpetuated? Why do we cling to them? Where can we ask such questions?

My suicide attempts were overcome by my curiosity.

In 1976, and after reading more books than any college curriculum would ever require, I began a formal study of ideas. I chose philosophy.

Why would a Native American choose to study philosophy? Isn't philosophy merely the elaboration of European dogma? What relevance should there be for a Native American in philosophy?[1]

Philosophy, unfortunately, has earned for itself the labels of dogma and inutility—but philosophy can do more than retell and reexamine the thought of various thinkers in the European tradition. Philosophy is an activity. It is the examination and analysis of belief systems offered up as "answers" to the dilemmas that human beings face. Philosophy can be dry and ethnocentric—there are times when it seems as if one is merely sifting through the cobwebbed attics of someone else's long-dead ancestors. But it is the questions raised by philosophy that keep one going.

What is the world? What is it to be a human in the world? And what is the role of a human in the world he defines? There does not exist one human group that has failed to raise such questions at one time or another. Our cultures, our values, and our goals are the various responses to the "answers" that diverse human groups have offered up to the main questions of philosophy. Those "answers" in turn provide the foundations of the actions and behaviors of our daily lives. We do not question these foundations. We take them for granted. The philosopher Martin Heidegger says of these foundations that they were once answers to "open" questions that are now "quiescent"—that is, we no longer ask questions concerning what the world is or what man is.

The Native American cannot afford to forgo those questions. The "answers" we have grown up with—our definitions of man, the world, and their relationship—do not rest "quiescent" for any of us. Our sense of reality—of what it is that is *real*—exists as reality through the daily reinforcement of others like ourselves. Our sense of reality is reinforced through our shared definitions of man and the world. The Native American's sense of reality is bombarded from every direction the minute he leaves his home or tribal ground to engage in the affairs of the larger, "non-Indian" world.

Our world is defined as Mother, and we grow up with a certain attitude to the Earth that penetrates all of our everyday thinking. Yet we walk out into a world that does not share our view of the Earth. Everywhere we look the Earth is covered, "paved," with asphalt, concrete, glass, and buildings that resemble from afar one of the European cemeteries with their projecting memorials.

On those occasions when we can look at the Mother or her offerings, we see "tamed" vegetation: the grasses are manicured, the trees pruned, and the whole is surrounded with fencing or signs that warn one away. "Keep Off The Grass." The domesticated bits of Earth lie like prisoners behind bars—contained, restrained, and isolated. The subjugation of the Earth is the product of another mind—a mind that shares few of our own definitions, or "answers," about what the world is.

The world is defined by Euroman as "hostile," "wild,"—something, that is, that is potentially harmful. It must be kept at bay. Even the "enlightened" view of the modern environmentalist or ecologist maintains Euroman's distance from the Earth. Man's duty, they might say, is to "keep guard" over the Earth—as if the Earth without their ministrations would deteriorate into chaos, or worse yet, become "unusable."

There is a definition of man in all of this, a strange definition: man is, at the same time, a pawn of the universe and its guardian. The paradoxical definition is resolved, however, when we explore the definition of man: a human being in the European sense is not a part of the world; in the religious sense, he is a creation of an extraterrestrial god who has set man up in an alien environment. In the secular sense, man is a being that has evolved beyond his former relationship with the Earth. In both cases man is seen as alien, a stranger, to his environment.

And did it take a decade of studying philosophy to come to these conclusions about Europeans? The definitions I have offered of the European American, after all, are neither unique nor unknown to the Native American. But there is something unique about all of this. A study of European philosophy brings out the relative "youthfulness" of Euroman. It brings out also that Euroman shares something with all the other peoples of the Earth: he is, as are the rest of us, the product of a specific belief system that originally provided him with "answers" that grew to serve as the unquestioned foundations of his world.

We have come to take Euroman for granted as a part of our landscape —we don't bother to raise questions about his "reality" or "validity." Instead, we question ourselves. We too readily fall into the judgments about ourselves that define us as "primitive" or "undeveloped." We treat ourselves as "specimens" and proceed to use the various "answers" to our existence as justification and explanation for the way we are. But Euroman should not be taken for granted. We should know who he is in order to know what we must coexist with. All of the methods that we are taught to turn against ourselves, the psychological, anthropological, sociological, and so on, can also be used to know Euroman.

The major ideas, or definitions, of Euroman did not arise in the far past. The view of man as a stranger on his own planet is only as old as Christianity. The idea that man's individuality is preeminent over his role in the group is only centuries old and that too can be traced to incipient roots in Christian thought. Euroman's treatment of human beings and of the Earth is essentially based on the views of man as an individual who is somehow superior to, or different from, the Earth. The definition of the Earth is generally that the Earth is a *thing* (as opposed to a "being").

It is not the insight into Euroman, however, that is the ultimately valuable lesson in the study of philosophy. It is the fact that through an exploration of the course of human thinking—worldwide—the Native American structures of thought come out to be not "alien" or even "primitive." Our views are the result of centuries of analyzing the world and our place in it. Our thinking is the mainstream of HUMAN thought.

But should you all rush out and sign up for a philosophy course? I cannot in good faith recommend it. If your intention is to translate Kant or Descartes into your own Native language or to give up your own views for those of the dominant culture, then the university will applaud and assist you. If, however, your intention is, as mine has been, to seek a method by which your own views can be articulated and examined, then you should be prepared for comments like these:

> "You must not make the mistake of attributing sophisticated notions to primitive minds."

> "The notions, if they are there, are not intentional."

> "Native American art is not a subject for an aesthetics course; the style is, as are all primitive styles, automatic (i.e., unintentional)."

> "The Greeks were not a primitive people!" (On my attempt to trace the similarities in Greek drama and Native American rituals.)

In other words, the Native American is not seen as a valid thinker. He is, at most, a living fossil through which Euroman can trace his own rise to his present stage of achievement.

The Native American remains, in the discipline of philosophy, something to be studied and analyzed and not someone who is capable from his own viewpoint to do any studying and analyzing. Yet Native American belief systems contain some of the most abstract notions in any philosophical system. Our ethical systems are certainly worthy of review, especially in a world facing environmental disaster. We, as human beings, are worthy of being taken as thinking beings.

There are at the moment, throughout the country, almost no Native Americans in philosophy departments at our universities. We have earned the right to become doctors, lawyers, scientists—we have not yet been accorded the right to speak for ourselves. Our "myths" and "legends" are explored over and over again in many disciplines and always the explanations seem inadequate to Native Americans. The time has come for American native peoples to give their own explanations. And that is the relevance of the study of philosophy for Native Americans: not to see ourselves as others see us, but to look at ourselves through our own eyes.

# Windows on Native American Philosophy

Philosophy, as it is practiced by philosophers, is an examination of ideas. Ideas, however, exist in a context. In order to fully understand an idea and its implications and ramifications it becomes necessary to understand the context. This is often overlooked in the new impetus to create a field called "Native American philosophy." The practitioners of the new specialty often come to the ideas drawn from indigenous cultures with very little knowledge of the culture from which those ideas originate.

The result here is that the practitioner pulls an idea out of a particular context and attempts to fit it into an idea from within his own cultural context; or, he can come to the alien perspective armed with his own concepts and attempt to find something in the other culture that matches his concept. It is very likely, however, that there are no literal correlates between concepts drawn from different contexts. An example here would be the futile attempt to find out what the "Huron's concept of the soul" might be, or the attempt to find out "what god" an alien culture worships. It is more likely to be the case that there are no correlates to the terms 'soul' or 'god' (perhaps, even 'worship') in the culture that is not our own.

To pretend that one can interpret a particular idea from an alien context without understanding that context is to engage in misinterpretation, that is, to make such ideas "plausible" only to those who think like ourselves.

Does this mean that it is impossible to do what is called "Native American philosophy"? Not at all. It does require that the approaches to doing this type of philosophical examination be quite different from the usual methods and approaches. We must first of all be aware of the assumptions that we bring to such a study: assumptions such as "all people believe in a god," or, "all people act solely from self-interest," or, "humans are naturally sinful." More suitable foundations for the initiation of a philosophical inquiry might begin with recognizing that all humans thus far encountered have described the world, they have described what it is to be human in that world, and they have prescribed a role for persons in that world.

Cultures differ as their descriptions of the world differ. The 'answers' that people create to the questions they pose about the world and themselves are in the philosophical realm of metaphysics.

One of the major obstacles to undertaking an examination of indigenous metaphysics is the result of another assumption that the researcher brings to his study: it is assumed that metaphysics is a philosophical activity that lies outside the capabilities of anyone other than "advanced" civilizations. An indigenous "tribal" culture, by virtue of not being a culture like that of the "advanced" West, is presumed to be on a different level of "development." Such cultures are assumed to operate in the realm of *superstition* or *imagination* as opposed to the "higher" activities of *observation, experience,* and *reflection.* That this is not the case should be obvious from the fact that numerous "tribal" peoples have managed not only to survive but thrive in very specific environments for thousands of years.

An interesting study done by Gerardo Reichel-Dolmatoff on the Tukano Indians of the Amazon basin bears out the intricacy of an indigenous belief system as it relates to the specific location of the group. He titled his research "Cosmology as Ecological Analysis: A View from the Rain Forest." In an abstract of his article, Reichel-Dolmatoff makes the claim that "concepts of cosmology represent a blueprint for ecological adaptation . . . ; acute awareness of the need for adaptive norms can be compared with modern systems analysis." The Tukano, it is pointed out, "have developed a set of highly adaptive behavioral rules," which among other things have allowed the Tukano to "maintain an equilibrium and to avoid frequent relocation of settlements."[1] The Tukano, on the basis of their own rules, manage to control the growth of population as well as the exploitation of their environment and interpersonal aggression. In other words, in the context of the Tukano system, they have managed to develop a cosmology and an ethical system based on an intimate, factual knowledge of their environment. Within the Tukano system there can be no doubt that there is an epistemological base as well as a system of logic and aesthetics.

When presented with Reichel-Dolmatoff's research, it seems absurd to assume that indigenous peoples operate only on superstition and imagination. It is equally absurd to believe that non-Western peoples do not engage in a wide range of "philosophical" endeavors. In a similar fashion, it would be necessary to understand the "cosmology" of the Navajo, for example, in order to understand what is meant when they translate a particular term from their language as 'beauty.' The philosopher would have to ask, "What is the basis of the Navajo aesthetics that underlies a claim to beauty?" What, in other words, is the *context* that lends meaning to the label 'beautiful'?

What is commonly presented as "Native American philosophy" is usually a reading of a particular myth or legend, and the events or characters are related to events and characters from the context of the presenter. Or a specific concept, say the concept of 'balance,' is taken out of its natural context and presented in a new context. A philosopher would have to ask, "In what sort of world would this concept make sense?" One should ask oneself whether the concepts of 'balance' and 'harmony' actually make sense when transferred over to a context in which the world is described as essentially chaotic. Where, in other words, and how, does the idea of 'balance' arise?

A concept, however, is merely a starting point. What would it be like to live in a world that we considered a living being? When we ask such questions as this we are beginning to get to the root of what a Native American conceptual framework might be. The implications involved in such an essential definition of the world are far-reaching. Our definition of what it is to be human will be grounded in the basic definition of the world. Our ethics, that task of claiming what it is that humans *should* do, are based on having a definition of what it is to be human in the world *as it is described*.[2]

We must, as philosophers, not lose sight of the fact that the reason for exploring alien ideas is to expand our understanding of the diversity of human thought and not to expand our own specific way of thinking so that it encompasses all others. It is common to examine the Other as a means of gaining understanding about ourselves, but we should not mistake the Other for a *mirror*. We can learn something about ourselves as well through a *contrast* with the Other.

One of the most important factors in creating a Native American philosophy is the inclusion of Native Americans in the activity. Many Native Americans, whether one wishes to believe it or not, have managed to survive the onslaughts of assimilation and outright eradication with an intact cultural identity. The Native American has, furthermore, been placed in the unique situation of having to understand two very different worldviews. He has been exposed, from childhood, to competing and often contradictory value systems. The average Euro-American lacks this experience of the competing worldviews and value systems. His "world" reinforces the dominant view; he cannot know that he exists within a self-referential system of thought.

Austrian-born philosopher Ludwig Wittgenstein declared that his aim as a philosopher was, "to shew the fly the way out of the fly-bottle."[3] Unfortunately, I doubt that he has managed to "shew" that there is a "bottle," that people live inside a set of beliefs and attitudes particular to their culture. They are the given of how we see and interpret the world. This failure is not, of course, from a lack of effort on his part. The Native American is in a unique position to realize that there is not only one "bottle," but several. In order to survive, he has become expert in flying in and out of two bottles.

It is, of course, much easier to explore Native American thought through early European contact accounts or from collected myths compiled by non-Native Americans, on the assumption that the contemporary Native American suffers from "intellectual pollution"—that he represents a degraded form of an "original" type. This attitude, which is not at all uncommon, leads to a situation where the interpreter of such thought has no "peer review"; that is, there are no checks of the validity of his interpretations.

A valid interpretation or explanation of Native American thought would require that the practitioner of that field explore the many facets of the cultural group he wishes to understand. It is not, perhaps, necessary to become fluent in the language, but it is necessary to know at least how the language works, its structure. It would be necessary also to understand how cultural transmission occurs through families, schools, and so on. It is not uncommon to find that some "expert" in a particular Native culture has never spoken to a contemporary member of that culture. Most philosophers wishing to learn about Chinese philosophy examine the language and the culture or at least spend some time in the company of Chinese philosophers. The greatest bridge between cultures is the person who is schooled in the philosophies and histories of both cultures.

Today the field of Native American philosophy is dominated by non-Native Americans. One reason is the small number of Native Americans trained in philosophical methodologies, but another reason is that often the Native American is seen as too *subjective*, too immersed in his own culture, to participate in an *objective* examination. On the other hand, the Native American trained in philosophical methodologies is excluded from dealing with topics that are "Western" on the basis that "since he comes from outside the culture, he cannot truly understand the full scope of Western thought."

In the one case "subjectivity" is a flaw, in the other, a requirement! However, a Native American with a background in philosophy—which by its present nature is necessarily a study of Western thought—is assumed to be fit to teach only Native American "philosophy." This double standard results in the situation we have at present: any Euro-American philosopher can teach a Native American philosophy course, regardless of his qualifications to do so, and very few Native American philosophers are allowed to teach Western thought, regardless of having the educational background or qualification to do so. "Qualifications," in each case, means something entirely different. The ideal situation would be to include Native Americans in the philosophical endeavors of non-Native Americans in both fields—Western and Native American.

I have often heard non-Native Americans speculate about how their culture would appear to someone from "outer space." I doubt that such a view would be any different from Native American views of non-natives now. Stanislaw Lem, a Polish science fiction writer, in his novel *Solaris*, postulates a truly alien intelligence that is beyond human understanding. One of the characters in the novel makes the statement that "man doesn't really want communication with the Other; he wants a mirror."[4] He wants self-affirmation.

The person trained in the field of philosophy, regardless of his or her background, should be expected to rise above mere self-affirmation. He is not, as is the missionary, looking for a ground of communication so that the indigenous thought may be eradicated through conversion to Christianity. And he should be well enough schooled in the tradition of "open inquiry" to be aware of the assumptions that he carries with him to another culture. Some of the assumptions that the Western philosopher brings with him are the view (1) that all human beings share a common set of beliefs, (2) that non-Western peoples are a less complex form of being, less developed than the Westerner, and (3) that indigenous peoples are incapable of engaging in philosophical discussions.

The first assumption, the "common set of beliefs," leads the philosopher astray in picking and choosing bits and pieces from the alien culture to satisfy the longing for a common theme. We make things fit from within our own context, whether or not they actually do. The human species shares common physical characteristics and sensory organs. This leads to many common symbolic forms drawn from sensation, but what those symbols mean is often very different in each culture. We should be prepared to ask of seemingly similar symbols: "This is what this means in my culture. What does it mean to you?" And we should question why we cling to the notion that there must be a commonality of concepts. We should be open enough to realize that this approach necessarily leads to viewing different cultural perspectives as either "right" or "wrong" based on a standard that is drawn from only one culture.

The second assumption, that non-Western peoples are less complex than those of the West, is a common assumption: our own cultural trappings seem more complex than those of the Other simply because of our familiarity with them. A broad inspection of another culture, language, religion, values, or historical sense quickly dispels the view of the existence of "simple" cultures. It is only through an exploration of the complexity that we find the identifying characteristics of specific cultures. There does exist a leitmotiv that runs through a specific culture, but it cannot be found if one simply picks up isolated bits of another culture and says, "This is just like that" (comparing one idea from one culture to an idea of another). Usually such comparisons are prefaced by, "This is a *less-developed* form of that."

The third assumption, that indigenous peoples are not sophisticated enough to engage in philosophical discussion, particularly concerning their own concepts, is simply not true. I recently spent the better part of an afternoon discussing the implications of a single term with an Anishinaube who spoke his language fluently. He gave me the literal translation of *engwaamizin* as "tread carefully." Some, he said, interpreted this as "be careful," but, he pointed out, it means much more than that. Unspoken, but understood, in that term is a whole worldview having to do with man's place in and effect on the universe. From my own experience, borne out through discussion with numerous other Native persons, I discovered that many of our family discussions around the kitchen table consisted of very sophisticated philosophical dialogues. Many of these discussions or dialogues revolved around trying to understand the vastly generalized terms used in the West; 'love,' for example, could be used to denote one's feeling toward apple pie, country, mothers, and members of the opposite sex. We discussed also the tendency to a reification of abstract concepts, as when the sacred was reified as an anthropomorphic deity; or 'motion,' 'change,' or 'duration' as *things* called 'time.' We did not use the language of philosophers, but the activity and the intent were the same.

The assumptions that serve as roadblocks to understanding the worldviews or philosophical stances of others can be overcome through methods that the philosopher has at hand: he has made a distinction between logic, epistemology, ethics, aesthetics, and metaphysics. Those are the 'tools' or 'approaches' that should be used in attempting to analyze the thought of others. He lacks only one other 'tool'—the need to concentrate, not on similarities, but on differences. It is by contrasting notions that one learns about the distinction between the self and the Other. Those differences are what make the Other an Other.

But even here there is an assumption that must be overcome. It is generally thought, in the West, that a concentration on differences is grounds for intolerance. "We should seek out our commonalities," I often hear. We are disappointed when disagreements arise. The disagreements are a result of the intolerance that arises out of the need to concentrate on commonalities. True tolerance consists, not of ignoring differences, but in acknowledging them and acknowledging with equal weight that even small differences carry tremendous import. But true tolerance also requires a recognition that there may not be a vast universal, absolute Truth (with a capital "T"). It may be that diversity, which appears to be the identifying characteristic of Earth's creativity, may extend to how we organize and explain our diverse experiences of the world. So the philosophic endeavor, philosophy as an *activity*, should extend its present perspective to an attempt to understand all of the possible ranges of human thought.

# Matrix: A Context for Thought

All peoples, regardless of whether they are labeled "primitive" or "modern," have described the world. They can be said to have a "worldview." This view, or description, consists of three very basic items: a description of the world, a description of what it is to be human in that world, and a description of the role of humans in that world.

The description of the world may have highly imaginary elements, but in order to have any validity for the group it must be based on the observation and experience of the group in a specific location and under circumstances specific to that location.

The three descriptions will be highly coordinated. All humans appear to have a knack for maintaining a high degree of logical consistency in their framework of explanations. The description of a human being will be consistent with the description of the world. The human's role in that world will be consistent with what a human is seen as capable of doing in that world.

The worldviews are shared views. There are no individualistic worldviews; an individual holding his own worldview would be defined as "not quite right."

The worldview is made up of several descriptions and explanations that expand the basic descriptions. There are many terms used to describe this set of explanations: "conceptual framework," "frame of reference," "presuppositions," "paradigms," even "worldview." I prefer the term "matrix," since it implies a web of related concepts.[1]

The matrix forms a foundation upon which all else is explained. Once established, the matrix is unidentifiable to the user. It serves, as the philosopher Ludwig Wittgenstein states, as "the inherited background against which I distinguish true and false." It is a "world-picture" underlying all of our inquiry:

> The propositions describing this world-picture might be part of a kind of mythology. And their role is like that of rules of a game; and the game can be learned purely practically, without learning any explicit rules.[2]

Furthermore, the matrix is not open to examination:

> It may be for example that *all enquiry on our part* is set so as to exempt certain propositions from doubt, if they are ever formulated. They lie apart from the route traveled by enquiry.[3]

The matrix serves as the given upon which all else hinges. For example, consider the "God question": A parent tells a child that God has made all things. The child, seemingly naturally, asks, "Who made God?" The child's question exposes a part of the matrix; the adult is uncomfortable and announces that "God" is where the questions stop. "No one made God." "God" is an example of "certain propositions" that are "exempt" from doubt.

A matrix is culture specific, but it need not be embedded in the language. A language can be expanded to accommodate shared notions. European peoples, for example, have many different languages, each having "meanings" that apparently evade literal translation into another language. Nevertheless, they have had enough common experiences to have a shared matrix.

A matrix is exposed when two people from different cultures come together. They find it difficult to communicate with one another—their frames of reference do not meet. Again, Wittgenstein has an enlightening comment on this situation:

> We . . . say of some people that they are transparent to us. It is, however, important as regards this observation that one human being can be a complete enigma to another. We learn this when we come into a strange country with entirely strange traditions; and, what is more, even given a mastery of the country's language. We do not *understand* the people. (And not because of not knowing what they are saying to themselves.) We cannot find our feet with them.
>
> They are not readily accessible.
>
> If a lion could talk, we could not understand him.[4]

There is a *context* underlying a "strange people's" observable actions that is inaccessible to someone from outside that field. Could we understand the context of a lion's field of meaning? Wittgenstein does not think so.

The lack of shared contexts, of shared matrix, leads to the notion of *incommensurability*, which is attacked from time to time by those who are threatened by the idea that there might be different explanations for similar phenomena. Anyone, however, who is fluent in two or more languages knows that there are some nuances in each language that cannot be translated. Jokes are an example.

An attempt to understand the matrix of another society is complicated by the fact that we try to fit the strange ideas of a "strange people" into our own frame of reference without realizing that no such fit exists. Another complication is an attempt to bring to the "other" concepts from within our own context. In the first case we see the other's actions and say "that is just like this . . ." In the second case we set out to see what the other thinks about a specific concept from within our own cultural context. In both cases one looks for similarities and ends by ignoring crucial differences that, despite apparent similarity, ensure continued lack of communication.

A society that has power over another is not in a position to understand the matrix of the society over which it exercises power. The less powerful society's matrix, however, is constantly under attack. Through this attack both matrices are exposed. Two frames of reference in the same place will be competitors for "truth" and "validity," as witness the former Yugoslavia where Roman Catholic, Orthodox Catholic, and Muslim are inhabiting the same area. The conflict between America's indigenous peoples and the European colonial is another example. Early in the contact between the two peoples, there was an attempt on the part of the colonial to "coexist." This was followed by an attempt to exterminate the other, then the incarceration of the other (in bounded locations), and finally the turning over of the indigenous to the religious missionaries. The attempt to convert the "other" to one's own matrix, regardless of how well intended or peaceable, is extermination by other means.

The existence of differing matrices among unalike people need not be a source of conflict. There are cultures that assume that the member of another culture will operate under a different matrix; this difference can be defined as a *natural* occurrence among the species. An *absolute* sense of truth then gives way to a sense of *relative* truth. The problem comes in when a culture has a sense only of *absolute* truth. All cultural groups not sharing the sense of truth with this group will be seen as existing in error. Or as Wittgenstein puts it, "Where two principles really do meet which cannot be reconciled with one another, then each man declares the other a fool and heretic.[5]

Among North American indigenous groups there existed a shared assumption that the group unlike one's own would have a different "truth" based on experiences and locations unique to the other. It is this notion of the assumed difference of the other that allowed the early European colonists to survive in countries unlike their own. The indigenous people, upon first encounter with the European, are portrayed as "helpful" and "generous." It is only when the indigenous peoples discover that the European does not share his sense of land and occupation that the troubles begin.

The linguist Benjamin Whorf claims that differences in language reflect differences in matrices, and both arise from the fact that different peoples focus on different aspects of the universe as most important. Peoples, according to Whorf, "segment" the universe in different fashions.[6] Their languages reflect this focus. Unlike Whorf, however, I do not think that the difference is a matter of language. A child, before the acquisition of language, is already exposed to a "worldview" that he will come to share as a sense of "reality" with the other members of the group. The child may, as Wittgenstein states it, learn the rules "purely practically, without learning any explicit rules." The child learns a way of being in the world.

The problem of discovering the matrix of understanding is a bit more complex than merely learning it in the course of infancy and childhood. I was made aware of the existence of different matrices in my own home. My father had one set of explanations and attitudes. My mother, Hispanic and Catholic, another. Outside of my own home there is another matrix. My father does not say that one is right and another wrong. There is no charge here of "fool" or "heretic." There is simply a method of doing that is ours and theirs. For the sake of survival, I learn from my father that it is necessary not only to know the different ways of being, but to know where they are appropriate. I gather also that I am free to select my own actions in the face of different ways of being.

Where there is no awareness of competing matrices, there is no awareness of the possibility of differing, equally valid ways of being. If I, as my father's child, act differently from my schoolmates, I am labeled "weird" or "stupid" by those children. But even though there is no reinforcement of my own way of being in the classroom, I have a refuge in my own home. It was not for nothing that indigenous children were taken away from their parents and placed in boarding schools. Where there is no reinforcement of a competing "paradigm," it cannot continue to exist. In most cases of the boarding school experience, children were forbidden to room with children of their own tribe. The reason given for this action was to promote assimilation into the mainstream. In actuality, it was to eradicate a way of being. Rapid assimilation did not necessarily follow. Suicide rates were high in boarding schools, and the attempt to replace one tradition with another too often led to an individual who did not know either.

Understanding the existence of two matrices in the experience of the indigenous person was a crucial component to growing up with any sense of identity at all. The child learns early that there are different expectations of his actions from within each group. The home group emphasizes the sense of the individual as a part of a whole; the European emphasizes the individual. My cousins and I, in the classroom, would have preferred to accomplish a task together. The teacher demands that each work in isolation. The teacher is authoritarian; the Native child's home life instills the value of self-directed behavior.

From each direction comes a set of contrasting stereotypes. The White Man is self-centered, greedy, acquisitive, unaware of the needs of others, unaware of the fact that he shares the world with other things, unaware of a living earth. The White Man gives orders and expects others to follow them; he asks for things and for favors: Bring me that book! Would you bring me that book? Would you do this for me? He announces his feelings: I have a headache! I am thirsty! I am tired! I want this . . . ! I want you to do . . . ! And so on. The Native child, on the other hand, is stereotyped by the following: he insists on socializing with his friends; he doesn't take care of his things (he lets others play with his toys). He is sneaky—he always seems to be watching everybody else. He never asks for anything. He won't do what I say. I never know what he is thinking.

I know now the reasons for my "weird" behavior. I know also why my behavior is labeled "weird." Here are the above-listed behaviors with their cultural opposites:

| | |
|---|---|
| self-centered | One should be aware of others. |
| greedy; acquisitive | What is the good of having anything if you can't share it? |

| | |
|---|---|
| unaware of the needs of others | No one should be reduced to asking something of others. |
| unaware of other living things | What other life forms am I disturbing? |
| unaware of a living Earth | One ought not take the world for granted. |
| ordering others about | No human being has a right to order others to do one's will. |
| announcing one's feelings | Everyone should be able to see that I am feeling sad, angry, etc. |
| direct | I must be aware of the needs and feelings of others. I cannot broadcast my feelings or needs; it would imply that I thought the other was unaware or uncaring. ("sneaky") |

Learning all of these things in the first few years of school is a daunting task for any child. Under threat of punishment or derision, the task is doubled. But it is just such incidences that call forth the awareness of the existence of competing matrices. Knowing the matrix of the demanding other would certainly facilitate the task of the indigenous child. The teacher, however, does not know why she does what she does: it is simply what one does, how one "trains" a child.

At the root of the teacher's demands and expectations is a worldview that is based on a very specific definition, or description, of the world, of human beings, and of the role of human beings in that world. Will exposing the source of that worldview, of the matrix, make the user of a specific matrix aware of *who* he is?

# Method: A Search for Fundamental Concepts

My approach to the study of Native American philosophy is based on the idea that all cultural groups have stories that "explain" the origins of the world, of the nature of man, and the ways man should conduct himself in the world as it is described. Philosophical method, first and foremost, should be, in its application to comparative philosophy, a search for concepts that serve as foundational notions for other ideas and practices observed within a specific cultural group. We have, for example, the Native American concept of the relatedness of all beings, and also, the concept of the Earth as a Mother. The questions here should be, "What *kind* of a world would it have to be in order to justify a claim that *all beings are related*? What description of the world would justify referring to the Earth as a *mother*? Attendant questions would have to involve a specific description of what it is to be human in that *kind* of a world. A focus should be on the interdependence of the answers to questions within a particular culture.

The original "answers" to questions concerning the world are based on observations of the world that inquirers inhabit. An "answer" must have some relation to the actual existential circumstances of a people in order that the "truth" or validity of the explanation might convince others to agree to its explanatory strength. Following a cue from Emile Durkheim's explanation of the origin of religious belief,[1] one might say that what first begins in the experience of human beings—in a specific set of circumstances and location—later becomes framed in sacred language. Once the sacred language and its accompanying rituals are set in place, it is no longer necessary to ask essential questions. The original "answers" become a *conceptual framework* that underlies all subsequent inquiry.

The ancient Greeks, for example, begin with a conceptual framework built around the actions of the gods in the present course of the world. With the appearance of the philosophers known as the *pre-Socratics*, the questions shift from trying to decipher the actions of the gods to a more basic question: What are things, really? The gods do not disappear, but the form of inquiry changes.

A similar change takes place in the Western world during the Renaissance. The conceptual framework offered the West by the Catholic Church becomes less satisfactory as the people are exposed to new questions concerning the description of the world. Eventually the explanations of the church must make accommodations to undeniable observations that serve to explain the world to its inhabitants. Science, in this case, replaces the church in its authority to define the world. This is not an overnight occurrence. The rediscovery of the speculations of the ancient Greeks begins its appearance in the West in the twelfth century; the years allotted to the Renaissance, the *rebirth of speculative inquiry*, are usually given as 1350 to 1550. The discovery of the antiquity of the earth and solar system does not take place until the eighteenth century, and Darwin's view does not occur until the nineteenth century.

A conceptual framework, once in place, is not easy to eradicate or replace—it requires more than merely substituting one concept for another. A major concept underlies many more and related concepts. To change a framework is to change a society. And societies resist change. In the West, today, and especially in the United States, there are still large segments of the population that deny the validity of Darwin's theory of evolution, despite its almost unanimous acceptance in the scientific community, and there are even some who deny that the earth is more than six thousand years old.

The indigenous American—despite five hundred years of concerted efforts by government, the military, and educational and religious institutions to eradicate a conceptual framework alien to the West—has managed to maintain a separate identity based on a conceptual framework that still seems to provide a better explanatory framework than that offered by the West. The philosopher's challenge is to explore those basic concepts that lend validity to the American Indian Weltanschauung[2] and find their origins, their force, the difference they make in how people live in the world.

# "They Have a Different Idea about That . . ."

The problem for the indigenous child lies not so much in his making sense of the facts that he must learn, but of making sense of the unspoken and alien context that his teacher assumes is inherent in the child. Because the new context lies unconsciously in the nonindigenous teacher's world picture, she cannot teach it to the child. She assumes he is stupid.

She does not, for example, begin her teaching with such phrases as, "I will teach you that . . . humans are superior to other beings, the world is a dead piece of matter floating in an empty universe, you are alone and in competition with each and every other individual in this classroom, there is something flawed about human beings and we will strive to surmount those failings." None of this is said because the teacher is unaware that such ideas lie at the root of her efforts. The child may know that the context is very different from what he is used to but he cannot articulate those differences. He assumes he is stupid.

The child cannot evade the educational system. It is illegal not to go to school. He is told he is going to learn; he is not told that much of that learning consists of proselytizing, or social conditioning for another form of social and cultural community than his own. If he has enlightened parents, they can assist the child in making sense of what he is taught at school. My own father prefaced most of his explanations about cultural differences with the words, "They have a different idea about that . . ."[1]

The Native American and the Euro-American see the world from two different perspectives. In general, the Euro-American conducts his attempts to understand his world on the assumption that there are definitive explanations to be discovered. He searches for what I call the "universal-absolute:" there will be one universal—all encompassing—and absolute—beyond question—Truth.

The Native American, on the other hand, understands the world as a more complex place. There can be no universals in the face of an infinity of complexity. There are no absolutes. The complexity is infinite because part of that complexity is change, motion. Whatever is, is in motion, and change is inevitable in the world. Motion, change, and complexity are absolutes. But they are absolutes that differ from the notion that there is one TRUTH that can be discovered.

A definition of a 'true' statement, in the Euro-American sense, implies a static state that will persist unchanging for all time. Statements of this sort are framed as "All mammals are . . . ," or, "Given that . . . , it follows that . . ." The purpose of the search for an absolute, universal Truth is the notion that such knowledge grants a high degree of control vested in the hands of the knower. A Native American cannot make such statements. He could, at most, say: "Mammals have a tendency to . . . ," or, "Since we have experienced (X) . . . , there is a probability that (Y)." Such an attitude, on the part of the Native American, does not lead to the view that humans are, or ever can be, in a position to exercise control over the world.

The goal of persons who envision themselves in a world of motion, change, and complexity is to create and work on maintaining stability in the face of all of that. The goal of the seeker for a definitive "truth" is to "lock in" something that is unchanging.

The paradox of the position of the "truth seeker" is that change, which cannot be denied, is then viewed as a directed motion toward the goal of achieving an unchanging *something*. In the West, the notion of *directed motion* is called "progress." "Change" is understood as a *necessary* marker for the arrival of (or at least, *approach* toward) the definitive, the unchanging. This notion is best exemplified by such claims as "the end of history," or the claim of physicist Stephen Hawking that his work will lead to knowledge of "the mind of God." No such claim could be made by a Native American.

The goal of the Native American, deriving from a different set of assumptions altogether, is to create an island of stable motion in a sea of random, but predictable, motion. An example of "random but predictable motion" would be the pattern of wood grain: there is always such a pattern (the *predictable*) but what that pattern will be is dependent on numerous, incalculable factors—this is the *random* element. 'Stability,' for the Native American, unlike its connotation for the Western thinker, is not synonymous with a static, unchanging state. 'Stability' requires action for its maintenance. 'Stability' denotes, for the Native American, a balancing act.

But there cannot be only one type of balancing act in a universe exhibiting numerous "motions." There will be numerous and diverse "balancing acts." There cannot be one all encompassing 'Truth' (or 'true' way of doing, or defining, anything) in the face of the diversity and complexity exhibited by the universe. Instead of 'Truth' there will be 'truths.' There will be *perspectives*—each dependent upon and relative to one's circumstances in the world. Each perspective, in its own environment, or circumstances, will be 'true' or 'valid'—in *that* environment, in *those* circumstances. He does not assume that the person from a different 'space' will share his notions. He does not assume the 'incorrectness' of the other's perspective when it does not coincide with his own.

Thus, a Native American confronts a problem when speaking to or writing for a non-Native American audience. The Native American, in any form of communication with someone outside his own group (Cheyenne, Cree, Pueblo, European, etc.) assumes that he is speaking from one very specific perspective and that he is addressing another coming from a very different perspective. He does not assume what the Westerner calls "objectivity"—that is, that there is a neutral ground upon which all perspectives cease to count. The Native American is speaking as 'subject' to other 'subjects.' His observations are *subjective*. The 'subjective,' however, has a very different meaning in this context than it does for the Western speaker. 'Subjectivity,' in the West, carries the implication of a highly personal, and most likely, *unshared*, perspective. The different concepts of 'subjectivity' rest on two very different definitions of what it is to be an *individual*.

In the West, the individual is assumed to be a subject of his own making: his views, his values, his *perspectives* are 'things' that he has come to of his own accord. He assumes that there is a world "outside" that which he makes for himself so that he can make such statements as, "Let's leave ourselves outside of this for just a moment . . ." The Native American assumes something quite different: his views, his values, his perspectives are shared notions. He shares these with the members of his family, his group. He speaks in the terms of "we" and not "I."

The "we" of the Native American (as in, "We believe [or 'say'] this about that . . .") would, perhaps, be more correctly defined as the *intrasub-*

*jective*. That is, there are qualities that I share with others of my own kind (views, values, etc.) and do not share with others unlike us. The Native American, just as the Euro-American, can make the distinction between what he personally believes (thinks, feels, knows) and what he shares with his fellows. But he recognizes that much of what he believes, knows, and so on is colored by who and what he is. The Euro-American does not acknowledge that he has an "inherited" worldview. An awareness of an inherited worldview is not necessary as long as *all of one's communication remains within a very narrow circle of one's like-minded fellows*.

The recognition of the rightful existence of the "other" is based on the metaphysical notion that the world consists of very different places and circumstances. Each place, each circumstance, contains within itself that which is accommodated to the specific place or circumstance. There is no assumption here that "all humans are alike," or that some such general notion as "mankind" can be used to apply to the human species except in a very superficial sense. The general term 'cats,' for instance, can be used to say something very general about a particular species. But to carry to any further extent the statements that can be made on such terms is rather difficult given that there are jaguars, lions, lynx, tigers, and domestic cats. To the Native American, the fact that lions and tigers and jaguars exist is equivalent to there being "Europeans," "Chinese," "Navajo," and "Anishinaube." Real knowledge consists of a recognition of the existence of *classes* and not merely the recognition of the existence of *species*.

It is not necessary for the Native American to identify himself as 'human' (one need not trouble oneself with stating the obvious). It *is* necessary to identify himself as a class, or "phylum": "I am a member of this family, this clan, this group, this place." The identifiers serve as notice to the alien *other* of difference and as an informal request for recognition as *other*. A person of the West need simply state a personal name; in doing so he makes an appeal to some understood, but unstated, sense of commonality. He expects also, although this too is unstated, to not have to deal with differences. The Native American gives notice of not only who he is, but where he is "coming from."

(I once read a text written for medical personnel preparing to work on the Navajo reservation. The text had a section on what to expect on meeting the first Navajo patient: "He will begin by telling you where he lives, what his clan is and who his family is. Only then will he tell you his name [if at all!].")

Without this stated perspective, the Native American feels, there would be no way for the speaker to know why he says what he says. 'Meaning,' for the Native American, is embedded in context—is, in fact, given meaning through context. I sat on the committee overseeing the thesis of a Native American master's student. She had prefaced her research with a chapter "about herself" (as the non-Native Americans on her committee described it). I, too, had faced such criticism as a graduate student. I tried to tell the student what it was that the rest of the committee members objected to in such an approach. She didn't hear me: "What sense could anyone make of what my research is about if they don't know who I am? How could they understand why I did this specific research and in this specific way?" Since we were not in a Native American school and certainly not in a Native American "world," I finally managed to convince her that her preliminary chapter, which we both understood as "essential," could be an addendum to her research chapters. "If you want the master's degree," I said, "this is the only way that you can receive this degree." The final presentation of her thesis—with addendum—felt as "wrong" to her as her inclusion of the "who-I-am" did to her non-Native American committee members. She did receive the master's degree.

In the *Philosophical Investigations*, Ludwig Wittgenstein addresses his questions about the possibility of different conceptual schemes in the following:

> [I]f anyone believes that certain concepts are absolutely the correct ones, and that having different ones would mean not realizing something that we realize—then let him imagine certain very general facts of nature to be different from what we are used to, and the formation of concepts different from the usual ones will become intelligible to him.
>
> Compare a concept with a style of painting. For is even our style of painting arbitrary? Can we choose one at pleasure? (The Egyptian, for instance.) Is it a mere question of pleasing and ugly?[2]

Wittgenstein stresses that it is not the "very general facts of nature" that guide us but rather our specific concepts of those facts of nature. If we are to understand peoples of a cultural perspective different from our own, we must first be aware that we, too, are driven by a perspective. Cultures differ from one another because they derive, or are based on, different understandings of the nature of the world. In the case of the "Egyptian . . . style of painting," the conceptual framework for the depiction of the world precedes the mechanics of painting. An "oriental" painting is not a matter of choice but a way of seeing the world—just as is a "Western" way of seeing or painting. The "style" is not visible to the artist as he creates his work—it is the picture through which he views the world. Westerners, taking themselves as the standard for measurement, are not aware that they, too, have a style that is unique unto themselves. All non-Westerners, however, can readily pick out a "Western style of painting" or thinking or seeing and interpreting.

From within one's own conceptual framework (the framework that is shared with the rest of the members of one's culture) it is possible to ignore the framework—as long as one communicates only with one's fellows. This is usually the case with Westerners. Their communication takes place within a closed circle—everything that exists outside that circle of reference is seen as "other" and is subject to understanding only after extensive interpretation. The interpretative network, however, is of their own making (or it would make no sense to them), so that the interpretations lead less to knowledge of the other as other than to an extension of one's own way of seeing: the new is made familiar.

From a Euro-American perspective the works of the Native American, before being put through the filtering process of interpretation, appear cryptic—there is much that is unsaid. From within the Native American circle of communication there is much that need not be said but is, rather, understood. It is not necessary for the Native American to say to his fellows (before each utterance), "Let us assume . . . that the world is dynamic, in infinite motion, and I can only make a statement through one of, perhaps, infinite perspectives." It is, likewise, not necessary for the Euro-American to say to his fellow, "Let us assume . . . that we are speaking for all humans when we talk about human nature; that we believe that there is one all-encompassing truth to which we all direct our research; that we are a superior species among inferiors; or that a semi-omniscient 'objective' perspective is possible." Our conceptual framework is a sort of shorthand that is assumed; it is what gives substance and meaning to our utterances; it is why it is so easy to communicate with those like ourselves.

Is it necessary to carry about a tract outlining the metaphysics of a particular group in order to "understand" what they are saying? Perhaps not. But it is certainly necessary, in the name of good scholarship, to have done some comparison of cultural *explanations* for some of the "very general facts of nature."

To assume that one's own conceptual framework or "explanations" are the only possible "answers" to the questions posed is precisely what the term *ethnocentricity* covers. A dialogue with an alien other requires, first of all, an acceptance that there is the possibility of an other as *other* (and not simply as a distortion of oneself). In the second place, one must be willing to accept the other as *equal*; that is, both parties have something to say and can provide their own explanations for their end of the dialogue. There lies still another problem in "cross-cultural" communication: the writer must grapple with the problem of determining which of the possible audiences one is writing for. A Native American must choose his "voice": will it be a Native American audience or a Euro-American? The Euro-American seldom has to consider this dilemma when setting down his thoughts. Beyond the fact that he might consider whether he is speaking to a generalist audience or one of specialists, he need not consider a cross-cultural, or "perspectival," approach.

# Language as Window

An exploration into a culture with which we are unfamiliar exposes us to more than new ideas and practices. We must encounter the language of that culture. In the case of North American indigenous peoples, we find that most of them speak English fluently and that some of them no longer speak their own native tongues fluently or at all. Nevertheless, the languages embody concepts that have survived the loss of a native language. Language is a window that frames a particular view of the world. Even when the window disappears, the view that it framed remains.

Benjamin Whorf,[1] a linguist working in the mid-twentieth century, explored the particularity, the incommensurability, of languages, specifically through an analysis of Native American languages. His work has been subject to much debate. Nevertheless, he has contributed to the awareness that other cultures, other languages, may not contain the same concepts. My own experience confirms this. In a conversation with a Shoshone speaker, I asked how the term 'God' was translated, since, from my own experience, there were no linguistic equivalents in North American indigenous languages. She said that they did not interpret the term; they simply used the known term, 'God.' In a similar fashion, the term that they used in her language to indicate the Shoshone idea of the sacred or divine was not translated into English. 'God' and the terms used to designate the "source (or force) of all things" are not equivalents—they are two different and incommensurable terms.

It may not be necessary to become fluent in a culture's language in order to understand the language structure, but it is necessary to have some knowledge of that structure. Even as a language conveys information through its structure, however, Whorf also realizes that language is based on some conceptual notions that are an integral part of a cultural group. He emphasizes that the languages of the Indo-European family—which are most of the European languages—can be as different as Norwegian and Italian. Nevertheless they share some common concepts. Whorf does not research the concepts themselves but is aware that these may be the source of differentiation:

Actually, thinking is most mysterious, and by far the greatest light upon it that we have is thrown by the study of language. This study shows that the forms of a person's thoughts are controlled by inexorable laws of pattern of which he is unconscious. These patterns are the unperceived intricate systematizations of his own language—shown readily enough by a candid comparison and contrast with other languages, especially those of a different language family. His thinking itself is in a language—in English, in Sanskrit, in Chinese. And every language is a vast pattern-system, different from others, in which are culturally ordained the forms and categories by which the personality not only communicates, but also analyzes nature, notices or neglects types of relationship and phenomena, channels his reasoning, and builds the house of his consciousness.[2]

Of the "vast pattern-system" that underlies our spoken language, Whorf says, in a note to the above passage, "much thinking never brings in words at all but manipulates whole paradigms, word-clauses, and such grammatical orders 'behind' or 'above' the focus of personal consciousness."

As an example of this "pattern-system" that may lie beneath our conscious awareness, consider the way that we "assume" a definition (or paradigm) of the planet we live on. We need not remind ourselves, if we are members of what Whorf calls the "SAE" (Standard Average European) group, that the Earth is an inanimate form of dumb matter; it is simply *there*, requiring no second thought on our part as we step onto its "surface." We are made aware of the Earth's "animate" character only when something unusual occurs, as in, for example, an earthquake. We are accustomed to assuming that we are walking and living on the surface of a ball that is more or less smooth.

Consider, however, another paradigm: What if we view "the Earth" not as a ball in "empty space," but like the inside of a raw egg? The Earth is the yolk, swimming in the egg white—which we know commonly as the "atmosphere," but usually disregard as part of the Earth. In this portrayal, or "paradigm," we do not so much *walk* on the surface of the Earth as *swim* in a narrow area surrounding the skin of "the yolk." The Earth, in this sense, is not a simple hard surface that we need not take into consideration when we plan our actions. The Earth becomes a more fragile "thing." Its permeability is exposed, its "surface" becomes less sure. In this scenario, we are like the creatures that dwell on the ocean floor; perhaps a fish in water is as "unaware" of the water as we are of the atmosphere that sustains us. We become aware of the equivalent of the Earth's "albumen" only when its consistency changes, in a wind storm, for example, or when the air is excessively polluted. The idea of being *in something* (the Earth as the inside of an egg) would result in a very different set of "forms and categories" underlying our languages than if we saw ourselves as existing on the surface of "a ball in empty space."

The egg analogy would not be so unfamiliar to many of the indigenous peoples of the American Southwest, who envision the female Earth as surrounded by a male fertilizing "sky." The reality of the Sky-Father and Earth-Mother in an unavoidable and eternal embrace would then "make sense" to those who presently see the analogies as mere figments of the imaginations. The philosopher Spinoza likened our existence to that of a cell in the bloodstream: the lone cell would be unaware of the fact that it is merely a part of a greater whole. The people with the imagery of the Sky-Father/Earth-Mother whole would be individual blood cells participating in a dance of existence and nonexistence, with one exception: they would be aware that this was the fact of their existence, a "knowing" blood cell, so to speak.

The work of Benjamin Whorf alerts us to the possibility of different ways of interpreting the world. Stuart Chase, in the foreword to Whorf's *Language, Thought, and Reality*, says that Whorf presents us with two major ideas: "*First*, that all higher levels of thinking are dependent on language. *Second*, that the structure of the language one habitually uses influences the manner in which one understands his environment. The picture of the universe shifts from tongue to tongue."[3] Whorf, in presenting the idea of linguistic relativity, and thereby bringing up the possibility of *cultural* relativity, "flatly challenges" the Western belief that all languages refer to "the same thing." Whorf's challenge consists of this statement: "A change in language can transform our appreciation of the Cosmos."

Chase explains the opposing view: "The Greeks took it for granted that back of language was a universal, uncontaminated essence of reason, shared by all men, at least by all thinkers. Words, they believed, were but the medium in which this deeper effulgence found expression. It followed that a line of thought expressed in any language could be translated without loss of meaning into any other language."[4]

But not all American indigenous peoples are fluent in their native language. This has been the result, first, of an attempt to eradicate "primitive thinking;" and secondly, an attempt to eliminate "the Indian" through total assimilation. When indigenous children were taken away from their homes to boarding schools, they were forcibly placed with children of another tribe so that they could not communicate in any language other than English. They were also provided with a new worldview through the ministrations of the missionaries who were often in charge of the schools.

Nevertheless, a view of the world that was "Indian" managed to survive all attempts to eradicate the paradigm. The reason that this was so is that behind language there is a "pattern system" of "forms and categories" that could be taught without full knowledge of the language. The "pattern" consisted of more than words and speech; it included also a way of being in the world. This latter is taught through attitudes, through practices, through teaching relationships between people and between people and the Earth. By the time the educators and missionaries abducted the child at about the age of five or six, such attitudes and relationships had already been established. The family, regardless of the educators, could reinforce such a pattern in the home and in the community. There was, in other words, beyond language, a *context* to being "Indian" that eluded the attempts at eradication.

# The Philosophical Questions

How have a people managed to maintain a worldview unlike that of those who now dominate their world? That there is such a worldview may be denied by some, but no Native American would accept this denial. The Native American differs from the Euro-American, not simply because he may have a different physical appearance, but because he interprets the world in a manner that is not consistent with the interpretation of the Euro-American. Whether the Euro-American wishes to admit this or not, the "paradigms," "model," or "worldview" offered by Christianity is the *implicit* model of the universe underlying the "modern" (read 'Euro-American') explanation of the world and of man that is offered up in the schools.

A Native American child does not encounter merely a new set of facts that he must accommodate into his lexicon of knowledge when he enters the school system. He also encounters a new set of expectations with which he is unfamiliar and for which there are no explanations.

The organization of the schoolroom is, to begin with, very alien. Unlike his home, the organization is one of extreme regimentation. Children sit in rows of seats that all face in one direction, toward the teacher. The teacher, alone, has a right to speak. She, or he, is the sole authority in the classroom. The student must not leave his assigned place without permission, and only the teacher grants permission. The Euro-American classroom is an exercise in authoritarianism.

The process of being and learning in a Native American environment is very different. First of all, children are not subjected to regimentation and adults do not represent authority that exists beyond question. What is taught at home is mutual respect: no adult has sole authority over a child and no child has authority over any adult. All human beings are equal, including children. Children, however, "*never having been here before*," are accorded a certain attention that is viewed as the responsibility of all adults. The child is understood to be in need of being shown how to act (or *be*) in *this world*. There is an assumption here that is missing in Euro-

American circles: that the child must be socialized into a particular pattern of behavior that is understood to be specific to the group of which he is a member. The pattern consists of showing what is involved in living within a community of others. Paramount in this involvement is how one's actions affect the others—the child is taught to be acutely aware of his own actions as well as the actions of others and the consequences of those actions.

The idea of the 'other' and of the 'community' far exceeds what is seen as "common" in the idea of a typical Euro-American nuclear family. The Native American "family" is the entire group. The "community" includes not only the family but the surrounding environment. One learns to be aware not only of one's actions and their consequences toward other people but toward the "ground" one inhabits. There is an assumption about *what* it is to be human that underlies all of this training of *how* to be human.

The assumption is that humans are not fully human when they come into this world—rather, they have the capacity to become a human *being*. A child has all of the faculties required to adapt to the group and to the environment in which they reside: he is keyed in to being a group-being, rather than an isolated individual; he is "programmed" to learn a language, which allows communication between members of the group; and he is naturally curious about the world around him. The child is not viewed as something that must be *allowed (given the freedom)* to learn, primarily through experience. With the assistance of the entire group, the child learns to become a human being according to how the group defines a *human being*.

There is another assumption related to this view: that each group is assumed to be different, to varying degrees, from one's own and will have a different definition of how one conducts oneself as a human being. 'Human,' in other words, is defined by specific groups in specific ways. The flexibility of a child's nature allows that he may be shown how to be an Apache, a Sioux, or an Englishman. For this reason, the first years of a Native American child are the most important years. In these few years the child is given a worldview—without books, without authoritarian means —and this is the child that is turned over to the official educational authorities of an alien society.

What may seem to be a digression into child-raising is very important here because it shows how it is that a worldview is inculcated, despite attempts to eradicate the Native American way of being-in-the-world. By the time the child reaches the age when he must enter the "American" school system, he already has a worldview. He knows his physical surroundings and what group he belongs to; he has learned to expect certain actions from others. He has also acquired a methodology of learning. The Native American child, when he enters the American formal system of "teaching" children, confronts not only a group of strangers but a system of *being* that is totally unlike his own. It may be argued that all children encounter an alien environment when they leave home to go to school. The Native American child, however, enters what could be described as a "parallel universe." The trees, the mountains, the air—the *physical* place— may be the same; the *philosophical* space is not.

An example might shed some light on this claim: My daughter and a non-Native American school friend both gave birth to their first child in the early fall. On a sunny spring day the two young women came together to give their infants their first outing. My daughter's friend has the back-seat of their car loaded with the paraphernalia she thinks necessary for the outing. My daughter has only her son. At a nearby park my daughter places her son on a grassy area and he begins to crawl and inspect the strange territory. The friend, on the other hand, leaves her son in a car seat while she spreads out a blanket for the child and then proceeds to dump onto the blanket an assortment of familiar toys. Once the child is on the blanket, he is admonished about touching the ground—the grass is "yucky," he will get "dirty"—and the mother distracts the infant from exploring by handing him various toys. Occasionally the mother takes the infant's hands and walks him about on the blanket. My daughter follows her infant as he crawls on the ground, introduces him to trees, flowers, clouds, the wind on his face.

The non-Native American mother introduces her child into a potentially hazardous and alien environment; she offers him "safe" alternatives through the presence of the blanket and the toys. Everything else is "dirty." My grandson, on the other hand, is encouraged to touch, taste, and explore a new and delightful place. The non-Native American infant is taught to *confront* his environment; our child is shown what the world contains. This is the stuff of which a worldview is built. Without language, without explanation, each of the young women is saying to their infant: this is where you live. Each child is introduced into the "real" world: one carries with him a man-made environment that proclaims safety amid a potentially hostile earth; the other into a strange but interesting place that he is expected to "know" intimately.

Ludwig Wittgenstein, in his work *On Certainty*, explores the means by which we come to have a foundational knowledge of the world we take for granted. "But I did not get my picture of the world by satisfying myself of its correctness; nor do I have it because I am satisfied of its correctness. No: it is the inherited background against which I distinguish between true and false."[1]

The experience of the world that my daughter and her friend introduce to their sons is a means of providing a *world-picture* that will constitute the "inherited background" that grants reality to all subsequent experiences of and in the world. The existence of these two unalike "world-pictures" is the basis upon which I make my claim that the Native American child confronts not only new physical surroundings when he enters the formal school system but a *different philosophical space*.

The confrontation of the two systems, or "games," as Wittgenstein would have it, leads to philosophical questions that even our children must entertain. Those questions are,

1. What is the world?
2. What is it to be human in that world?
3. What is the *role* of a human in that world?

## III  WHAT IS THE WORLD?

How did the world come to be the way it is?
Do the stories we tell about the origin of the
world make any difference to who we are and
how we live? What is the relation of human
beings to the rest of creation? What is the world
made of—matter or energy, stones or songs or
spirit, the breath of the wind, beauty, harmony,
or some relation among these? Does time flow
like a river, spiral like a whirlwind, float like
ice on a pond—and what difference does that
make? What is real, after all? Are there
many realities, or one?

# How It Is: A Native American Creation Story

*There are many ways of knowing. We can learn through textbooks and academic articles, but also through poetry, dance, stories, music, loving attentiveness, art, experience—so many ways into the human understanding. What follows is an extended poem that Viola Cordova published as a chapbook illustrated with her pen-and-ink drawings. The poem introduces her metaphysics, her understanding of the nature of the world. (The Editors)*

## How It Is

Before there was any thing
There was something
It was mist.
And in the mist
   was absolute Motion.
Some call this circumstance,
   Plasma;
Some call this Energy
We call it,
   Wind.
We call it,
   Sacred.
Because it is Wind
   it is not static
   and because it is
   Wind
   there are fluctuations.
We call these fluctuations,
   Things.
We call these fluctuations,
   A Universe

A Galaxy
A Solar System
And in this field of Motion,
    there are smaller
    and smaller
    fields
and when the fields are dense enough—
    they hold themselves together.
We call them
    Stars
We call them
    Suns
We call
    One Star—
    *Ours*
We call it—
    Holy Sun.
Oh, Holy Sun
    the Mother Earth
    is in your debt.
From it she derives
    her creative energy.
And from deep within
    her own energy
    she derives us
    All.
From life
    from the living something,
    that always is
    and always will be,
    comes more life.
We call it Holy Wind.
There is not anything
    that is not suffused
    with Wind.
    We call the wind's creations
    and sub-creations

"objects" and things—
they are, more properly,
fields.
A field is a vortex of
Wind
a whirlpool, a whirlwind.
We know that this is so because
at our fingertips,
at our toes,
at our hair,
are the vortices
that connect us
to all the other things
the air
the water
the rock
the tree
the grass
the deer
the Earth
the Sun
the universe.
What we see and call
"Things"
and, "Many Things,"
are in actuality
only one thing.
We call it
WIND.
We call it
Holy.
Some call the wind
"energy,"
and they call the
many things
"matter"
and so they see

two things
where we see
only one.
   It is *matterized*
   *energy*.
   That we call
   WIND,
   when it becomes
   THINGS.
There is no absolute space—
   if Wind is everywhere
   how could there be void
   and emptiness?
There is no absolute time—
   if Wind fluctuates
   how could there be
   anything but motion?
Time is the counting
   Of motion.
Space is the discounting
   Of the in-between.
And so it is.
   How what is was
   and how what was not
   came to be.
And so
   there came to be
   She,
   She we call Mother,
   Woman,
   Ground,
   Area,
   Na'ho'dzaan.
She is *not*—
   a dead rock
   a blue ball,
   suspended,

in empty space.
She is fiery egg,
    the yolk—
    a smoldering cauldron
    separated from the misty
    albumen of atmosphere
    by the thinnest of crusts
    the shell—
    a permeable barrier
    receptive, enveloping.
She is a minor sun,
    following, like a child,
    the grandparent.
    like a child,
    connected
    round and round
    and round.
But, unlike a child
    and, like a woman
    She produces, from within
    the living fire
    all manner of things.
WHITE SHELL WOMAN
WHITE BUFFALO WOMAN
CHANGING WOMAN
SHE WHO SPEWS FORTH
    POSSIBILITIES. POTENTIALITIES.
From deep within
    through layers of being
    out of the yolk
    and into the albumen
    come the potentialities
    to be finished
in the shadows of stones
in the rays of the sun
in the warmth of the waters
in the cool of the mountain

in the heart of the desert
    come the myriads of things.
like a living being
    she makes no two things
    exactly alike.
    a jaguar is not a tiger
    a tiger is not a lion
    a lion is not a cheetah
    one cheetah is not another cheetah.
She it is who creates
    In the light of the sun
    In the path of the wind
    In the belly of fire
    She
    The Mother.
diversity is her signature.
And there is motion.
If something exists
    it is in motion
    and if there is motion
    there is life.
    Everything that exists
    is in motion
    Therefore, everything that exists,
    is alive.
Picture a landscape of shifting sand
    Nothing stays still
    yet it is the same.
    The sand ripples
    forms dunes
    shifts.
This is the way of the Universe:
    Stable shifting
    Shifting stability.
This is the way of a human:
    Stable shifting
    Shifting stability.

In harmony,
Balanced.
We are not rocks,
we do not know of what
a rock has awareness.
We are not grass
nor water
nor bees.
We are not those things
but it is by those things
that we are.
We are no more than a blade of grass
and we are no less.
We all partake,
by virtue of our being,
in that which is sacred.
We are all equals
for how could inequality arise
if we are essentially
the same?
We are all siblings
of the same mother.
We are all children
of the same father.
connected
related
through
the one
wind.
The same, but different.
I am not a rock.
I am not a bear.
I am not water.
If a rock falls
it is what a rock does.
If a bear is hungry,
it eats what it likes.

If the water floods
　　it does what water does.
I, alone, can know
　　the consequences
　　of my actions.
I, alone, am responsible,
　　and, I am not alone.
Humans are animals of the herd
Language is the bonding mechanism
Empathy is the cause.
Because we are not alone
　　there are no meaningless actions.
I affect the universe
I bring into the universe:
　　poverty
　　wealth　　　　kindness
shame　meanness
pride　ugliness
　　beauty　　　　envy
pain　　sharing
pleasure　　respect
　　hatred　　　　knowledge
horror　　　　ignorance
calm　apathy
　　caring　　　　tolerance
loyalty　　　　intolerance
jealousy　　　　competition
　　cooperation
I am a co-creator
　　I
　　can
　　enhance
　　I
　　can
　　detract
　　I
　　alone

am
   responsible.
BEAUTY
   I can make it.
   But what is it, this thing—
   we call Beauty?
Price, but not arrogance. Strength, but not forcefulness. Courage, but not
foolhardiness. Caution, but not cowardice. Softness, but not weakness.
That is beauty.
And
HOW IT ISN'T.
In the beginning
   (it is said)
There was: Nothing
But how can
   SOMETHING
   arise from
   NOTHING?
It is postulated
   IT WAS GOD
   said some.
   IT WAS VACUUM
   said others.
And God said
   Let There Be
And the vacuum
   that was nothing
   EXPLODED!
The big bang
   It is said.
And that which was nothing
E X P A N D E D
into nothing
which is space
and time began
before which
there was nothing.

It is said.
And I whisper
Is not "GOD" a mere name
    a euphemism
    a metaphor
for . . . SOMETHING?
Is not "VACUUM" a mere name
    a euphemism
    a metaphor
for . . . SOMETHING?
Of course NOT!
    It is a Miracle
    said one.
    It is Mystery
    said another.
(Or . . . A BLACK HOLE).
There must be secrets
    so that we can find them
So that we can say
    "I found it!"
    "He found it!"
So that
    there can be
    medals
    honors
    awards
    elevations
    HEROES
The universe is a machine.
The deity is an engineer
    or perhaps, a chemist.
It all works according
    to laws:
    of ratios
    and forces
    maybe even
    action at a distance

(or by inverse proportions?)
Anyway: $E = mc^2$
And there is a purpose
for the mechanism
 It was made
 so that man
 could rule—
 or at least
 be foreman
 of the maintenance
 department.
Residing in the somewhat
flawed mechanism called
 "BODY"
is a somewhat less flawed:
 "MIND."
The mind operates the body.
It analyzes input,
It creates output.
It is immortal.
It is immaterial.
It is the "ghost in the machine."
The ghost is spiritual
as opposed to the
 mundane
 crass
 material
 and
 functional
It is where the "higher order"
of things happen.
 ONLY HUMANS HAVE "MINDS"
 THEREFORE, THEY ARE NOT—
 AS ARE ALL OTHER THINGS—
 MERE *MECHANISMS*.
Each knows only
its own mind.

It does, however, assume
   that other things
   exist.
Other things may be
   consumed
   used
   led
   organized
   analyzed
   categorized
   and
   other-wized.
All things exist in a hierarchy—
   culminating with the
   Ghost.
The ghost is the culmination
of 4.5 BILLION years of
progressive evolutionary
DEVELOPMENT.
or—
The ghost is an alien infusion
   into an alien and hostile
   environment.
HEADS OR TAILS.
IN ANY CASE—
The goal of the ghost
is to
   surpass
   overcome
   transcend
   supercede
NATURE
   (that which is
   red in tooth
   and claw)
To bring CIVILIZATION
   to the stars

(And, *incidentally*,
   find new resources
   to feed the voracious
   mechanisms of the
   civilized man).

# What Is the World?

All human beings, regardless of whether they are labeled "primitive" or "modern," have a "story" about the world, how it came into being and what it is.

We have become accustomed to believing that such stories are based on imagination and laced with superstition. We are willing to grant that such stories might be based on factual circumstances only in the case of the "story" the modern, Western world has to tell—in which case the term "story" is considered inapplicable. Nevertheless there exist various explanations of how, or even why, the world began.

The term "world" includes the descriptions we give to our immediate geographical surroundings, the planet, and the universe that surrounds us; in this sense, the term more appropriate here would be "worldview." The worldview a people develops provides the foundation for all subsequent knowledge about that world. Human beings, aside from the capacity to communicate with one another through a spoken language, also seem to show a capacity for logical consistency; that is, the definition and/or description of the world that we develop provides the logical ground that gives meaning to our further descriptions of ourselves, as humans, of the other beings with whom we share a planet, and even of the role we declare for ourselves.

Benjamin Whorf says that all human beings, in social groups and sharing a common language, *segment* the world.[1] That is, they see the world around them, choose a few characteristics of that world, and expand on those to build for themselves a portrait of the entire world. In the Standard Average European (SAE) worldview, this world, he says, is portrayed through a language dependent on static nouns. It is a world of cause and effect. Other peoples, and he uses as an example the Hopi Indians of the American Southwest, segment the universe in a very different way. Rather than the static worldview of the Europeans, the Hopi depict a dynamic world of ceaseless and uncaused motion. To portray this world, the Hopi have developed a language largely dominated by verbs. Other American indigenous languages also are dominated by verbs.

How does one develop such different views? The universe exhibits many different characteristics. There are stars that seem static and unchanging; one cultural group may focus on this quality and take it as the "real" aspect of the world. Another may focus on those same stars and notice that there is movement to them, despite their consistency in appearance. The motion becomes more important than the consistent, or unchanging, quality.[2]

The worldviews we develop must have some grounding in a people's factual circumstances in order to acquire validity or credibility. The worldview provides, aside from a simple explanation of our physical circumstances, a strategy for survival. Once this worldview is in place it is very difficult to eradicate, precisely because it provides the structure for everything else we have to say about the world. It becomes the ground upon which we make all of our determinations of truth or falsity. A threat to a specific worldview is a threat to the culture that entertains it. Witness the threat that the theory that the Earth was not at the center of the universe posed to all facets of Western thought. Again, in the mid-nineteenth century, Charles Darwin threatened the standard worldview by proposing a new theory for the origins of human beings; his theory, though accepted by scientists, is a continual thorn in the side of those who have held that the original Christian creation myth is "sacred."

The cosmological theory that a culture adopts serves as a matrix into which all other theories about the world and human beings are woven. To remove the major 'thread' is to threaten all of the others.

The origin of the Western worldview has been made relatively accessible by virtue of having a written history. On the other hand, tracing the origins of a Native American worldview is fraught with several difficulties. First, the Native American cultures of the "New World" were, with the exception of the Aztec and the Maya, nonliterate, or 'oral,' cultures. The majority of attempts to record myths and practices of the Native American were undertaken by people outside the circle of the indigenous peoples. The interpretative network of the outsider could not begin to probe the beliefs of an alien people.

We see this in the early recordings when we come across something that claims to discuss what the indigenous peoples think about "God" or the "Soul" or "Heaven" or "Hell." There is an assumption made that the concepts of a Western society will have direct cognates with the concepts of the indigenous American. But there are many ideas that do not have their counterparts in the clashing cultures. Native Americans, for example, are seen to worship in strange ways—the means of worship are quickly dismissed as "devil-worship," and attempts are made to eradicate, not only the practices and rituals, but the concepts on which those rituals are based. Moreover, the relationship between the Native American and the land is very different from the relationship that Westerners have with their concept of 'land.' The missionaries are originally given the task of 'converting' the natives from one belief system to another.

Secondly, there is a mistake that the early colonists made in believing that they were dealing with a singular group. Since all Europeans in the sixteenth century held a similar worldview derived from Christianity, it was believed that all indigenous persons shared with one another the same ideas and practices. But there were no such thing as "Indians" on the American continents; there were as many as five hundred different cultural groups with their own languages, practices, and geographical groundings. If there were similarities to be found among the indigenous groups, they were not based on any of the views that the European colonists brought with them.

There is no lack today of literature dealing with the various 'creation' myths of American indigenous peoples; ethnographers and anthropologists have had a field day in the Americas. The diversity of peoples has been diminished tremendously; entire groups were eliminated, and among those that have survived, there has been a loss of those very people in whom the culture's knowledge was held, as well as a loss of fluency in the languages of America. Rituals and other practices, educational techniques, for example, were banned by the U.S. government until only recently. Nevertheless, there has been, of late, resurgence in attempts to revive Native languages as well as rituals.

If, at the beginning of the colonization of the Americas, there was no such thing as the singular notion of all indigenous peoples being "Indians," there is now such a thing. This has come about through the fact that Native Americans find that, despite forced attempts to assimilate them conceptually as well as physically, they have more in common with other indigenous groups, regardless of their obvious differences, than they do with the conceptual framework of the European colonizer. So it is possible to identify some of the conceptual commonalities shared by Native Americans.

## There is Something, Rather than Nothing

Today, the major metaphysical view of the West can be depicted by one philosophical question: Why is there *something* rather than *nothing*? There is an assumption here that at one time *there was nothing* (no-thing). Things came into being out of nothing, but that is not possible, therefore a cause is sought. The original metaphysical view postulates a creator-being that *causes* something to begin; the current view, regarded as less metaphysical (meta-physical: beyond the physical) is that the world *begins* out of *nothing*—with a "big bang."

The idea of "nothingness" exists for other peoples also. It is called "the void" by some, and in some instances depicted as "the blackness" (Apache, Pueblo)—but there is a difference in this void: it is not empty. "No-thing" in this depiction is best described as "without definite characteristics"—it is the void out of which arise "the ten thousand things."[3] For the Eastern Apache, one of the indefinite contents of "the blackness" is energy, which is depicted by lightning. It is the action of the lightning on the rest of the blackness that brings distinct things into being.

For some of the ancient Greeks, the idea that something could arise out of nothing seemed absurd: "Out of nothing one can get only nothing." Their major philosophical statement was more on the order of, "There is *something*." And their major concern was to understand *what* that *something* was. One of the intriguing answers is that of Anaximander, who postulates that the *something* is an infinite but indefinite quality out of which all other things arise. He sees a world of ceaseless changes; even humans, he thinks, must have come from some other form, since their present prolonged infancy would not have allowed them to survive. The "forces" of this indefinite "something" mingle and borrow from each other, thus creating the things of the world.

Like the ancient Greeks and Romans, the indigenous peoples of North America believe that *there is something*, rather than *nothing*. A general idea of something that manifests itself in all things is common throughout North America. Different peoples have different names for this, but they are in agreement that it is beyond the gods or spirits or things. The concept of the *something* that manifests itself in all things is difficult to comprehend. Nevertheless this concept does exist. It is variously called "nilch'i" by the Navajo, "natoji" by the Blackfoot, "usen" by the Apache, "manitou" by the Ojibway. Regardless of the names applied to the concept, it is generally thought to be that something that drives, sustains, and is the universe. Nothing exists without the participation of the thing in *natoji*.

Just as the foundational thought of Western societies is the idea that "once there was nothing and then something was brought into existence," the indigenous Americans believe that "something" always has been and manifests into the many diverse things of the world. Each thing is, in a sense, a "part" of the greater whole. Diversity is its hallmark.

## There Is a Diversity of Creations

Taking diversity as a hallmark of "the something," Native Americans do not argue over differences in how the world is described by various groups of human beings. The reason is that each description is assumed to be *local*; the stories of origin (of how humans came to be in their portion of the planet) are assumed to refer to a definite bounded space.[4] One of the unifying factors that Native Americans share is the idea of separate creations. Each group has a creation story that tells only of their unique creation. No one group claims to have the one, and absolute, story of creation that concerns all peoples everywhere. The Christian mythology does have this view: there was only one Adam and only one Eve; there was only one creation of 'man' and 'woman.' All human beings, in this account, stem from one set of parents. There is, similarly, only one account of the creation of the world—before this creation there was *nothing*.

No Native American groups have such a story. If there are creators, and some groups do have such beings, they construct what comes to be the world out of material that is ready-to-hand. There are numerous 'creators,' one for each of the groups. No one argues over the truth or validity of one group's story over another. It is understood that the story being told is a localized creation. There were, in other words, numerous creations. The story of each group postulates a creation not only in time or space but in a specific place. Each group views itself as being created for one specific place.

Some groups have a creation story that proposes human beings as being 'produced' by the Earth out of her womb. They propose also theories that humans had other forms before they took on their present physical characteristics. Some theorize that they have come through several *transformations* or *metamorphoses*—that they now exist in a third, fourth, or fifth 'world.' Some would say that this depiction of various life forms and their transformations portrays the various migrations of a people from one place to another. What is significant here, despite the fact that the transformations may have been migrations, is that the people see themselves as *rightfully* occupying a place that they are intended to occupy and to which they must adapt themselves.

The other significant factor here is that each group recognizes that there will be other groups in other places. The diversity of the world, and thereby the diversity of peoples, is a concept that all Native Americans share. Each group *rightfully* occupies a place for which they were created, produced, or into which they emerged. No one group sees themselves as the one and only correct group; nor do any have a myth that postulates themselves as the owners of an entire planet. Christianity, of course, with its story of a singular creation, postulates that the entire planet is "made for" a specific people. The 'other' exists only as competitor, as enemy, that must either be converted, that is, made Christian, or destroyed—if not literally then in sufficient numbers that those remaining might serve as slaves to the "rightful" people.

## The Earth Is a Living Organism

Perhaps the most distinctive difference between the Native American's definition of the planet and that of the non-Native American is the description and/or definition of the Earth as living organism. The Earth is given a gender, "she," though she is certainly recognized as a being quite different from human beings. The 'she' gender signifies that the Earth is seen as the producer of all things. The Sun, or "grandfather," is less of a 'being' than the Earth and is symbolic of a greater force in the Universe that provides the fertilizing power that entices the Earth to produce its many things. The Earth is seen as a primarily necessary being upon which humans, as well as all other "things," depend for their survival. She is essentially "good" but subject to mistreatment by humans.

The Earth is not, as it is in a Western worldview, a potentially harmful place made up of "inanimate" or "dumb" matter. She is alive, but different from human life forms. The term 'mother,' which so many indigenous peoples use to designate the planet, correctly acknowledges the dependence of all things on her own existence. Plato, in the *Timaeus*, refers to the Earth as "a nurse to mankind" and as being "divine" and "immortal." The West, unlike the ancient Greeks, sees "nature" as essentially hostile, stingy, unstable, dangerous.

The description of the Earth as a living being is one of those concepts that is fairly well distributed among Native Americans. This description has implications in how human beings are defined or described.

A response to "what is the world?" includes not only a description of the universe and the world we occupy but also a description of what it is to be human in that world. A worldview is not simply a description of the world—the description serves as the foundation of all subsequent concepts concerning the things in that world. It really does make a difference how we describe the world.

It is a commonplace among many Western researchers to propose that all diverse cultures, and their worldviews, represent merely so many variations of a general theme. They search for commonalities among the diverse accounts. The Native Americans take some general commonality for granted—we are, after all, all manifestations of the ONE thing. But it is the differences that intrigue us. An assumption of difference has built into it a tolerance that is absent from those views that see only one possible way of being-in-the-world. My difference, it can be said, is based on our mutual tolerance for our essential differences. Without it we would all meld into a field of sameness without distinction. The signature of the One, however, is to manifest itself into as many things as possible. The Earth produces as many things as she is capable of producing: There is not such a thing as "man" but there are "men," no "human" but "humans." There is no such thing as a "cat." There are, instead, jaguars, lions, ocelots, tigers, leopards, and so on. The world is a fulsome place.[5]

# *Usen*: The Unidentifiable *Is*

The term *Usen* is derived from the Jicarilla Apache, an Athabascan people of the American Southwest, specifically, the state of New Mexico. The term signifies a concept that may be "pan-Indian"; that is, it may be widespread throughout Native America. It signifies something "of a substance, character, nature, essence, quiddity beyond comprehension and therefore beyond explanation, a mystery; supernatural; potency, potential," in the words of Basil Johnston, Anishinaubae.[1] The concept of this mysterious "force" also shares the notion of its being all pervasive, that is, it is everywhere and in all things; perhaps *is* all things. Again, Basil Johnston: "[Scholars] . . . continue to labour under the impression that the word . . . means spirit and that it has no other meaning. . . . They do not know that the word bears other meanings even more fundamental than 'spirit.' "

The term *Usen* may or may not contain all of the features that the individual tribal groups use throughout North America. It does, however, share in the notion of something that simply *is*, that remains unidentifiable, mysterious, supernatural in the sense that it is beyond pointing to. Nevertheless, this mysterious *something* precedes everything else; it serves at the same time as the *ground* of things and the manifestation of itself.

The American aboriginal concept of *Usen* is a term of such abstraction that it has, thus far, proven too complex for Europeans to understand. The idea of *Usen*, or its other manifestations, was mistaken by early Christian missionaries for the Western concept of God. "Great Spirit" is the name the missionaries gave it.

I imagine something like the following to have taken place: The missionary tries to tell the indigenous person about his focus of worship—the extraterrestrial deity that creates but exists outside and apart from its creations. The missionary talks about "the Great Father" in the sky. The indigenous person says, "Yup . . ." and points to the Sun.

"No! No!" insists the missionary and he tries another tack. He tells a story about God the Son. Again the indigenous person can relate to that idea: he points to some geographical feature of his landscape and proceeds to tell how a mythological figure became that mountain or rock or ravine. Again the missionary is frustrated. "No! No!" and he tries again.

This time the missionary describes the "Holy Spirit," which seems, only *seems* to the indigenous thinker, to approach the abstract notion of *usen/waken/Manitou/natoji*. The missionary finally breathes a sigh of relief, "At last!" and he proceeds to tell the potential indigenous convert about what it is that this Great Spirit wants him to do. "Wants?" The indigenous person shakes his head at the missionary. Wanting is a human desire. To credit *Usen* with any anthropomorphic characteristics is a bit further than the indigenous thinker can go.

The imaginary missionary, in this instance, illustrates a typical response to the indigenous person's attempt to explain a concept that is very crucial to understanding everything else that follows about Native cultures and traditions. Some contemporary Western researchers have actually declared the concept of *Usen*, or "the all-pervading force," to be "too abstract" and thereby beyond the conception of indigenous peoples.[2] In actuality it is the Western thinker who cannot deal with the ultimate of abstractions—the concept of *Usen*.

European thinkers pride themselves on being masters at the art of dealing with the mental act of abstraction. Abstraction, by its very definition, means to take away everything from a certain idea, a process that allows only the essential to stand out. A good example of abstraction is a simple line drawing of a vase. It may be only one continuous line, but there is no doubt in the eye of the viewer that the line depicts a vase. The viewer does not then make the mistake of seeing the line drawing *as* the vase of all vases. The abstraction remains an abstraction, a "standing-for" something that is much more complex.

But the Western thinker suffers from a tendency to reify all of his abstract notions, think of them as real things. Another example of the Western proclivity to reify is the idea of time. For most of the world's peoples, time is an abstraction derived from the fact that there is motion and change in the world. For Aristotle and Plato, time was the measure or "number" of motion. But time itself was not a thing. For the Western thinker time becomes a thing, a dimension, something that is itself measured. A reification of the concept of time allows Westerners to speak of traveling "in" time. They can postulate traveling into the future or into the past as though the future and past were places or things that exist somewhere out there.

Yet one more example of Western reification can be drawn from the Western concept of God. Joseph Campbell, a philosopher of religion for whom I generally have little regard, said something very interesting in one of the last television programs in which he was featured before he died. When asked about the concept of God, he pointed out that the term was a metaphor. We see all around us, he said, the vastness and the mystery of space. This experience frightens us and awes us at the same time. Out of our terror we make a metaphor. The metaphor is the term 'God.' Once having made the metaphor we need never be troubled by the original terror and awe that the universe inspires in us. We can control 'God.' We define the metaphor and give it attributes. We call it "Him" and give it desires, needs, purposes, and, in some circumstances, even claim to talk to "Him." The awesome universe has been made manageable. The West has come to worship a metaphor. The terror has been *reified*.

The Native American's response to the terror and awe inspired by the universe is to call it sacred. Its mysterious qualities are maintained. It is sacred precisely because it is beyond reification. To assign anthropomorphic qualities to such a substance would be to reify human nature. Of course we are all familiar with the results of this reification: there are numerous conflicts over the descriptions of the god and over what it is that the god wants of human beings; there is certainly conflict over what the god has allowed to be written as "his" word, as we can see by the development of numerous sects within the Christian fold.

In spite of the European inability to be comfortable with pure abstraction, there have been instances where the notion of the mysterious sacredness has surfaced in the European context. Most prominent in this vein is the seventeenth-century philosopher Benedict de Spinoza. Spinoza, born a Jew, was excommunicated from his community of relations and religion because of his views about the world. Spinoza believed that whatever it is of which the world is composed can only be one thing. He called this one thing God, Substance, and Nature. To European thinkers accustomed to the belief that God was extraterrestrial and thereby separate from his creations, Spinoza's concept was an absolute threat. His theory meant that if God/Nature/Substance was all of one piece, then, in effect, everything *was* God! Some referred to Spinoza as a "God-intoxicated man"; others called him an "atheist." Most contemporary philosophers refer to Spinoza as "too complicated."

What Spinoza did was a very thorough logical analysis of the views of others, primarily the French philosopher René Descartes. By tearing away all of the extraneous factors that he showed as untenable, Spinoza showed that there could logically be only one thing in the universe. Furthermore, he insisted that this one thing was material. And he claimed that he saw no problem with calling this matter 'sacred.'

His use of the term matter did not come to be clarified until the twentieth century. Albert Einstein, when asked whether he believed in God, replied that he "believed in the God of Spinoza." What Einstein did was similar to what Spinoza had done. He narrowed down the field of what there was in the universe. The difference between Einstein and Spinoza was that the hold of the churches on the exploration of the world in which Westerners found themselves had been loosened by the time of Einstein. Knowledge of the world did not need the imprimatur of the church in order to be declared valid as knowledge (although it was not until the 1990s that the Roman Catholic Church gave its approval of Galileo's proof that the universe did not revolve around the Earth).

What the findings of Einstein, as well as the investigations of many others in the fields of mathematics and physics, did was to offer us a world that was composed not of the dualities of matter *and* energy but of something that was more clearly explained as "*matter-energy*"—there was only the one substance. This was the information encoded in his famous equation of $E = mc^2$. Energy and matter were two facets, apparently interchangeable under certain circumstances, of one "something." The fact that scientists have since gone on to find that that something may be made of more than just "atoms" (there are "quarks" and other "ultimate" building blocks of the universe postulated) did not negate the findings of Einstein, who saw himself as exploring the world of Spinoza's God.

The fact that people usually seen by Europeans as primitive relative to their own intellectual sophistication could hold a view that is only now coming to be examined by Westerners is very threatening to Westerners. Linguist Benjamin Whorf claimed that the language of the Hopi actually might be a "better vehicle" for explaining the modern views of twentieth-century physics than European languages.[3] He rested his claim on his examination of the Hopi language, which was based, as are many American aboriginal languages, on the concept of motion. He said that the Hopi language depicts a "dynamic" universe and contrasted this view with the "static" universe of the European languages. In the static universe, nothing happens unless there is a cause. In the dynamic model of the universe, something is always happening without an agent having to cause anything, because that is what the universe, by its very nature, does.

This view of the universe as dynamic rather than static is not solely described by the modern scientist. The ancient Greeks and Romans also occupied a dynamic universe, despite the existence of thinkers within their ranks who denied that there was any motion at all, or any substance.[4] The Chinese systems of thought also depict a dynamic universe. One notable ramification of a dynamic universe model is that there need be no anthropomorphic creator deity who must himself be explained as "uncaused"; nor is a human being the goal toward which all creation is striving (especially as Ortega y Gasset points out, a *European* human being).

Regardless of the fact that the concept of *Usen* can be shown to be present in Western thought, it remains true that the Western culture and tradition are not much affected by this concept. Despite the findings of physicists about the existence of "matter-energy" that would deny the dualities typical of Western thought (matter/energy, mind/body, material/immaterial, animate/inanimate), common notions about the world and human beings in that divided state would persist. The new physics insists on presenting a world of interrelationships and interdependencies just as do the theories of *usen/wakan/natoji/nilch'i/manitou*. Ideas that the North American aboriginal peoples arrived at through their observations of the world around them have finally arrived in the West. Whether it will take four hundred years (as in the case of Galileo) for Westerners to adapt to a more realistic view of the universe is not, at present, answerable.

Deeply held notions of the constituents of "reality" are not easily given up. Such notions serve as "givens" of a culture that no longer questions the validity of certain explanations. At one time it was hotly contested in the Western world as to whether the universe was infinite or not. Those who declared that it was were burned at the stake. Today, a person who persists in saying to the "missionary" that he fails to understand our notion of *Usen* is no longer likely to be burned at the stake. He is, however, most likely to be dismissed as showing "a lack of understanding" or to be exhibiting a persistent type of "ignorance" owing to his "undeveloped" state of being.

As more Native peoples engage in the methodologies of philosophical analysis, perhaps there will be a greater clarification of Native ideas and concepts that are the product of Native context. Equally important to Native thinkers is the need to study the Western culture and tradition. It is as important for us to say what we are not, as it is to say what we are.

# Mother Earth

A belief does not exist in isolation; it carries with it numerous implications —that is, accompanying beliefs that can naturally be inferred from the basic and most common belief. It is an accepted notion that American aboriginal peoples believe in something they have called the "Mother Earth." The notion, however, except for somewhat superficial definition, has not been thoroughly explored. What does it mean to believe that the Earth is a mother?

The belief has been superficially explained as symbolically expressive of the idea that the Earth is sacred. The notion of the Earth as mother is explained as a symbol. That is, the concept of mother as applied to the Earth is *symbolic* of the creative forces inherent in the planet. On this interpretation, 'mother' does not literally refer to the planet but to a force that exists outside of and apart from the Earth itself. To the American Indian, however, the notion of this particular symbol is alien.

I had occasion to present the idea of "Mother Earth" as symbol to a well-informed and articulate Indian college student. When he denied that the concept of the Mother was merely symbolic, I asked him to explain his understanding of the Earth as Mother.

"The Earth," he explained, "brings us into existence—literally. Our own mothers—our biological mothers—are the vehicle through which the Earth spews forth another creation." He went on to explain how the Earth creates and sustains all existing things on the planet. "Without the Earth," he said, "there would be nothing."

"But what about the ultimate creative force that we are told underlies our belief in the Earth as Mother?" I asked.

That there is such a force is not questioned by American Indians. But the "force" (or "power" or "energy") does not take the form of creator, and especially not that of a paternalistic deity. The universe is taken as "the force." The argument for such a force goes like this:

There is *something*.

That something is dynamic, that is, in motion.

Motion is equated with life.

What has motion therefore must be *alive*.

Only that which exists has motion.

Therefore, there is something that exists.

The "something" is a life force; it has no beginning or ending. The life force manifests itself into many forms—but the forms once in existence can in turn direct that life force to specific things. The Earth becomes "mother" when she directs the life force to its numerous creations. This Earth, this planet, will create its own unique beings out of its own materials. The life force is essential and therefore not to be discounted in any manner, but the Earth becomes "parent" not only because of her act of creation but because of her continued sustenance of her creations. In this latter sense the Earth exists as a literal mother.

There is, of course, symbolism involved in the belief systems of the American Indian. The Sun, for example, is referred to as "father" or "grandfather" and figures prominently in American Indian legends and explanation systems. But the Sun "develops" into mere symbol. The Sun is symbolic of the life force that is the universe. The Sun represents the whole because it is a visible manifestation of the "force" or energy that is believed to be a characteristic of all that there is.

As I am using it in this book, 'universe' implies a totality of all that there seems to be in existence. 'Universe' as it is used in scientific circles, speaks of "this" universe, that is, that which is visible, or perhaps *hypothetically* visible, to the scientist. The scientist can speak of "other" universes. The American Indian could not. To speak of "other" universes implies that there is something larger in which those universes appear. To the American Indian, talk of the universe necessitates talk of something infinite—it is the background upon which whatever happens *is* happening. There is *one* universe in which numerous things can and do become manifest.

The American Indian is a *monist*. That is, everything that exists is perceived as being the manifestation of one particular thing. In effect, everything that is, is *one* thing. The *oneness* is ascribed to the fact that everything is, essentially, *Usen*, the life force. It is not uncommon to find an Indian making the profound observation that "Everything is one thing." For the Christian and perhaps for the modern Jew, God and his creations are never "one thing." God exists always outside and apart from whatever it is that exists. The concept of the Sun as "father" is closer to the concept of the Christian concept of God, but the similarity between the two is often offensive to Christians. If the Sun is a symbol of something greater, then the equation of Sun and God is wrong. Some Indian peoples, however, do credit anthropomorphic characteristics to the Sun that are akin to those credited to "God."

The concept of the Earth as Mother has received less attention from philosophers and writers, perhaps because there is no near equivalent in the conceptual framework of the predominantly European explorers into the belief systems of Native peoples. James Lovelock in his Gaia hypothesis[1] comes closest to the American Indian concept of the Earth as a living being. Also numerous "environmentalists" have latched on to the concept of the Earth as "mother." In this latter sense there is an attempt to acknowledge human beings' dependence on the planet. There is however, accompanying this "environmental" notion, a very European (and Christian) notion of man as "steward" to the Earth. Stewardship implies a superiority of man over the planet—a notion that is decidedly absent from American Indian views. The American Indian gives preeminence to the dependency notion rather than the stewardship notion.

From this, it should be clear that the concept of the Earth as Mother is not mere symbolism, and that the life force that is the universe is different from the Earth. What, then, are the inferences that must be drawn from a belief of the Earth as a mother?

First of all, though the life force is suffused throughout the whole of whatever exists, the Mother Earth exists as something apart from man. Just as there is a distinction between mother and child, that is, they are two separate beings, there is nevertheless a relationship that is, to the Indian, undeniable. The creature, man, stands at all times to the earth as an infant child to its mother. The child is a product of the mother and dependent on the mother for sustenance and life itself. The relationship is a good one, and the mother is a good mother.

This view should be contrasted with the Genesis account of creation. In the Biblical account, man is created from the clay of the Earth but is created as something apart from the earth, apart and superior. Man resembles not the earth and its other creatures but the extraterrestrial god that creates man. Man is created and placed in a specific and slightly unearthly place: The "Garden" of Eden implies a place that is separate from the normal earth—it is cultivated, trimmed, and so on—it is a *garden*. When man is ousted from the Garden, he is confronted with a harsh and stingy land—he is furthermore cursed to struggle for a living "by the sweat of his brow."

By contrast, in American Indian legends, man is placed on Earth within specific boundaries but he is not given anything specially created to make his life easy. He is given the "sweet grasses," the waters, the animals as both food and medicines. Man is not placed in a harsh environment, nor is he cursed by his maker. There are areas that become "forbidden" to man—but not because they are "evil," rather because they are not places for man, nor places where he might survive in comfort. But overall, the Earth is seen as a good and rightful place for man to be.

Secondly, the sense of being in the "right" place is essential to the understanding of the American Indian's concept of the Earth as mother. Man was created by the Earth and belongs to the Earth. He does not think of or postulate another or "better" home.

The belief that man is rightfully created by the Earth, for the Earth, does not however provide an excuse for complacency. The Indian knows that he is dependent on the Earth, but he realizes also that he exists in a reciprocal relationship with the mother. At some point the human being grows to a maturity and, rather than realizing a sudden independence from the mother, he realizes that he must also give something back to the mother in order to have her continue her productiveness. The Indian may see the Mother as Sacred, but he is first of all of a very pragmatic nature. He cannot long survive if the mother does not survive. His relationship to the mother becomes not one of mother and independent offspring but a relationship of reciprocity—a giving and a taking.

# Time and the Universe

Indians and Euro-Christians hold very different views of time and the universe. These lead to different answers to the question, What is the world?

## The Universe

From an Indian perspective, the universe is infinite; it had no beginning. It is, by definition, in motion, and change is inevitable. Motion/change are, overall, harmonious, balanced, and stable despite occasional and temporary suddenness.

Because the universe is dynamic, changing, creative, infinite, and full, there is no idea of a static or empty space in which things exist. The universe would be best described as an energy field with no gaps. What we interpret as "things" are concentrations of energy. The concentrations are a result of the motion of the universe (dynamic energy) and are viewed as temporary but necessary.

Motion and existence are necessarily interrelated for the Native American philosopher. What exists has motion; what has no motion does not continue to exist. The universe is one "thing," that is, energy, although, whether the quality of *thingness* is applicable in a Native American context is doubtful. This "energy" seems to have a natural tendency to "pool," that is, to gather in various degrees of concentration. The "pooling" causes the diverse "things" in the universe. Thus, for the Hopi at least, there are not "things" but rather the world consists of "events": *being, peopleing, mountaining,* and so on.[1]

For the Euro-Christian, on the other hand, the universe is finite; it had a beginning—either through Creation from "nothing" by a being that exists outside the finite universe or by a "Big Bang" that occurs "nowhere" and sets off a process of progressive movement. The idea of 'progress' is somewhat like an unfolding of something, like a seed that will grow into a definite something. The completion of the unfolding process is always in the future.

## Time

The concept of time is tied to the concepts of the universe held by each group. For the Euro-Christian, the universe is what some call a "block universe." Imagine a square box that is divided off into three sections. One section represents the past, another the present, and the third the future. All three—past, present, future—coexist at the same time. The sections of the box are not equal—imagine the present to be a moving section that travels from the section of "past" into the section marked "future."

Because of these qualities and the *thing-like* nature of time, Europeans can speculate about traveling *in* time or *through* time. Time can be spoken of as changing, slowing down, speeding up. Objects and events exist in portions of time: they can be in the past, in the present, in the future.[2]

The religious aspect of this view of time depicts the future as bounded —that is, there will come a 'time' when the boundary is met and con-fronted. The secular aspect has added a touch of the infinite in that it tries to envision the future as boundless. The future, for the religious, is already there, waiting for the present to reach it. The idea of 'progress' comes in because the present is making progress in its movement toward a goal. This is the idea of a 'teleological' universe—it is set on a course toward a particular outcome or goal. 'Time' is a thing that serves as the stage upon which the drama of the universe is played.

"Indian time": 'Time' means something different when it is based on a concept of an infinite universe. Time is merely a measure of motion: of the motion of the sun, stars, and moon through the sky, of changes that are visible and can be predicted. Time, as a *measure*, is not a self-existing "thing"; it is not even a *dimension*—it is a *human construct*.

There is no idea here of a "block universe." Imagine, instead, a ball to which one slowly adds a layer; each layer is a "present" that is laid over a steadily growing "past" that supports the present. There is no preexistent "future" into which one moves. Many Native American groups portray themselves as active participants in the making of the present—we are, in effect, "cocreators" with a natural process in constructing the future. The future is not "there"—we are creating it through our present actions. The future can be foretold through reading the signs that exist at present and are imagined—with their implications—as building the coming layer of the world (the "ball" that is 'time'). This view may be the origin of the idea that we are cocreators of future conditions. We do not exist in a preordained universe; our actions bring the "future" universe into existence.

## The World

The two opposing descriptions of time and the universe held by Euro-Christians and Indians reflect two very different views about the world. The idea of progress that is so important in the West could never have developed in Indian America, just as it could not have developed in ancient Greece and Rome. The Greco-Roman world depicted the universe as infinite but cyclical. The best analogy here would be to organic growth; there is an initial germination of a 'time' or 'era,' then a blooming, and finally a decay. They portray themselves as having descended from a mythical "Golden Age" (the "blooming") and are on the downward cycle of the process. The end of a cycle initiates a new germination—like a seed from an oak tree bursting into life to begin its process again.

Some even postulated that the new cycle would repeat exactly the old cycle. The philosopher Nietzsche dubbed this "eternal recurrence"—we were doomed to repeat our entire life and its circumstances through eternal recycles. There is, in this view, a scent of fatalism in that we are preordained to do the things that we do. We can catch a glimpse of this preordination in the Greek dramas; Oedipus, for example, is preordained to kill his father and nothing can forestall this—it is "written in the stars."

This sense of inevitability is also present in the Euro-Christian view of the universe and time. The Judeo-Christian god is omniscient—he knows all things—past, present, and future. The future circumstances of people are not in their own hands but already laid out. The circumstances are inevitable. In the secular version of this mythos, there is still a sense of inevitability: the future is there and we are on our way toward it. We can even measure our progress toward it—everything moves from a state of simplicity to one of greater complexity, from a "lower" stage to a "higher" stage.

"Indian time" is of a different sort. Since we are *participants* in a process of motion and change, we know that we can affect the future. If we chop down all the trees, we will live in a world without trees. If we have too many children, we will live in a state of overpopulation. There is no glorious 'future' out 'there' waiting for us to arrive. We build the future through our present actions. We do not, however, "build" as gods but as participants in certain circumstances—not all events are of our own making. The universe is a process of which we are but a small part. In such a process the goal is more likely to be *stability*. Our survival depends on maintaining a certain degree of stability, which we know more familiarly as "balance." 'Stability' in the West is synonymous with *stasis*, a state in which "nothing happens." Stability, however, is something that can be achieved only with tremendous effort. Imagine yourself on a sea of shifting sand. On this sand there is a ball upon which we place a balancing board. We stand on that board and try to balance ourselves so that we do not fall when the sand shifts the position of the ball. Stability, in this sense, requires constant adaptation to changing circumstances.

In this way, the universes that Indian and Euro-Christian inhabit are two different "worlds"—parallel universes, so to speak. We occupy the same space and the same time but we live in different "worlds."

# What Is Reality?

The main focus of psychological theories is not "What is man?" but "What is reality?" This focus is illustrated when we speak of the insane, or "mentally ill," as "losing touch with reality." In the case of the Native American it is appropriate to ask, "Which reality?"

'Reality' is assumed to refer to factual (empirically verified) knowledge about what the world and man are like. Reality is that truth that lies beyond question. However, reality is not identical for the Native and the European. The fact that it is not can account for the characteristics of "mental illness" that seem to befall Native Americans.

In his novel *One Flew Over the Cuckoo's Nest*,[1] Ken Kesey presents to us a Native American inmate of a mental institution. The "Chief's" problem is a feeling that he is surrounded by a consuming fog that slowly absorbs his existence, or person. The "fog" serves also to veil or obscure his presence from others, especially Europeans. The fog has, the Chief says, already consumed his father.

In *Ceremony*,[2] a novel by Native American Leslie Silko, the main character, a Native war veteran, is also subject to being overcome by "fog," a sense of unreality about the world he finds himself in. In both cases it is not the world of the white man that is taken to be unreal, but that of the Native American.

Silko's character's problem begins with his inability to distinguish the enemy, a Japanese man, from himself. He sees not the "enemy" whom he has been trained to destroy, but a man who physically resembles himself and his relatives. The "oriental" is "the enemy," but the real enemy surrounds him. The real enemy is the white man, but it is their uniform he wears, their cause he is sacrificing himself for, and their company he shares. He disappears into the equivalent of the Chief's fog. His reality is consumed by the reality of the European who calls himself 'American.'

The remainder of the novel is an insightful exploration of how the main character escapes the fog, which is actually the 'reality' of the European that seeks to supplant his own sense of what is real.

The key to his cure is not in the institutions of the white man that he has experienced and is threatened with, and certainly not in the psychology being practiced there. Old, known remedies of Native Americans are not sufficient either. This is a new problem; until the forced association with European systems, the Native American's reality, or worldview, had never been threatened. Silko provides, however, an unorthodox medicine man. He is unorthodox because he uses strange and new methods of curing. The methods are calculated to deal with the sense of unreality that strikes the Indian forced to associate with the European world.

The cure consists of reinforcing the validity of Native American reality and emphasizing the ill effects of European reality upon the Native American. He does this by encouraging the "sick" man to pursue a Native lifestyle and goals, while at the same time showing him those Natives—drunken, whoring, selfish, and cruel—who exist at the fringes of the European world. There is an implication that this "fringe" existence is all that exists for the Native who forgoes his own reality.

Silko's 'mentally ill' Native is encouraged to see the dual nature of reality that confronts him and is told that it is acceptable to choose his own reality. This is not a choice that is available to the Native subjected to analysis and therapy based on European models of man and the universe.

The European reality that threatens Native reality consists of seeing man as an isolated, potentially self-sufficient unit of existence. This model is manifest in the belief that man, the individual, is in competition for survival against every other man; he creates himself, not through others, but in opposition to others. Man is isolated from nature; he is superior to it. Nature is a hostile force opposed to human beings and ever ready to absorb the unwary individual. Nature calls him to succumb to its oblivion, and man must fight this by continually striving to "develop" his isolation and self-sufficiency.

In the reality of most Native Americans, however, man is not an isolated and self-sufficient unit of existence. Man is a group being and dependent, not only on others, but on the Earth. Survival depends not on competition but on cooperation. Man is not a being in opposition to nature but a part of it. Nature gives him his subsistence; the group gives him his identity. Just as man "owes" something to his fellows, he feels indebted to the Earth. Earth is the context of his being. He and the context he exists in are one—there is no existence for man outside of that context.

The ethical system of the Native American extends beyond man's relationship with others and the institutions that men create. The Native American includes the Earth and everything in it in his ethical system; this is a very important fact in determining the well-being of a man.

Silko demonstrates this extension of values when she has her main character blame himself for a drought that covers his home area. He is convinced that his behavior (consorting with the enemy, the white man, by participating in his war) has led to his failure to observe the ceremonies and behaviors that would have ensured the earth's fertility. He is guilt-stricken.

The universe of the Native American is based on the concept of Harmony. This leads to the idea that man, a part of that universe, must adapt himself to and be responsible for the continuing harmony he sees about him. There is no sense of man needing to war against nature or having to purchase his existence in competition with his fellows. Harmony, evidenced in the benefits of cooperation with his group and in man's ability to adapt to changing circumstances in his environment (the seasons and the change of lifestyles required year in and year out), is in his eyes the right behavior. The war against nature is seen as wrong—futile and destructive. Competition with others is wrong because it leads to disharmony—isolation, selfishness, pain to others.

The psychological theories of the European do not take into account these particular realities of the Native American, because they are outside the frame of reference of the European. European psychological theories are directed to adjusting the mentally ill person to a European reality that stresses man's superiority to nature, his self-sufficiency, his independence, and the need to acquire (enforce) these latter two through conflict with others.

European psychologies are predicated on the alienation of the individual. Ironically, near total self-sufficiency and independence are methods developed to deal with the effects of alienation. But since they are themselves also a cause of alienation, their reinforcement serves merely to provide a buffer for the individual against the inroads of others. These methods do not eradicate alienation; they provide one with the strength to accept, and live, with alienation.

The Native, when confronted with such "cures," is actually being coerced into participating in the cause of his own distress. Alienation is not a part of his mental makeup, as it is in the European. The Native's own reality of oneness with nature, of responsibility to the Earth and to man, is overlooked, discounted. It is irrelevant to the therapist and the world he is committed to; he literally does not see the world of the Native.

The "fog" that rises between the Native American and the European world is a clash of realities. There is much support for European reality; theirs is the dominant culture. The Native confronts this "alien" reality from an early age through a system of compulsory education. He is taught that the Earth is raw material, an enemy to be conquered and used. Each of his fellows is a potential enemy, a competitor in a war of survival. Cooperation, when it enters at all, is not a way of life, but a means of compromising in order to achieve the ends of the isolated individual. The Native is subjected to these denials of his reality through all his classroom days.

Outside of the classroom, his reality—the sanctity and meaningfulness of the Earth—is literally covered over. More concrete, more asphalt, means progress. This covering of the Earth provides a guarded path on which the European may tread without fear of the wildness and vagaries of the hostile planet. What natural vegetation is allowed is trimmed, controlled, subjected to man's whims. In the process of paving the earth, the reality of the Native is covered over, made insignificant. "Meaning" is presumed to lie in concrete, glass, iron, measured geometric spaces, and artificial suns to ward off the night. Little wonder that the Native begins to be consumed by a feeling of invisibility. His reality—his world—is literally lost from sight, and since his identity is so intricately wound into that of the earth, so, too, is his identity threatened.

Too often, the Native American responds to this rising "fog" by seeking oblivion in alcohol, drugs, and suicide. He responds by striking out in violence, battering at the fog he sees enveloping his world, his loved ones. Still another response is to go through the fog to the reality that it represents—the white world, committing oneself to an endless denial of what once was.

There are no psychologies directed to making the Native aware of the existence of two realities in his field of choices. The European psychologies make him aware of (1) his primitive, uncivilized, nonprogressive nature (an unreality in the eyes of the European); and (2) the civilized, progressive, alienated lifestyle that the European calls reality. In this frame of reference there is only one choice: European reality. Native reality is not a choice but a "regression." A European psychologist can no more encourage this than he could the "reality" of one of his own who has slipped into a world of "paranoid fantasy."

"What is reality?" is a question dealt with only superficially by the European psychologist. He "knows" what reality is, and is barred by that sense of reality from being aware of another. In fact, a confrontation with another reality would be threatening to him. European man is no more capable of coping with threats to his reality than is the Native. But Euro-man has more "tools" with which to bolster and "prove" his reality—the most important being the "education" of Natives, that is, emphasizing the reality of European knowledge over that of the Native. The Native's existence, if dealt with at all, is usually relegated to being an anachronistic example of "previous" and "less advanced" lifestyles. European man copes with other realities by absorbing them into his own frame of reference, thereby eradicating what he might interpret as being threatening to his own reality.

The ramifications of Euroman's clinging to his own reality are detrimental to the Native when the two must confront one another. They lead to extermination of cultures and judgments about the behavior of Natives based on a value system that is alien to the Native. The examples of this are many: The "Indian" who fails to accept European ideas is "less developed" than one who does. The Native's need to synthesize knowledge into one holistic system, which is consistent with his holistic view of the universe, is seen as an inability to be "objective" and "analytical." A Native who, committing a wrong and believing that there are consequences to "disharmonious" behavior, readily admits to his behavior or adjusts his response to the expectation of his inquisitor (in order not to pile up "disharmonies") is viewed as "without conscience." The Native, who sets a great value on self-discipline, is seen as "cold," "lacking in emotion," because he does not act in conformance with the behavior of his European conquerors who depend less on self-discipline than on "law," or external discipline. The list is endless and serves merely to point to those confrontations that are a result when two realities clash.

The solution may possibly await the enlightenment of European psychologists, finally able to confront the relativism of what is called 'reality';

or the entering of Natives, already so enlightened, into the field. Perhaps, also, Leslie Silko might divulge the identity of her unorthodox medicine man who so successfully brought one Native American out of the fog and into awareness of the choices open to the Native. I eagerly await her next novel, for the poet often points to a truth that escapes the scientist.

# Artesian Spring: A Poem

*Along with her academic articles about the nature of reality, Viola Cordova left us a poem that brings her ideas beautifully to life. After all is said and done, here is what is real: the laughter of horses and cold water flowing from the ground. The real world, the ground under our feet, is full of wonder and meaning. (The Editors)*

Towards the end of May, when Spring was safely in place,
The snow given way to the first wild flowers,
We hiked over the ridge, which hovered over the small Wyoming town.
Over the ridge were the artesian springs where wild horses wintered.
The neighborhood children gathered in the early morning,
Comparing foodstuffs, knives and thin rope,
Our survival gear for a day's hike.
The older children gave admonitions to the younger,
Discouraged the youngest with descriptions of extreme rigor ahead.
And then we were ready.
The wild horses, covered with clumps of falling winter coats,
Had, we hoped, not yet embarked on their summer travels.
Every step of the way was described beforehand:
There's Camel Rock, remember when we found the Jerusalem Cricket
    nest?
And the old twisted Juniper growing out of the sandstone?
And the Sage Grouse mating grounds
Where the males paraded and stomped and flapped their chest sacs?
And the Lava Tube?
The Lava Tube was an ancient remnant with a collapsed roof.
We hiked over sharp rocks, clinging to equally sharp sides
And laughed gleefully over the surviving snow on its floor.
"Even in July, the middle of July," claimed the older children,
"There is snow in the Old Tube."
The younger, in awe, believed the tale.

Outside the Tube, silence prevailed.
Instructions, softly whispered,
So as not to scare the horses.
We heard our heartbeats, felt the warmth of our excitement,
And heard the gentle burbling of the Artesian Springs,
The soft contented snorting of a feeding horse . . .
They were here! They were still here!
Silently, ever so silently,
From an embankment of weathered sandstone
Which would cover, we thought, our presence,
We peered at the small herd.
Their manes hung over their eyes in matted clumps,
From their bodies, the winter coat clung to freshly appearing summer
    hair.
They pawed at the damp ground for fresh greens
Then grew alert at our presence.
There was a whinny, a toss of a head,
One or two moved away from the embankment.
We watched, in silence and in stillness.
Equally silently, now cramped from long immobility,
We crawled, in pairs, in single file, back to the Tube.
And our voices came back:
We saw them, we actually saw them!
Did you see the Pinto with the clumpy feet . . .
Like bedroom slippers . . .
And the black one that looked like it had rolled in the mud?
And the water?
The marvel of water appearing out of the ground,
Clean and clear and singing . . .
Where did it come from?
"Out of the ground," the older children solemnly pronounced,
"It comes, by itself, out of the ground."
Can we drink it?
"Afterwards," they said, "after the horses move away."
And then we started home, sharing horse stories along the way.
Once, I said, when we first moved here,
We lived in the very last house, on the top of the hill.

My mother was recovering from diphtheria,
She couldn't walk across an entire room,
She woke up, in the middle of the night, I thought,
But it could have been in the early morning hours.
She was crying and my grandmother was holding her,
My mother thought someone was laughing at her,
Because she couldn't walk. She heard the laughing.
Shhh, my grandmother murmured. It was horses.
The Wild Horses.
And I heard them, too, and my mother crying softly.
My grandmother brought us each a glass of cold, cold water.

# IV   WHAT IS IT TO BE HUMAN?

Who are we? How do we become human? Of
what memories and stories, relations and
responsibilities, affirmations and refusals,
substance and spirit are we made? How do our
relationships to others shape who we are, or
our relations to the earth and the sun and the
web of life? How are a Native American's views
of himself or herself different from Christian
views? Who has the right to define who Native
Americans are? Noble Savages, injuns,
archetypes, artifacts, subjects of
anthropological study. How can we
reclaim our identities and the right
to shape our own destinies?

# Who We Are

## An Exploration of Identity

*The text that follows is the second of Viola Cordova's illustrated chapbooks, intended to introduce her views to a larger and more diverse audience than might be reached with academic articles. It is a powerful introduction to her philosophy of personal identity, her answer to the question, What makes me who I am?*

It is as if
before 1492
   we did not exist—
   that we sat around
   eating fruit off the trees
until we were "discovered"—
   by accident.
Columbus thought
   he'd found
   "Sypango"
   or China
   or India
or, at least—
the Spice Islands
and then, he thought,
he'd found Eden
the mythical home
of Adam & Eve
from which they'd been
   ousted
   for messing up.
"Don't eat from that tree!"
He said—
The god said—
"Or you will become like us

Like Gods."
But they did
She made me do it
He said
It was his fault
She said
Old serpent
He just slithered away.
Columbus thought
   he was in paradise
The people, he said,
For he thought they
   were people—
are kind and generous
and share all that
   they have.
And then
   they became savages
   cannibals
   devil worshippers
   heathens
   Indians
but
   they had souls
   said the Pope
   and if they had souls
   they could be converted
and if they could be converted
—from heathen to Christian—
they could be used
   as beasts of burden
   to plow their own fields
   which were no longer theirs
   of course
and to build edifices
   for the glory of god
   and

civilization
a brick
at a time
A couple of generations
later
    "Indians"—for that is
    what we came to be called—
    were seen by some
    as
    Noble Savages
We graced their coins and imaginations.
Except
—of course—
where we still
outnumbered them
    Out west
    where
    the buffalo roamed
    or
    used to roam
    and the only
    good injun
    was a dead injun.
"Nits make lice,"
    said an otherwise
    respected officer,
when asked about the children.
And, finally,
when the numbers
had fallen
they, too
out west
became noble savages.
For the purposes
    of missionaries
    anthropologists
    psychologists

ethnologists
painters
sculptors
and
Edward S. Curtis
We were the trophies
white folks
hung on their walls
their museums
and placed on their
coffee tables
next to the stuffed animals.
They think
we're dead
and if we're not
soon will be
If we exist
exist at all
it's as living fossils
of their own dead past
We represent
an archaic form
of their own
glorious rise
to
Modernity
In the eyes
of modern man
we are specimens—
of Jungian archetypes
of hunter-gatherer
of his own lost innocence
of quasi-mystical
supernatural
spiritual beings
They know everything about us
what we eat

what we dream
who we're related to
where we came from.
They've lived among us
been "adopted" even
or done "field research"
learned our language
and even braided their hair
and worn turquoise.
They build sweat lodges
and pound drums
ladies smoke peace pipes
and they talk about
    the Earth Mother
    draw pictures of her
    offer up sage and
    sweet grass
hang imitation eagle feathers
on the rear-view mirror
of their VOLVO.
But REALLY
They don't know much.
They don't know
That the Mother of us all
made many kinds of human beings.
Some she made for mountains
others
    for rivers
    and deserts
    and plains
    and lakes
She made us with the capacity
to live in specific places
for specific reasons
    and she gave us
    the capacity
    to say

why we are each
in a specific place
and not any other
The story of the mountain people
will not be the story
of a desert people
and their story will differ
from those of the lakes.
In the east
will be one story
in the west
another
and all of them
the stories
will be true.
FOR
BUILT IN
BUILT IN TO OUR TRADITION
IS TOLERANCE
A TOLERANCE
FOR THE TRUTH OF THE OTHER
SIMPLY *BECAUSE* HE IS
THE OTHER
WE KNOW THERE ARE SIMILARITIES
BUT WE ALSO KNOW THAT
IT IS DIFFERENCES
SOMETIMES SMALL DIFFERENCES
THAT MAKE US UNIQUE.
It is those differences
that have allowed
our survival
in the mountains
the prairies
the forests
the arctic
the deserts
and we have survived

for thousands of years
    without
despoiling the waters
    the air or the land.
We did so because
    in our stories
    in our actions
    we know
that we are temporary
    transitory creatures
    inhabiting
    a less transitory
    world
"At my feet,"
say some Eastern tribes,
"and connected to me
are seven generations."
I came into existence
    and found
    a world of beauty
I will go out of existence
    and must leave
    for those who come after me
even to the seventh generation
    a world of beauty
    a fertile world
    my world.
We are not creatures
of an alien being
tossed into an alien
    environment
We are the production
    of Mother Earth
    produced out of her fertility
    into a specific region
    for a specific purpose
We are exactly what

She meant us to be.
WHOLE
COMPLETE
GOOD
As much
a part of her
as a fish
  a bird
  a tree
  a stone
  the mountain
  the cave
  the snow
  and the sand
We are the children
  of the earth
  of the sun
  we belong here
There are those who say
that the life of a human
is "solitary, poor, nasty,
brutish, and short"
  that every man
  is enemy
  to every man
That humans have
  engraved on their foreheads
  as it were—
  the following words:
"Every man acts so as to
enhance his own well-being."
We know well this picture.
It is the story
  of the solitary
  individual
But we are not solitary
  nor poor, nasty, and

brutish
by nature
We are a part of a whole
The "I" is a unique combination
of the group
that brings the "I"
    into existence
"I" am the sum
    of the memories
    of the group
    of its experiences
    its knowledge
"I" become "I"
    when I have learned
    my place in the group
    when I become aware
    of the fact
    that my actions
    have consequences
    on others
    on the whole
    only then
    am "I" a person
A WHOLE PERSON
"I" am born only humanoid
    "I" become human
    when "I" know
    when "I" am aware
    that human actions
    are not meaningless
    but consequential
    knowledge
    real knowledge
    is the ability
    to know before
    I act
    the possible consequences

    of my actions
on myself
on others
on the whole
I am a pebble on a unitary universal pond.
"I," said an old man,
    "do not speak much
    to white people—
They are in too much of a hurry
They are like cars going
    70 miles an hour
    I am being careful
    watching
    where I am going
    I can only go
    15 miles an hour!"
THEY—
    rush to the future
    which they think
    is already there
from a past
    that is truly past
through a present
    that is measured
into a future
    that is waiting
We
We know another universe.
We are our past
and in the present
we make the future
    As long as the past
    exists in memory
    —it is the present.
    And the future
    is what we make it.
We occupy

the same space
the same time
but we live in parallel universes.
How can we say
to them
that we are not
specimens
frozen in test tubes
caught in a time warp
pinned to a wall
living testaments
of their own rise
from amoeba
to MODERN MAN?
Through definition—
SELF-DEFINITION
WE
will tell YOU
who we are
and
we are not
specimens        fossils
archetypes        anachronisms
relics
evolutionary dead-ends
mystical beings
primitive man
or
even
artifacts
informants
and subjects
alternative developments
part of the diversity
the variety
which is the signature
of the Mother

which makes
no two things
exactly alike.
We are instead—
CHILDREN OF THE EARTH.

# What Is It to Be Human in
# a Native American Worldview?

In the basic Western creation myth, an extraterrestrial god creates human beings out of, essentially, *dumb* matter drawn from an inanimate planet. He places his creations into an area that is presumed to be "perfect." They are subsequently exiled from this "natural" abode of human beings and the land into which they are thrown is cursed. Human beings are consigned to leading a harsh life in a harsh land. They are, nevertheless, still creatures "made in the image of God." The image includes license for "naming all things," "multiplying" their numbers, "holding dominion over all living things," and "subduing" the environment in which the ousted couple find themselves.

In what some call a "post-Christian" world, the story changes, but the details do not differ in any of the important details. Human beings arise out of a primeval mass and become human by virtue of surpassing all other life forms in an evolutionary "struggle for survival." The Earth is still *inanimate matter*, and all living things exist only for the use of man and for the exercise of his creativity. The Earth is not perfect, whole, or complete; it is in need of transformation. Only humans, like God, are capable of doing this.

In the original myth, God deals with his human creatures as a group of specific people, the Hebrews. After the advent of Christianity, the allegedly same 'God' deals only with individuals; they are told, through scripture, that they "shall not be saved through the traditions of their fathers;" they have no families except among those who join the "brotherhood" of Christianity. What we would label a racial or ethnic identity ceases to be of any importance in the newly founded Christian church. The "Old Testament" God makes promises to his people *as a people*. The "New Testament" addresses itself to individuals who are required to make a choice between their former identities and the new Christian identity. Despite this group membership, salvation is awarded to individuals for individual deeds. The ethnic identity of a group is no longer relevant.

In a Native American worldview there is no divinity that exists outside the universe—primarily, because there is no "outside." Whatever *is*, is an indivisible, infinite, and divine *something*. All things are perceived as either *participating* in this one thing or being *manifestations* of the one thing.

There is no sense of causation here as there is in Western thought. Whatever *is*, is in many forms. The Navajo feel that *wind* is symbolic of this force; what we perceive as "things" come into existence through some sort of specific wind; a vortex of some kind becomes a "thing" that exists for a time and then falls back into the "mainstream." Some manifestations of this wind, *'nilch'i,'* may be harmful to humans but not intentionally so. Some Pueblo people credit the Milky Way as the inseminating "potion" of whatever it is that brings the different things into existence. The Apache credit *lightning* as the initial event that causes other "things" or "events" to come into being. The 'wind,' the 'Milky Way,' the 'lightning' are all manifestations of the one thing that is dynamically transforming itself. A blade of grass is as much *Usen* as is a human, a mountain, or a molecule of oxygen. All are infused with divinity. In Christianity, this would be blasphemy.

The stories that are told about the appearance, creation, or emergence of humans are specific to a group. The story tells of their entrance into the world, and it is specific to a place. There is an assumption among Native Americans that each group will have a different story since they occupy different "niches." Each group is seen as essential to the place in which they find themselves. It may be that they are, overall, only oxygen absorbers, or perhaps the nerve ends of the universe. They are not, however, "meaningless things" in a "meaningless world." They fit in a particular place for a particular reason.

Individuals are not created, except as "first man" or "first woman," but they are, in their inception, a group, a *people*. Humans are first and foremost defined as social animals. Aristotle expressed this idea, saying that "a man alone is either a god or a beast." Humans, like some other animals, exist in a herd or flock, but beyond this similarity there is an even stronger bonding mechanism, language. Humans can communicate with each other in order to inform each other of intentions, planned actions. Moreover, humans, unlike most other animals, have a greater memory. Memory is what allows the humans to remember the consequences of their actions upon others and other things and places. Intelligence may be said to consist of knowing consequences in many different circumstances.

The issue of "consciousness" that so bedevils the Western philosopher is not a great issue among Native Americans. Consciousness, awareness, is assumed to be a characteristic of the universe. Communication may be limited to specific groups of living beings, but consciousness is everywhere. We simply cannot know other consciousnesses because we can communicate only within a limited field. There is no doubt, however, that even stones, water molecules, trees, and other animals have some kind of consciousness. The Native American universe is not made up of "dumb matter."

A philosopher, aware of the view that Native Americans hold of humans as "group" beings, asked me if I thought that Native Americans had "self-consciousness." The question was absurd on two levels: (1) Since self-consciousness is seen to be that characteristic that separates humans from animals, to ask if Native Americans have this characteristic was an insult to the human status of Native Americans; and (2) since "nature" does not create multibodied things with only one sense of awareness (or "brain"), it stands to reason that all things have a concept of self as distinct from other things. All "beings" are seen as essentially unique, that is, "individuals." It is not, however, individual uniqueness that grants anything a special status; instead, its existence as a manifestation of the divine something grants individuals a status that is worthy of respect.

The unique view of individuals held by the majority of Native Americans leads to a paradox: How is it that in an individualistic society—such as the United States—the individual can become anonymous; while in a "group"-oriented society such as the Native Americans, the individual is never anonymous? In an American society, the individual often feels that his individuality is threatened by the group—he might become "just a number," or "submerged" into an anonymous "mass." In a Native American sense, the individual is always a part of something greater than himself, a family, a clan, a tribe, a place. He can be "located" in a larger whole. It is not the group that threatens the individual, it offers him a *sense of belonging*; it is, instead, the individual that poses a potential threat to the group's survival.

The unattached individual is merely humanoid. This is the state in which the infant appears to the group; he must be shown how to be a human being according to the definition of such as held by the group. The child is trained to be an Apache, a Sioux, and so on. The adult lone individual—or 'individualist'—could be likened to the "rogue elephant" that is 'rogue' by virtue of some anomaly that causes him to be separated from his "natural" state as a part of a herd.

The idea of humans as herd animals is very insulting to most Westerners. The 'herd' represents a mindless and chaotic conglomeration that lacks the ability to reason; the herd is equivalent to a 'mob.' This fear is based on the assumption that individuals without a leader to tell them what to think simply take on the thoughts of those around them. This doesn't say much for the individual's capacity to think for himself and does say a lot about the authoritarian cast of Western perspectives about man and society. The human, in a Western sense, must be told what to think, how to act, and he must be placed under some sort of external restraint at all times. The idea that society is always a form of restraint differs sharply from the idea of society that is held by Native Americans. The society, as a whole, is held together in the Native American context by individuals, all thinking for themselves and contributing to the greater whole. This perspective has very deep implications for how children are taught to become *persons*.

J. Douglas Rabb and Dennis McPherson, Canadian professors in Native American philosophy at Lakehead University, have written on the method of creating autonomous actors within a Native American society.[1] They make a claim that, on the surface, seems incredible to those who are not familiar with child-raising techniques among Native Americans. They claim that the methods that eighteenth-century German philosopher Immanuel Kant proposed for making adults into autonomous thinkers and ethical agents are the same methods used in raising Native children, with one very important difference.

According to Kant it is necessary for an individual to go through a period of *heteronomy*—of dependency wherein one is guided by external rules and authorities—before one can become truly autonomous. Rabb and McPherson, backed by numerous and varied research into the cultural learning styles of Native American children, show that the Native child is allowed to be an autonomous agent from "the age of mobility." The Native child, in comparison to the Western child, is considered to be "a person" when he begins to be "mobile"—that is, when he becomes capable of encountering the world. The child is given freedom "to explore his own environment," whereas the Western child "is watched and controlled by parents throughout childhood." The "independence and autonomy" of the Native child exists in contrast to the state of the non-Native child, who is "dependent and controlled." The Native American child is not subjected to routine or to physical punishment or its threat. He lives in a "child-determined" environment. For example, "meals are served on demand, bedtimes vary with sleepiness and family activity." The Native child is also offered countless opportunities to make decisions and, it is assumed, to encounter the *consequences* of those decisions, which provide the primary form of learning experience.

Another important factor in the child's learning is the fact that he is introduced to a world where the concept of 'person' is much more extensive than that of the Western child, or adult. "I try to teach young people respect for everything: other people, trees, water and the spirits," an Ojibwa elder is quoted as saying; the others, the nonhuman part of the child's world, are also 'persons'—though the term used here would be more likely 'beings'—which are equally deserving of the child's respect. The worldview that the child is being taught is that which places him in a world that he is "*a part of*" rather than "*apart from.*" There is, according to Rabb and McPherson, an "enlarged sense of self" that is being granted the child in this view of what it is to be human. There is, here, a sense of oneself as involved in an *interrelationship* rather than a mere *relationship* with the 'other.'

In the Western context of "human nature" there is thought to be a dualistic nature, that is, that the person consists of a mind and a body. This is not as complicated as the view held of humans in a Native American context. It has been explained that the "world" (everything that is) is essentially the manifestation of one single "thing." In this sense, there is no divisibility possible—humans are constituted of two aspects of one same thing. Rabb and McPherson quote here an Ojibwa scholar, James Dumont, who uses the term "soul-body" to define this state. Dumont further refers to the fact that the human "moves about in both ordinary and nonordinary reality" and, as an adult, will be keenly aware of this reality that is at the same time one and two *realities*.

Another explanation of this facet of "human nature" might be explained through the use of a term from physics, 'matter-energy.' A person is both "soul"/mind and body at the same time, both "spiritual" and nonspiritual at the same time, as in the state of *matter-energy*. One state, in this case the "state" of being a human body, cannot exist without the other, and, in fact, if dissolved, dissolves into the energy state. The energy state, however, is not a dissolution into a state that bears the unique history of the "matter" portion. Something may dissolve into an energy state, but "matter" without the involvement of energy is not conceivable within this framework. It is this view that disallows the use of the term 'inanimate' as a description of the universe and everything in it. It is also this view that allows Native Americans to see themselves as a part of a greater whole.

Thus, being human, in a Native American perspective, requires having an "enlarged sense of self," as McPherson and Rabb have described. The self, in other words, does not suffer a dilution or eradication as is so feared in the Western view of individuality, but, instead, an "enlargement" of the sense of what one is.

There is, however, one more aspect of being human that must be mentioned here: The human being does not come in only "one flavor." There is no single "correct" or "real" way of being human. All human groups are believed to be "created" or "produced" to fill a particular niche in the Earth's environment. Therefore, it is assumed that each specific group will differ from all other groups. The fact that there are similarities between humans as a species is not as relevant as the fact that as *groups* they will differ in markedly important ways. This understanding of difference as a natural occurrence leads to a stance of toleration that is absent from a Western view. Western views tend to be based on absolute and universal truths that disallow the existence, or "correctness," of those who do not conform to the "truth" (in this case, of what it is to be human) as defined by Western thinkers.

# Credo: This I Believe

What is it to be human? How do humans differ from other life forms? The following is a list of beliefs to which many Native Americans would ascribe.

1. Human beings are a part of a whole that is greater than the individual. A human is not something *apart from* the Earth and the rest of its creations, including rocks, trees, water, and air; he is a natural *part of* the Earth.

2. A human is first and foremost a 'herd being.' He is such even more so than other beings by virtue of the bonding "mechanism" of a common language that allows for shared traditions, rituals, and histories. No other life forms have an equally strong bonding mechanism. The individual has value because of his uniqueness (there has not been nor will there be again another just like him or her) and because of the potential gifts he brings to the group. But the group is preeminent. The sense of "we" dominates the sense of the "I."

3. Human beings are not alone in having "intelligence"—all life forms are understood to have intelligence in one form or another. However, humans differ from other life forms in that they have a greater capacity for memory. This larger memory capacity allows humans to understand the consequences of their actions. Wisdom, or intelligence, consists of being able to see how our actions and their consequences affect the greater whole, not just the group but also the world around them.

4. Human beings, unlike, say, bears, have the capacity to change their behavior. They do not, in other words, act only from instinct.

5. Humans are not "fallen" creatures; they are what the Earth intended. Most of all, they "fit" in this world because they are products of it. A sense of alienation from the world and its many beings would not, in this context, be seen as the common malady of individuals but as a psychotic disruption, an illness.

6. A human is both spirit and nonspirit, mind and body, matter and

energy at the same time and requires both to exist in unison in order to *be* (as opposed to nonbeing) anything at all.

7. Humans are not superior to other life forms. They are simply different. This difference is natural in a world that displays a vast variety of diverse life forms. Humans are one among many others, and all are "equal" in the sense that they all depend on some very specific conditions of the planet Earth in order to survive. All of the diversity, together, forms a complete whole that is what the Earth *is*. She is what she is "meant" to be; humans are what they are "meant" to be. They "fit" into the pattern that Earth exhibits. Moreover, no group of humans is "superior" to another. They are produced to fill a certain ecological niche and are therefore each different. Tolerance is built into the notion of different and separate "creations." Each group plays a specific role in a specific part of Earth's "environment." Each group has its own story of "beginnings" and each of them is true in its own context.

8. Humans are not "meaningless bits of cosmic dust floating about in an infinite universe." They are an integral part of the whole. However, just as the butterfly may be unaware of what role it plays in the general scheme of things, humans also may be unaware of their role in the world. Knowledge and wisdom consist in learning about what that role might be and acting so that one's actions become a balanced part of an essentially harmonious whole.

9. Humans are born "humanoid," that is, with the capacity to become "fully human" through the exercise of all of their faculties. This includes not only "intelligence" but also the emotional component of being human: for example, guilt, which calls us to rectify what is wrong, and sympathy and empathy, which call us to be aware of the other as someone like one's self. Humans have many qualities that must be fostered for one to become fully human. We have a broader range of capabilities through our physical structure: our ability to walk upright, our easily manipulated hands, our stereoscopic vision with a broad color range, our ability to adapt to a variety of geographical environments, our ability to respond to our environment with awe, reverence, or even fear.

An infant is seen as becoming "human" when he or she demonstrates the fact that he is aware that his actions have consequences on others and on the world. Becoming a human is a responsibility of the group that teaches the new being what it is to be human in *this* group of beings. In many tribes the new being is not seen as fully human until he or she is five to eight years old (many official naming ceremonies take place at this time). It is at that age that a human being can discern the consequences of his actions on others. He is taught to be human by showing him that he is one human among others. Because he shares the world with other beings, there is an emphasis on cooperation rather than competition; sharing rather than accumulating.

10. Humans, as part of a greater whole, become part of an ever-changing and ongoing process that is the Universe in process of *being*. We have the capacity to change the course of that whole—for good or evil—through our actions.

This is only a partial list of what it is to be human in a Native American sense. The implications and ramifications of such descriptions and definitions of human being are vast and lead to social structures and cultural perspectives that differ tremendously from that of the mainstream. An understanding of Native America necessarily requires an exploration into what it is to "be human" as described by Native Americans.

# Critiques

## I. Against Individualism

When Aristotle commented that "a man alone is either a god or a beast," he intended to point to the fact that a human, unlike "a god or a beast," is a *social* animal. Humans, by definition, in the Greek mind, could be likened to "ants" and "bees"—other species that exhibited a "social" nature.

The contemporary West, on the other hand, sees such an analogy as an insult. The mention of ants and bees calls up visions of a mindless mass swarming through mere instinct, waiting to be led to whatever fate awaits them. There is granted the awareness of a human social factor, but it is explained as a factor that is artificially forced on an essentially independent, autonomous, singular *individual*.

The individual is defined as having some inherent quality that guarantees that he is not *naturally* a social being. He is something separate from the group and what he is must be guarded from the group's intrusion. The group is always, in this view, an intrusion. Group values are an imposition on the individual. The individual has a "true self" that he must guard against the demands of the group. His membership in a group, and there is always such, is seen as a necessary imposition. It is necessary in order to guarantee the survival of the individual.

This view of the primacy of the individual is illustrated by the vision of a human first drawn up by the seventeenth-century philosopher Thomas Hobbes. Hobbes portrays man as a singular being existing in a state of competition: a state of war of each against all, each against each. Human life, according to Hobbes, is short, brutal, and solitary. The life of the individual is driven by self-interest in the name of survival. That Hobbes's vision of the individual is not "outdated" is borne out by the fact that today the discipline of economics operates on a very specific law: "Each man acts so as to enhance his own self-interest." This view of "human nature" is not simply an observation but is seen as having much the same weight as the "law" of gravity. It is presented as the major fact of human existence: humans are "solitary" and exist in a state of competition with all other humans.

The notion of the competitive individual is again strengthened in Western society when Charles Darwin offers his evolutionary theory. Darwin, himself, does not depict the Hobbesian worldview, but he does see a hierarchy from single-celled animals to angels. It is Herbert Spencer who is responsible for what has come to be called "social Darwinism." Spencer revived the Hobbesian state of competition with an added twist: the war is a "survival of the fittest." The world is depicted as *naturally* existing in such a state that each and every life form survives only because it does not allow another thing to exist: "Eat or be eaten." "The law of the jungle." "Dog eat dog." The phrases that are well known in the West depict the worldview that is held by most Westerners as "reality." The fact that humans always exist in a social setting is not an argument, in the West, for a natural bent to be a flock or herd animal. Existence in a group merely extends the metaphor of "survival of the fittest": groups exist in a state of competition for scarce resources with other groups.

How much of this is drawn from actual observation and how much from justification for how Western man does indeed operate?

The argument for competition, for the "winner take all" atmosphere, would seem to imply an evolutionary process that strives for a lack of diversity. In fact, however, we have proof all around us that diversity is the hallmark of nature. One can grant that the individual human is absolutely unique: barring twins, no two individuals are alike. That diversity extends to snowflakes and elephants and it certainly extends to groups. There are hundreds of cultures on the planet and perhaps thousands of languages. Languages have a tendency to become local—they diversify from a major language group and proceed to even greater diversity with regional accents. The attempt to depict a state of affairs in the world that leads to one massive "monoculture" would seem to be unrealistic in the face of the diversity displayed on the planet.

It seems even somewhat paradoxical to be arguing that a state of competition exists whereby there can be only one "winner" and then to argue for the autonomy of the individual. An argument for the uniqueness and solitary condition of the individual is an argument for the ultimate form of diversity.

Individuals who accept that they are "group beings" are seen in the

West as at an "undeveloped" stage of the species. "Tribalism," and its accompanying label "nationalism," are seen as archaic notions. I encountered a textbook in a political science class years ago that dealt with the issue of "development." It outlined the necessary steps that must be taken in the process of moving a nation from an "undeveloped" stage to "modernity." The first step was to eliminate "tribalism," the sense of the individual that he is a part of a greater whole. If the individual could be shown, according to this theory, that he was something separate and apart from the group, then he could be shown to operate "in his own best interest." The tribe, itself, need not be destroyed—the process of separating out the individual as a separate unit would be the tool of destruction of the archaic notion of "tribalism" or "group identity."

An individual, set apart from his group, can be more easily manipulated by others. He has no value except "self-interest." The former stake of working for the survival of the group as a necessary condition for the survival of the individual as a specific type of individual is eradicated. The sense of oneself as an Apache, or a Watusi, or any other cultural group, is replaced by a sense of autonomous existence. The individual exchanges a group identity—"I am Watusi"—for a name—"I am John Doe."

I have always found it curious that the autonomous individual with an unbearable name is often hesitant to change that name, the excuse being that the name signifies who he is. Barring membership in a group with a shared identity or culture, perhaps all that is left to the individual is a sense of self as a *name*. He cannot place himself into a larger sphere of meaning. The autonomous being is seen as a higher state of being. But such beings seem to spend an inordinate amount of their lifetimes trying to find out "who they really are."

The respect granted the integrity of the individual, as an individual, is so great in some Native American groups that private names are not bandied about. I very seldom heard my father use my mother's name or even that of his children. When he did use names the occasion had some great import. Our sense of identity is not tied to a name; however, the name can be a very important symbol. There were no such things as "family names" before the arrival of the European. Names were earned or granted or taken and were subject to change as the circumstances of the person changed. A very strong sense of personal identity is necessary to allow the change of a name. As an instructor in various universities, I have learned to memorize my students' names because I know that the name carries great importance in Western societies. I am, however, always just a bit astounded when others use my name with any sort of frequency.

A sense of oneself as a part of a greater whole does not lead to a loss of a sense of self. There is no such thing as a "herd mentality"; instead, there is a greater sense of oneself as a responsible human being. The consequences of an individual's actions carry much more weight in small groups. One is never anonymous. One can never claim 'rights' that demand that others exercise responsibility. *I* must be responsible—for myself and to others.

I have often encountered Native Americans who have lived apart from their relatives and find the lack of anonymity when they are with relatives or clan members to be uncomfortable. "At first," said one woman, "I really like the fact that I am a part of something, that I am responsible to everyone else. But after a while I long to be anonymous." On the other hand, she finds herself exasperated by the self-centeredness of the "Anglos" in her non-reservation home. "You can't have it both ways!" she says. She, as do many others, shifts back and forth from one "world" to another.[1]

The myth of the autonomous being has many other pitfalls with important consequences for the explanation of individual identity. To imagine that the individual is "self-made" or that he comes into the world with a ready-made identity requires a denial that the individual is modeled by the group.

Take any infant, from whatever cultural group, raise him in another group, and he will grow up with an identity totally unlike that of his siblings left in his original group. Human beings appear to be highly malleable. Long before the question over personal identity arises, the individual has already been "imprinted" with a very definite identity. He can also be taught (or "imprinted") with the idea that he has no group identity. This latter course seems to be the method of child-raising most employed in the West.

What is it that constitutes the group identity, or the sense of oneself as being a part of a greater whole? An infant receives a set of values, a set of approved behaviors, a language, perhaps a religion, and certainly a worldview. He comes to share this set of characteristics with his group. A sense of sharing such characteristics with others allows for a sense of self as a part of a greater whole. Believing that one's values are "self-made" is an act of delusion.

I often encounter college students who claim to have "their own values," "their own worldview." No, I say to them, you do not. The person with his very own worldview is what we call a madman—a "crazy" person. That is the usual definition of madness in any culture—someone who does not share the worldview of his peers is seen as "insane." "Sanity" is measured by one's ability to communicate with others; an ability to communicate assumes some shared notions.

An example: A professor points out to me my use of the term 'we.' "What do you think . . . ," she asks in a class on the philosophy of 'time,' and I reply, "We think. . . ." I reply that same way for each question: "We . . . think . . . say . . . believe. . . ." She responds, "Who is this 'we'—there is only one of you sitting in that chair!" I am startled. I am assuming that she and the rest of the class are discussing views from a particular perspective—the Western perspective on space and time. I assume that they know that I am also speaking from a perspective—one that is unlike their own but not uniquely my own. I say "we" to indicate my awareness that my view is a result of shared notions, notions that are not shared by the professor and the class.

They, on the other hand, believe that they have no perspective, that their discourse is not conducted within very narrow boundaries. The professor wants to know what "I," the autonomous being, thinks, says, and believes. She and the students imagine themselves to be conducting an unbounded discussion. From my own perspective, I can see that they are doing no such thing—that their discussion is predictable. Within my own context, or "language-game," my responses would be viewed as "predictable" also—if someone were aware of that context and had come from outside that context. Standing within a context one sees only the unbounded complexity of discourse; standing outside a context and looking in, one sees the boundaries of discourse. That is why one can pick up a written text and without seeing the title identify a particular work of an author with whom one is acquainted: "That is Kant's *Metaphysics of Morals.*" The key is the familiarity. If one assumes that others from a culture unlike one's own do not think, or that they have only erroneous ideas, or that there are no "language-games," then it is easy to see why one would come to believe that one's thoughts are unique to an individual.

I believe, in contrast, that there are no self-made persons. There are only those who cannot (or refuse to) acknowledge their debts.

## II. Against the Singularity of the Human *Species*

The idea that human beings developed in a single way, with a shared "beginning" and a shared teleological course of development, is a uniquely Western idea. It is an idea that is seldom, if ever, questioned. Yet none of the other peoples of the world hold to this idea.

An incident that happened some years ago will serve as an illustration. Upon discovery of the ancient tomb in China that contained thousands of replicas of soldiers with their weapons, accompanying possessions, and their horses, an American history magazine featured a cover depicting the musical instruments found in the tomb. The cover of the magazine proclaimed, "Our ancient musical heritage." The "our" in the title was to be understood to stand for "mankind." The point here is that American readers did not see the find in China as demonstrating the unique cultural heritage of the Chinese people. By emphasizing the "mankind" aspect, there was an attempt to co-opt the historical significance of the tomb's content to China alone.

The accomplishments of all other cultures, particularly as they are distant in time, are claimed as part of the "heritage" of the West. One need only pick up a child's "History of the World" to see that the history of the West begins in the ancient Middle East. The child is taken through a route that begins with Babylon and Sumer, goes through Egypt to Greece and Rome, and culminates with contemporary America. The child need not be faulted if he walks away from such a text believing that coursing through his veins are the memories of having been Sumerian, Egyptian, Greek, and Roman. All of the histories of the world, he might think, have been the forming ground for his own existence.

Another illustration can be drawn from the charts made up to depict the evolutionary course of "modern" man. The chart will begin with the lemur-like primate and proceed through the apes to the proto-humanoid *Australopithecus* and on to the Neanderthal and the Cro-Magnon. The chart culminates with the depiction of a "modern" human who is, invariably, a northern European male. There is never, at the end of that chart, an African, an Asian, or even a southern European. Usually the charts depict the creatures prior to the appearance of the northern European male as being smaller in size than the "modern" man. Again, we could not fault the contemporary child seeing this chart for believing that northern European males represent the latest evolutionary stage of the human species.

No other people except those of the West write "history" in such a manner. They may, as has China, have a long recorded history of their own, but they do not presume to be writing the "history of the world." Nor do other peoples rush to collect the artifacts of ancient civilizations far from their own lands to house in their museums as the "history of *mankind*." The Chinese do not house the artifacts of Egypt as part of their "heritage."

Few Westerners would see the act of collecting the artifacts of the planet's people as a bit odd. Their need to document the "history of the world" is seen as a noble act that they alone undertake because others "fail" to see that there is a "history of *mankind*" to be written.

Westerners have gone so far as to point out the place where "the mother of mankind" was born: it is in eastern Africa.

The problem with visualizing "history" in this manner is obvious to non-Westerners: the actual fact of human diversity takes second place to the notion of singularity. If all of the world's peoples are not exactly like the northern European male, then something must be *wrong* with those others. Here is where the "developmental" charts fit once again. This time we will compose a chart of "human development," somewhere between the space that exists on the evolutionary chart between Cro-Magnon and the northern European male. This chart is also familiar to the child student. We begin with the simple gatherers of fruits and nuts wandering about the savanna and proceed through the addition of hunting by the gatherers on to nomadic wandering after the herds of wild animals. On we go through simple agriculture, the discovery of metals and the rise of urban centers, culminating, again, in the cities of the largely northern European male. The various "stages" of human development are given names: "Stone Age," "Bronze Age," "Iron Age," and so on. They have other labels also: "primitive," "feudal," "medieval."

If, in the midst of "modern man's" presence, there exist human beings who do not share his particular lifestyle, they can be labeled according to the scale of "gatherer," "hunter-gatherer," "nomadic," or "medieval." They are referred to by the West as representing "undeveloped" peoples or as existing in various "developing" stages. The idea that all human beings exist in a stage either as "modern" (read: European) or on the way to becoming so is a "fact" of Western "knowledge." There is no awareness here, by the Western thinker, that other peoples are denied the claim to be pursuing a *valid* lifestyle by virtue of having been placed on the Western hierarchical scale of being.

The actual diversity of the human species is denied. There is only one *correct* lifestyle: that of the contemporary European.

The concept of a singularity, such as the term 'mankind' signifies, is a pernicious concept. It flies in the face of the actuality that human beings do exhibit different means of adapting to the diverse circumstances offered by the planet. The concept ignores also the fact that the Earth exhibits tremendous diversity, not only in environmental circumstances, but in the plethora of creatures and vegetation that occupy those environmental niches.

Western scientists, in the 1930s, began to look at the fact that the world operated in a carefully balanced manner. Out of this perspective the science of "ecology" has been developed. The most recent contribution to arise out of this science is a recognition of the necessity of diversity for the health of the planet. "Monoculture," in agriculture and in forestry, has been found to lead to a less healthy environment. Monoculture in the ranks of human beings has yet to be viewed as equally harmful.

The concept of the singularity of 'mankind' prevents recognizing also that the diverse cultural adaptations exhibited by humans throughout the planet also improve the health of the planet. How could a people that justifies its manipulation of the nations and lifestyles of others on the basis that they are "helping" in their "development" suddenly say to themselves, "Maybe their lifestyles are valid . . ." How could the "modern man" acquiesce to the fact that—maybe—it is necessary to allow "a handful of savages" to maintain control over a vast area of rain forest in the deep of the Amazon? For the health of the planet?

What would happen to the "modern" lifestyle if access to more and more resources were halted on the basis that the people occupying the lands holding those resources had a right to their lifestyle—which does not include the removal of what the modern man calls a "resource"? At one time, before the "age of exploration" began, most of the world's peoples led a self-sufficient lifestyle. Today, most of the world's non-Western peoples lead lives of hunger and misery. They suffer the displacement from ancient homelands. The ancient homeland has been harnessed to provide "resources" for the voracious modern lifestyle. The residents of the formerly self-sufficient homelands now swarm into the cities in search of a means of survival. The world's people grow accustomed to seeing this displacement called "progress." We grow accustomed to the forced change of lifestyle referred to as "development." We acknowledge that though the present lives of millions and millions of people are lives of hunger, poverty, and desperation, this is merely a necessary stage on their way to "development."

The consciences of the sensitive are smoothed through the various charitable organizations that gather food and cast-off clothing for the world's hungry. We do not acknowledge that the price of "progress" is the misery of other peoples—that the hunger of others is the price paid for the West's access to the world's foodstuffs and the world's ores.

The pernicious quality of the concept of the singularity of the species prohibits seeing the other as a form of life of value equal to that of the European.

All contemporary human beings have been on this planet for the same length of time. Each group has a history of tens of thousands of years and is therefore as 'modern' as is the European. The European has dismissed the lifestyles of others as mere "artifact." In a recent television program on the life of the "bushmen" of the Kalahari Desert in south-central Africa, the commentary records the former lifestyle (pre-European invasion) and contrasts this to the present circumstances of the "bushmen": they cannot adapt to the "changing world" that encroaches into the places and acres required to sustain their former lifestyles. There is no call here for the establishment of an area that will be beyond encroachment for the sake of the continued existence of the "bushmen." There is, instead, a tone of the inevitability of that change, an acceptance of the demise of the "bushmen" as though their demise were as natural as the disappearance of the blooming of a flower. And, as with the recording of the blooming of a flower, the commentator dispassionately ends his discourse with an air of having accomplished something rather grand: the death throes of a people captured on film.

This perspective on the inevitability of the demise of non-Western peoples has particularly harmful effects on those indigenous people now surrounded by Europeans on the North American continent.

The coffee tables (probably made of exotic woods from a tropical rain forest) of the middle class in America are graced with expensive photo essays published (in time for Christmas, no doubt) on the various "Indian" tribes of America. While the Native American, as an *artifact*, is undergoing a resurgence of popularity, the Native American as he actually exists is ignored. Today, in the United States, the average life span of an indigenous person is around forty-seven years. The indigenous people have the highest unemployment rates, the highest incidence of diabetes, and their children have the highest suicide rate in the nation.

The bored youth of the Euroman middle class engage in quests to learn ancient Indian mysticism that will lend meaning to their ennui-filled lives. They decorate their rearview mirrors with "Indian-made" *dreamcatchers* as talismans, perhaps, to protect them from the disease of their fathers. Academics make their livelihood in the analysis of ancient Indian cemeteries and abandoned homes. Native American myths and legends have provided a new discipline for the European practitioners of academic analysis. Whole careers are built on "understanding" and "interpreting" the indigenous cultures—as *artifacts*. None of that research lessens the suicide, or alcoholic, or diabetic rate among the indigenous people. The contemporary indigenous people serve in the place of the "bushmen" of the television commentary. There is little attempt to communicate with the indigenous persons beyond recording their accounts of myths and legends. It is assumed that the viewpoint of a contemporary, live "Indian" could have no value for the "modern" researcher.

Again, another television program, this one about the ever-popular "mystery of the Anasazi," the abandoned sites of the indigenous peoples of the southwestern United States. Only once throughout the entire hour-long program does anyone bother to confer with a contemporary descendant of "the Anasazi." He is allowed to recount the story of his people's migration from the "Anasazi" area to his present homeland for less than two minutes. No questions are asked of him either by the researchers or the television host. Yet these same people will probe the legends in the Bible for the "truths" to be ferreted out of ancient place-names and locations. On indigenous ground, the researcher will walk past the poverty of the contemporary indigenous person to find the burial grounds of indigenous great-grandparents. The artifact, in this case, and as always, has more value than the contemporary presence.

Here, again, the assumption is that there can be nothing learned from contemporary indigenous persons. They do, after all, represent on the hierarchical chart a lifestyle—a life form—that is archaic, irrelevant. The contemporary indigenous person is, at most, a living fossil of "modern man's" own rise through the evolutionary scale. All knowledge that could possibly reside in the contemporary indigenous mind has already been experienced by the "modern" person—experienced and discarded as useless. The "modern" mind has "risen" above the thought patterns of the indigenous mind. No account of migration provided by a contemporary indigenous person of the American Southwest could satisfy the European fascination with "the mystery of the Anasazi": if there is a "secret" there, it must be found out only by the European in order to be granted validity.

The experience of the contemporary indigenous person is valid only insofar as he is granted validity by the European researcher. The early sixteenth- and seventeenth-century accounts of the American indigenous groups by the explorers and missionaries carry more weight in determining what a group is than all of the words of the contemporary Native Americans. The only value of the contemporary Native is as a possible corroborating source for a European researcher's theoretical construct. Should such a person, however, question the correctness of the researcher's theories, he would be ignored. How could he, centuries removed from the "original" people, know anything? He doesn't, a researcher might snort, even know his own language!

There is an argument that the indigenous person cannot know or interpret his own culture because he is embedded in that culture. However, if that same indigenous person should make a study of the European in his midst, he would be chided for being too unfamiliar with the European to make any valid judgments. The European researcher claims, with a stay of six weeks, six months, or six years, to understand and interpret a non-Western culture because he is armed with "objective" methodologies. The point of this inquiry into the concept of 'mankind' is to show that such "objectivity" does not exist.

I remember sitting between two persons from different nations at a mini-UN conference at a university. On one side was a man from Sri Lanka, on the other a man from India. We were listening to one of those "One World, One People" speeches that Europeans are so fond of giving. The speaker noted that the concept required that each of us give something up in order to live together in harmony; he likened the "one people" to passengers on a ship. "Guess who," asked the Sri Lankan, "gets to be the captain of this ship." "Guess who," asked the Indian, "gets to give something up." All three of us knew that we would not be "captains." Each of us knew that the European would not give up anything; he was, after all, the standard by which he measured all others.[1]

The concept of the singularity of the human species prohibits seeing the *other* as truly *an other*. The *other*, under this "method" of interpretation, remains an undeveloped form of life, a form of life that has failed to become fully human, that is, European. The fatal quality of this line of reasoning is that Europeans fail to see the diversity of which the human species is capable. How many different ways can humans understand and adapt to the world as they find it?

# Becoming Human

A definition of what it is to be human presents not so much an illumination into 'humanness' as an enigma.

The encounter of the European with the inhabitants of the Americas in the late fifteenth century can best be compared to what would happen today if an inhabitant from another star system were to land in one of our cities. If this alien were at all humanoid, chances are that his appearance would be like none with which we have become familiar. The European was not totally isolated from the existence of peoples that did not bear a physical resemblance to himself; he was familiar with the "Negro," the "Oriental," and the Semitic peoples. There was also a broad variety of countenances within the European group. The peoples of the New World, nevertheless, represented a form of humanity never before encountered. A very major question arose from this unfamiliarity: Were they to be counted as human? And if they were at least *humanoid*, did they have *souls*?

The answers to these questions were provided in the famous disputations of Bartolomé de las Casas and Sepulveda.[1] The church had less of a problem considering the newly discovered peoples as human, complete *with souls*, than did the minimally secular forces then in existence. Sepulveda, taking his cue from Aristotle, preferred to grant the 'Americans' a degree of humanity: they were a lower type of humanity, fit more for slaves (as 'beasts of burden') than for incorporation into the family of man. Las Casas argued that the natives were rational beings, capable of learning, and certainly capable of understanding the tenets of the Catholic Church. Las Casas's view was the official view of the church, and the effort of the church remained to convert as many of the natives to Christianity as possible.

To be *human* in the fifteenth and sixteenth centuries was to be capable of reasoning and to have a soul. Animals were thought to lack both. The definition of a human, within a Western context, has not changed from the definition put forth by the Catholic Church. This has not, however, eradicated the view held by Sepulveda, that is, that these newly discovered beings are lesser forms, or types, of a more highly endowed or evolved human type. Today, even though the attitude toward humans unlike those known in Europe has become less derogatory, there still exists the view that some peoples are "representatives" of "man's" earlier stages of development. There is no longer a distinction between 'beasts' and 'primitives' or 'men' and 'modern man'—there is now a distinction between humans made on the evaluation of whether the non-Western native of another country is *undeveloped*, *underdeveloped*, or *developing*. The standard for the evaluation remains the same: European Man, who is, of course, *fully developed*.

A human is, by definition, a *thinking* being. But the process of thinking does not, in itself, guarantee that a human is a rational (reasoning) being. The view of the thinking animal has taken a circuitous route over the centuries. For the ancient Greeks, the awareness of humans as thinking beings posed a philosophical problem. What was it that caused thinking? The idea of an animating force within the human led to an idea of a soul (*psyche*), but this had no personal characteristics. For Plato the soul might have been memory. He shows this in the *Meno* when he has a simple boy work on a mathematical problem; through trial and error the boy comes up with the only rational answer. Plato considers this proof that the boy had the answer all along, he had merely to *remember* it. Thinking, in this case, seems to be a matter of remembering. We must ourselves do a bit of remembering here: We must remember that Plato thought souls might be immortal, traversing a series of indefinite reincarnations. The soul carries memories through the various form changes.

Thinking, in the Christian era, is not a matter of 'remembering.' Saint Augustine offers a theory of *illumination*. In his *Confessions*, he prays for God to illuminate his reasoning abilities, so that he can come to some sort of truth about the topics he puts to inquiry. This can most simply be illustrated by the cartoon character who is shown with a light bulb blinking on over his head as an idea "strikes" him. Eventually, this notion comes to a new formulation in the introduction of *innate ideas*. God, for Descartes, places ideas in the mind of humans. These ideas then serve as a foundation for *true thought* or *certainty*. A subtle change comes about with Descartes: we now have that aspect of humans that causes thinking transferred from a *soul* to a *mind*. This transformation leads to another dilemma: how is it that the mind and body seem to communicate or correspond? This is the problem of *dualism* and remains a problem to this day. There is, if not an actual expression of dualism, a reference to dualism that is seemingly ineradicable from the Western conceptual framework. The *soul* is seen as something separate and disconnected from the physical body; the *mind* is seen as something equally separate from brain function.

In the twentieth century, the terminology changes once again. The term 'consciousness' comes to replace talk of *mind* or *soul*, most specifically, *self-consciousness*. As an awareness has developed that beings other than humans exhibit consciousness, it has become necessary to distinguish human consciousness from animal consciousness, hence "*self*-consciousness." Other animals, it is proposed, lack awareness of themselves as individuals. My view is that *individuality* is a 'given' rather than something that comes to be discovered. What distinguishes human from other animals is the awareness of the fact that *individuals* exist within the context of a group. What makes humans *human* is the recognition that the individual is a part of a greater whole. This view is, of course, entirely counter to the prevalent view in the West, in which the individual is not truly human until he "discovers" his givenness as an *individual*.

We have already ventured into the question of how two different groups can define a human being. I think that, in a Native American context, all things in the Universe seem to have a uniqueness that is summed up in the statement, "no two things are exactly alike." The "signature" of Earth's creativity seems to be a tremendous diversity. Even "identical twins" appear not to be exact copies of one another. The very fact that there are two beings precludes exact identity. It is in this sense that I can claim that the uniqueness of the individual is a *given*. The individual, however, seems to be "programmed" to be a social being in the normal course of development to adulthood. We, unlike other animals, have a prodigious capacity for speech. However, if speech is not developed before the age of puberty, and there are such rare cases, it appears that the ability to develop speech disappears altogether. Children at an early age have a tremendous capacity to use more than one language; the facility with which one learns a "foreign" language in childhood also allows that the child will have an equal facility in learning other languages as well.

An interesting, but little explored aside here is the ramifications of *interlingual* capacities among indigenous peoples in America. All groups seemed to have rules against marrying within a small group. Spouses from other groups were often sought out. The "foreign" marriage partner provided a means to communicate with another group, extending the sense of relatedness between groups. The "pure" group, existing in isolation from other groups, may be a figment of imagination perpetuated by anthropologists; it may be merely a means by which the researcher could categorize and distinguish between peoples.

One example of how this interlingual, and intercultural, exchange takes place can be drawn from northern New Mexico. The indigenous people of this area have been intermarrying with the Hispanic population for hundreds of years, yet the two groups have maintained their separate identities. This is done through choice. The partner going into the "alien" groups chooses to live a different lifestyle while at the same time maintaining sufficient ties with the "home" group to allow the ability to interpret between the two groups. There is intermarriage also with the "Anglo" population that has come into the area, but the Anglo population seems less open to the maintenance of separateness. "It is easier for the child," one might hear in this situation, "if he learns to speak the dominant language," which would, of course, be English. Bilingual ability is not generally valued among the Anglo population, yet in northern New Mexico it is not unusual to run into persons (most likely they are indigenous persons) who are *trilingual*. That is, they are likely to be fluent in three languages, English, Spanish, and one of the indigenous languages. The acceptance of "bi-(and poly-)culturalism" that results from this language usage is a topic that deserves an exploration that is important in itself.

What all of this points to is a flexibility of the human character that is not often taken into account when one attempts to define what it is to be human. Furthermore, becoming human is a responsibility of the whole; a child has to be taught the language of the group, as well as the mores of the groups, so that he can participate in the group. Many indigenous peoples see this membership as beginning when the child undergoes an official naming ceremony, usually between the ages of five to eight years. Until that time the child is being taught to be perceptive about his role in the group. He is taught to be aware that his actions have consequences for others and that he has a contribution to make to the group. Creating a human being is, in other words, the responsibility of the whole group.

Contrast this with another perspective on what it is to be *human*. In Western societies, more so in some than in others, the newborn child is recognized as fully human at birth. The child comes into the world with a full personality (the "true self" that is the subject so many attempt to "find") that is then thwarted by the group. For an indigenous society, the group offers the individual the possibility of rising to his fullest potential in a manner that helps to maintain the survival of the group; in a Western society, the individual represents a potential burden to the group unless it is coerced in some fashion. In both cases the child is seen as in need of socialization. The ends may be the same, but the means are very different and lead to a very different definition, in each case, of what it is to be human.

# Time, Culture, and Self

When we define "human nature," we also set forth certain expectations of a human being. Different cultures define human beings according to other beliefs about Life, Time, and the Universe. The definition is set, so to speak, in a matrix of related beliefs.

As an example, we might look at the different definitions of human beings offered by Christianity and the secular West. In the first instance humans are defined as "fallen creatures;" they are so because of a willful act on the part of the first ancestors. All human beings inherit the willfulness, or "sinfulness," of the original pair. In the secular version of human nature, humans are described as essentially laden with "instincts" that have not kept pace with other aspects of human evolution. In both cases human beings are not "what they are meant to be." In both cases, it is "human nature" that is to blame for human shortcomings.

What we expect from human behavior is colored by the definition we have given of human nature. Human nature, on the other hand, is defined in the matrix of other beliefs about the greater world that humans occupy. In the Christian version of human appearance, an extraterrestrial being creates the universe, the planet, and then places humans at the center of concern. Their command is to "subdue, and hold dominion . . . over every living thing." The Earth and all of its characteristics is an object, a *thing*. Humans hold a position of superiority over Earth and its other occupants. In the secular belief system, Earth, too, is mere object. Humans, by virtue of having evolved from a lower stage to a higher, are also superior to other beings and the planet itself. The secular version offers a humanistic version of the Christian mythos: What God has failed to do, through not restoring humans to their rightful place (the perfection of Eden), Man can now accomplish. He can transform the Earth, establish proper order, and guide his own "development." The Christian version gives a limited time for the rectification of humans so that proper order might be restored; there is a sense of an "end time." The secular West postulates a near infinite scale of progression from one state of being to an ever higher and more complex state.

Time is the stage upon which the Western drama is enacted. It has been so since the days of the firming of Christian beliefs, especially in the work of Saint Augustine. Time, in Augustine's sense, is not the "mere measure of heavenly motions" as the pagan Greeks and Romans would have it; it is something else altogether. Time exists as its own dimension. Augustine offers as proof of this claim the biblical account of the battle fought in God's name in which God allows time to stand still (the sun does not go down) until the battle is fought to its proper end. If time were not something separate from heavenly motion, would not everything have come to a standstill along with the sun's passage? asks Augustine.

We are more accustomed, today, to hearing of something called the "space-time continuum" than we are of biblical accounts. Nevertheless, Augustine's re-formation of time is the Western sense of time. Time and the Universe are set out as in a closed block—the past and the future are all laid out by, perhaps, "the hand of God." The present merely marks out the passage of humans through the past and into the future. The future is when everything will work out—either God returns through his avatar, Christ, or man himself will bring the glorious future. It is *out there*, waiting. The best analogy for this sense of time is the cinematic film. If we stretched out the film from beginning to end, we would see the outcome of the "play," frame by frame. We could imagine ourselves as actors in a play who imagine that they make up the dialogue as they go along. Only the playwright knows different. God holds past, present, and future in his vision. There is nothing new under the Sun.

Time is culturally constructed. The Muslim believes that the future is not yet created; Allah creates the universe second by millisecond. The Westerner exists in the "year" 2001, for example, by virtue of a time system based on a specific event, the birth of Jesus. The Chinese and the Jew exist in a time frame counted in the six thousands, again based on culturally specific events.

What if, however, there is yet another means of "telling time"? Native Americans are not usually questioned about their theories of human nature. What could they possibly have to say that has not been said before? In the Western scenario of time and the Universe, the Native American exists as a living fossil portraying earlier stages of Western man's singular climb to complexity on a teleological evolutionary path of the Universe. If so, it is no more acceptable to engage a Native American philosopher in discussions of time and human nature than it would be to engage a single-celled amoeba.

But such discussions do go on. The Native American exists in a world not of his own making, and in order to survive he must learn other ways of "dissecting" the world. He arms himself with Western concepts so as not to alarm his potential non-Native American listeners. He maintains his own view for discussion with his own kind:

Human nature does not revolve around a fall from a deity's favor. There is no prisonlike sentence of a specific time in which he must redeem himself in the eyes of a deity. Human beings are beings of the flock, like geese. He, more so than any other being, is tied to his group through language. The Earth has produced him, as part of a group, to occupy a certain area. There are other groups occupying other areas. Each new being is trained to be a specific kind of human being, according to the group's definition of what it is to be human.

Despite such views of singular "creation" of specific groups, there is much accord among Native American groups. Contrary to the anthropologists' view of Native Americans living in isolation, in a state of genetic purity apart from other groups, there was in fact much mingling between groups. The northern part of America was crisscrossed with ancient trade routes. Copper from the Great Lakes is discovered in the ruins of the Southwest, and coral from the Caribbean is found in ancient mounds in the Midwest. There were intermarriages and ready interpreters between different peoples. There was a well-established and now, perhaps, forgotten sign language that dealt with concepts that allowed people of different tribes to communicate with each other.

The idea of a human nature, though existing in various guises, revolved around the fact that humans were creatures of the hive, the flock, the "we." Humans were but one of many species of beings that coexisted equally, all dependent on the Mother, the Earth, for their sustenance. Humans differed from other flocks in that they had language, the better to bond the group. They saw themselves as existing in a web of highly interrelated and interdependent "substances": air, water, other beings, the land. They maintained their life force by ingesting the life force of other beings. No less respect was due a wild onion than a deer. "Eat it," my father would say to us; "we took its life that we might continue our own." Eating was a holy sacrament; a thanksgiving to the creatures that provided us life.

Above all, humans had prodigious memories. Memory provided the awareness of consequences. All actions came with consequences. To know consequences was to exhibit knowledge and learning. And to know the consequences of actions of those before us was to display wisdom. The past was not a dead and unknown time—for so long as there were people to remember it and hand it down to others.

And with mention of the past, mention of the future cannot be avoided.

Many Native American languages are languages of verbs. The noun depicts a world of stasis—*something* is. The verb portrays a world in perpetual motion and change—*is-ing* occurs, *being* happens. Time, said Aristotle, is "the measure of motion;" Plato called it the "number" of motion. The Native American could say, "Time is the measure of *relative* motion." "I once heard a man say," Augustine informs us, "that time is simply the movement of the sun and moon and stars. I did not agree." Time, for Augustine, as for the majority of the West, is not a measure of motion; it is that, instead, by which motion is measured.

Augustine is plagued by the views of the pagans. They insist that there has always been motion and that the Universe is infinite. Augustine must explain the creation of the world out of nothing and at the same time explain the eternity of God. Things did exist prior to God "speaking" them into existence, says Augustine, but they existed in *eternity*—in the mind of God, as a poem exists in the mind of the one who has memorized it. The poem is called into existence "out of nothing" through the poet's recitation. What word, asks Augustine, did God utter to bring things into existence? As for those vexing questions posed by the pagan thinkers as to what God was doing *before* he decided to bring the Universe into existence, Augustine offers an explanation all too familiar to modern-day thinkers more predisposed to a big bang theory than to Creation: there was no *before* before things came into existence.

The Native American philosopher could have joined the ranks of the ancient Greeks and Romans: perhaps the Universe is infinite as well as is motion. Picture another "version" of time: imagine a spinning top, a child's toy. In this case, however, it is a top spinning in a perpetual motion. One cannot *go back* to a previous spin—it no longer exists. One cannot go into a *future* spin—it has *not yet* come into existence. Now imagine tops among tops, vortices, if you will—so that there is no space between the spinning tops. And imagine also that all of the things on the top, in the top, have an effect on the spinning.

The legends of Native Americans that portray humans as cocreators of the spinning Universe should be taken deadly seriously: Time and the Universe have everything to do with expectations of what it is to be a human being. I AM RESPONSIBLE. My actions in the world are not meaningless; they may be no more than a drop of water in an ocean, but at some point that drop triggers a deluge, or a weather pattern, or myriads of other "relative motions." The future does not exist. "I" have not yet made it, contributed to it. My present actions are making it. Present actions are like layers of snow added to a snowball—the shape of the present outer layer determines the future shape of the whole.

Whether any of these accounts of time are true or not, they do affect the actions of humans in their world. A view of the Universe as on a collision course with greater forces will affect a Christian sensibility; a view of the Universe as set on an inevitable progressive course through time will affect the sensibility of secular Westerners. A view of a Universe in the making will affect the actions of a Native American, who understands that "what one sows, one will reap."

The ancient Hebrews had only to exercise patience toward the fulfillment of a promise made by a god: someday they would be led to their proper home. The Christian invented a new sense of waiting for that fulfillment. The secular, post-Christian Westerner invented a new theory of time: the idea of Progress is a product of the Enlightenment.

Who questions the reality of something called 'progress'? I know of no work to match the critique in J. B. Bury's *The Idea of Progress*,[1] though today evolutionary biologists question the idea of a progressive evolutionary process. They offer, instead, the concept of change in the face of other changes. A Native American philosopher could agree with that: what I change can change me. The first oxygen-breathing being changed in response to changes and caused, in turn, other changes to the world. The Universe is about interrelationships and interdependencies. In a world of change and motion, *stability* becomes an important goal. In a world that asks, "Why is there something rather than nothing?" a fear of falling into nothingness, motionlessness, is something to be feared. The ancient Aztecs, fearing that the Universe would slow to a stop if they did not sacrifice pulsing hearts to augment its own pulsing, fought with their neighbors to obtain sacrificial hostages. What price is paid in the name of Progress, and who pays the price? Who are the sacrificial hostages of the superior beings who mark the acme of a teleological process?

Time, Culture, and Self are intricately tied together. It is not possible to determine human nature, or the concept of a self, without taking into account a theory, or theories, of time. Nor is it possible to determine with any finality what it is to be human, if all "stories" are not laid out on a table for the perusal of all comers.

# Cowboys and Indians: A Story

*With a short story, Viola Cordova shows us how an old woman's relation to a place fundamentally shapes who she is and how she ought to live. The story brings her philosophy of personal identity to life and invites others to consider their own relation to their place and their own sense of right action.*

Manuela Tsosie rises early every morning. She has to get her sheep down into the arroyo after yesterday's rain. But her sheep are not the only reason she rises before dawn.

She is of the SunBringer Clan, as were her mother and her grandparents for untold centuries. The major responsibility of her clan is to welcome and thank the rising Sun. She thanks the Sun—for the dew on the sagebrush and the dawn flowers. She joins in the waking of the Earth, *Na'ho'dzaan*, from a night's sleep.

"Like a child's breath upon waking from a nap," thinks Manuela, as she becomes aware of *Na'ho'dzaan*'s morning breath, aware of the warm moist scent emitted by the Mother through her plants, her stones, the dust. Manuela distinguishes between the odor released by the dampened trunk of the sagebrush and that of the more acrid leaves. Sagebrush is the carpet that surrounds Manuela's home.

"Home" is the area Manuela's family has inhabited since the time of the Emergence. It is home despite the recent frequent oustings by Europeans. She knows the legendary tellings of real events: the herding of her people to Fort Sumner; the directed attack of Kit Carson pursuing his assigned task of "exterminating the Navajo and the Apache;" the diaspora of fleeing relatives among the friendly Pueblo people of Jamez, S'Ildifonz, and San Juan.

Manuela knows the boundaries that mark her home: the mountains of the Four Directions. She knows even more intimately the immediate area that she, through maternal inheritance, has received as her specific responsibility. Manuela's two daughters and her granddaughters have hoghans nearby. "*This,*" she can say, as she waves her arm across the horizon, "this is who we are."

Manuela, having surveyed the atmosphere of the early morning and welcomed the Sun, knots her headscarf under her chin and sets off to saddle her horse. "Horse," she calls the old mare, for she doesn't know what the horse calls itself. "Horse, horse, horse," she murmurs, as she strokes the horse and sets the blanket on its back. In the small corral, sheep bleat comfortably. Her daughters allow her only "a handful," which, in reality, amounts to around thirty sheep. Her horse saddled, she leads it outside and opens the door of the sheep pen.

"Sh, sh, sh," she lulls the sheep as they run from the pen. From a small pouch around her neck, Manuela gathers a pinch of pollen. This she offers to the Sun, to the Four Directions, to *Na'ho'dzaan,* as she releases the pollen through a movement of thumb and forefinger. "Eh," she murmurs, deep in her throat; and "*hozhoni,*" pronouncing the day, the area, good.

Manuela has not gone more than a mile from her hoghan when she spots the furious dust cloud coming at her from the northeast. She pauses her horse. She knows, from the speed, height, and consistency of the dust cloud that it is some white man coming across the landscape. Din'eh teenagers drive like that, she thinks, but their speed is not so consistent; they get to feeling ashamed and pull their foot off the gas pedal. They know that *Na'ho'dzaan* knows, feels, senses, the travesty being forced upon her. Does the white man feel, Manuela wonders, any shame for what he does to the Mother? She notices that the path of the furious truck and her own will intersect in some few minutes. She dismounts and begins to fuss with her horse. The sheep, sensing a break in the steady routine, pause for a search of the ground for fresh vegetation.

The truck halts some quarter of a mile away. Like a lightning clap, the slamming of the truck door by the driver as he alights from his vehicle shatters the slight soughing of the breeze. The dust, which followed the vehicle, slows and seems to try to gather at the truck as though trying to collect itself at the foot of that which called it into action.

Manuela can see that it is a "Ranger" that heads toward her. He comes, she believes, to count her sheep, to gauge their health, to take notice of their footprints around the brush, amid the dust.

"Howdy!" shouts the Ranger as he approaches Manuela. He says "Howdy" as though he means to impress her with the fact that the term is part of his everyday language, but she knows that it is an affectation. He thinks (she thinks) that by taking on a folksy attitude that he will disarm her suspicions over his intentions. Little does he know that "folksy" is more likely to be coming from those who dislike Indians most of all.

Ranger wears a proper shirt over his dirty and worn denim jeans. His long hair is tied back with a dirty string. He must be one of those "natural" people, thinks Manuela. She is familiar with the "natural" types, the "earth people." They are the spoiled youth of the white conquerors who now posture aghast over what their parents and grandparents "have done to the earth." Usually the type is relatively harmless except that they tend to want to linger. They do not simply greet one and move on. They seek approval. Manuela looks at him stone-faced. He is a hindrance in her day's activities.

Ranger introduces himself with his boisterous voice. He gives one of those singular anonymous names that they think serve to identify them. The impatience of the white man is too forbidding for Manuela to introduce herself. How long would he last, she wonders, if she began with her place, her clan, her born-for clan, her parents, all those things that serve among the Din'eh as markers of identity. No Din'eh has the luxury of anonymity. She is answerable to a horde of people for her actions. Who is Ranger responsible to? What keeps him in a state of respect?

Manuela's response is to focus on the shoes the Ranger wears. Tightened laces, squashed feet. She can imagine the way those feet would look once released from their casings. She nods her head in acknowledgment of the Ranger and makes ready to mount her horse.

Suddenly, out of the mouth of the Ranger, comes pouring a swarm of words accompanied by wild and uncontrolled gesticulations. Manuela climbs onto her horse. Ranger approaches. He smiles, the teeth seeming strange surrounded by facial hair. "Butt-faces," the kids call the white men. Facial hair is strange when confronted by those who have no or little body hair. The long hair on the Ranger's head seems matted compared to the smooth look of her husband's pulled-back hair. He ties the long hair behind his neck in a "chongo" and fastens this with a clean cloth. The Ranger offers a contrast to her husband's "chongo" hairstyle. She spurs her sheep into motion; knowing the routine, the sheep fall into place. Manuela turns in her saddle and waves good-bye to the Ranger. He stands in place for a few moments and then, as though jolted into action by some outside force, thrusts his whole arm upward and shouts, "Bye, see you!"

Poor man, thinks Manuela, as she pats the side of Horse's neck. "Sh, sh, sh," she murmurs to Horse and to Sheep. Sh, sh, sh. And, once again, she gives herself to the landscape, to the sheep, to the horse, to her world of wind and sand and sagebrush and stone. The breathing world. *Na'ho'dzaan.*

## V WHAT IS THE ROLE OF A HUMAN IN THE WORLD?

What are right ways of acting in the world? How do our relationships to place and community shape our responsibilities? What can we learn from Native American philosophies about how to live on earth without damaging the social and ecological systems that sustain us? How can we find a new reverence for the good earth, honoring our obligations to the generations that came before and will come to be? How shall we live in a sacred world, with what gratitude, what reverence, what respect and care?

# What Is the Role of a Human Being?

Any discussion about the role of humans in the world necessarily incorporates discussion about the ethical dimension of human action. Most ethical discussion begins with the grounds for justifying one's actions toward others. In a Christian worldview, humans are seen as tied, first and foremost, to a relationship with an extraterrestrial god. The relationship is between an 'I' (an individual) and the god: if the 'I' follows the rules of the god, he will be rewarded; failure to follow these rules results in punishment.

In the secular version of this view, an individual is alone and separate from other human beings. "Right" behavior results from a contract between humans that is based on self-interest: "I won't harm you at the waterhole if you won't harm me." An important conception of what it is to be human in both the Christian and Western secular views is that humans are seen as existing in a state of competition with one another, even within the group of which they are members. Human membership in a group is not understood as a natural state; there can, therefore, be no "natural" explanation for ethical behavior between human beings. Moreover, since a human being, in the Western/Christian context, is defined as separate from "the world," there is no need to include the Earth in one's ethical calculations.

The Native American view of human beings and their role in the world is very different from that of the Western/Christian view. It could be said that human beings have an *instinct* that draws them to others. It is this instinct that provides the basis for cooperative behavior. Cooperative behavior is "right" or "normal" behavior. Persons act ethically because they *want* to maintain their membership in the group. In order to maintain membership in a group, the survival of the group is as important as is the survival of the individual, perhaps more so. The individual is dependent on the group for his survival, and the group is dependent on its individuals for its survival. The group, in turn, as well as the individual, is dependent on the particular conditions of the area that it occupies for its continued survival. Other areas contain other people equally dependent on the conditions of their area for their survival.

One very important fact here, a fact that is missing from the Western/ Christian perspective, is that humans are seen as groups occupying specific *niches*. The existential and geographical circumstances of the group will provide the basis for the ethical considerations of the group. Since each group occupies a specific area, each group will have its own "code of conduct."

The ethical rules of Native American societies would seem to be based on two assumptions:

1. Humans are not alone.
2. Humans occupy a specific place.

What follows from these two assumptions is the following:

1. If humans were solitary individuals, as are some animals, then there would be no need for cooperative behavior and there would be no social groups. But humans do exist in groups and do not automatically compete with each and every individual. Therefore, it is "natural" for humans to be cooperative.
2. If our survival is dependent on certain conditions prevalent in our area, then we must maintain those conditions in order to continue our survival.

The consequences for behavior that is not conducive to the welfare of the entire group is a failure to survive, either as a group or as an individual. "I am *good*," in other words, "in order to maintain my membership in the group." And, "I must be mindful of what I do to my environment because I am dependent upon it."

An article by McPherson and Rabb,[1] which deals with the training of Native Americans children to act autonomously, points to the fact that such training leads to individuals who need no written rules or rewards and punishments with which to gauge their every action. The internalized perspective derived from the view of humans and humans in the world becomes, perhaps, the *unconscious* ground that guides individual behavior: each human being, in this context, becomes the judge and jury of his own behavior. The individual who is perceived as having done something "wrong" is also perceived as *knowing* that he has done so and is expected to engage in self-correction. Repeated wrong behavior is seen, not as criminal, but as *abnormal* ("There is something *wrong* with him"). Ostracism ("throwing him away") or exile (as in the ancient Greek societies) is the most prevalent means of dealing with an individual who persists in wrong behavior that results in harm to other individuals or to the group.

# Bounded Space

## I. The Four Directions

The fact that the Four Directions have some symbolic importance to the Native Americans is commonly known. What those directions symbolize is not always very clear. There is a general notion of the Directions that seems to grant them a somewhat amorphous character: that is, that the Directions, themselves, are "sacred" and, therefore, out of the stream of ordinary understanding. The fact that, in most instances, there are actually six directions considered sacred is not so generally known. Aside from the East, West, North, South Directions, included also are Up and Down. The six-directional grid is to be seen from the position of a particular viewer. The viewer in this grid is, in actuality, positioned at the "center of the universe." This is not, however, an egocentric interpretation: the viewer is only a small aspect of the entire directional system.

My claim here is that the Four Directions have a very definite signification that, in turn, serves to lend meaning to the addition of the other two directions.

Most known North American indigenous groups have a very definite sense of place. The "sense of place" is distinguished by the fact that there are very explicit boundaries to which the people can point in order to describe their "home" or "place." The sense of place is a sense of *bounded space*. The fact that the Native American sense of place is characterized by very definite boundaries is important to understanding the sanctity accorded to the Four Directions.

When the Europeans arrived in North America there were hundreds of very diverse and distinct groups of indigenous peoples. There were also hundreds of languages spoken by the various groups. In order for the diversity of peoples to have survived the thousands of years of occupancy on this continent, there had to be some "mechanism" to allow the persistence of diversity.

Today, each Native group knows the boundaries, or former boundaries, of its homeland. Many indigenous groups have been displaced from their original homelands, but the memory of the traditional home is not forgotten. "Home," in a Native American sense, is much broader than that of the nonindigenous Americans. In my own case, my father could point to our former boundaries: to the North was the Arkansas River (present-day Pueblo, Colorado); to the East were the plains of eastern Colorado where the people could go only so far as it took to find the buffalo; the people's "ground" extended as far South as Taos Mountain; and to the West, only so far as the homeland of Utes began (approximately Pagosa Springs, Colorado). These directions and places would, today, be equivalent to pointing out the town in which one lived.

The recognition of the home area was accompanied by another awareness: that beyond the larger home area was the home area of other groups. To the North and East there were various "Plains Indians;" to the South, the Pueblos; and to the West, the Utes. The home area also included various and related groups of "Apaches."

It appears to me that the sense of bounded space is the source of the granting of sanctity to the "Four Directions." There were boundaries that delineated the "proper" space in which a specific group could comfortably range. Within those boundaries there were other boundaries that signified "home" to smaller clans within the larger group. To go beyond the designated boundaries was to encroach on the homeland of others, to *trespass* on the rightful spaces of others.

The Four Directions may not have been, in origin, amorphous religious principles. The recognition of the existence of boundaries may derive from recognition that all people have a "right" to a specific home ground. The "mechanism" for the maintenance of the continued diversity of peoples on the North American continent could well stem from this very sense of bounded space that survives intact even to this day, five hundred years after the disruptions created by the European colonists.

The sense of existing within specific boundaries is not easily acknowledged by many European peoples; they do, nonetheless, tend to occupy bounded spaces. There are within the European group many distinct groups: French, German, English, and so on. The majority of wars fought on the European continent have been based on the trespassing of one group on the "homeland" of another. The reluctance of Europeans, in general, to acknowledge the existence of peoples as distinct groups may be the result of a mythology—the story of Adam and Eve—that is at odds with the actual existential circumstances of human beings.

Today it is common to hear Europeans and their colonial "modern" descendants speak with disdain about "petty nationalisms," as though the sense of a people as a distinct group is somewhat anachronistic. The fact that people cling to their national language, traditions, and beliefs, as well as to bloodlines, geography, and history, is seen as merely stubbornness. It seems forgotten that one of the "advances" made by Europeans in breaking away from the dogmatic authority of the one and "universal" church was the use of local languages for written matter. Dante, for example, wrote in Italian rather than Latin. The invention of printing led to translations from the Latin of the upper classes into the languages of the various groups throughout Europe. This "national" self-assertion was a threat to the dominance of the Catholic Church. Today, the contemporary United Nations organization recognizes the existence of diverse peoples and their right to "self-determination." The UN Charter forbids the elimination of diverse peoples through what is called "cultural genocide." It is not uncommon, however, despite the willing membership of European or "Western" groups in the UN to hear the impassioned plea (usually from a Westerner) for a "One World, One People" outlook.

One of the primary differences between Europeans and Native Americans consists of the recognition, by the Native American, that human beings occupy specific locations that are their "rightful homes." The Native American view is not, however, simply an "instinct" of territoriality. It is commonly known that the Native American found the concept of holding ownership of parts of the Earth quite alien. They did not think of their homelands as something they *owned* but instead as something that they *belonged* to. They thought of themselves as being "created" for one specific part of the planet. In an extension of this view they also included in their belief systems the idea that other peoples, those unlike themselves, were also "created" for their own places. Each group was viewed as having a set of "truths" that pertained to their own unique circumstances and locales.

An awareness of belonging to a specific place carries with it numerous ramifications that have not been thoroughly explored. The idea of being a part of a bounded space becomes the ground upon which a very intimate knowledge and understanding of the homeland is acquired. The people's goal is to adapt to the place that they see as, not only a home, but an extension of themselves as people. An awareness of the resources available within the bounded area becomes the means of survival. There is not an indigenous American group that did not develop rules for the use and management of those resources. The use and management of resources—rules for hunting, an awareness of proper planting and gathering seasons, an awareness of community in the sharing out of resource availability—is also accompanied by an awareness of how the numbers of the group affect the resources of the area. The need to control one's population is necessary when the world one inhabits is seen as consisting of bounded space. The entirety of the world is not at their disposal. Moving to another place in search of accessible resources is not an easy option—someone else occupies the other places.

The world is not a world of scarcity but of fertility and abundance. Human beings are not viewed as competitive animals who consume an area and move on to another to continue the practice of "take and leave." Each group recites the history of their group within a certain bounded area that has been "home" for hundreds of generations, or, as many say, "forever." They see themselves as having "emerged" into a specific area and as having a responsibility to that area—they are a "natural" part of the area.

The various "territorial wars" between groups can be ascribed to the coming of the European: as the Europeans displaced Native groups, the groups found themselves driven into territories of others who, in turn, displaced other groups. Enmity was not always the only solution. Alliances were formed, or a people assimilated into the cultural mores of the other groups—both became possible solutions to untenable circumstances. The fact that "home" groups were sufficiently accommodating and understanding to the needs of newly appearing groups is borne out by the reception that Europeans received from indigenous groups when they first arrived. It was the Native American who showed them what to eat and how to harvest the foodstuffs that indigenous peoples had "engineered"—they also seem to have granted the newcomers places to which they might adapt themselves. The lack of cooperation and the idea of accumulation of lands that came to be exhibited by the European was an alien concept among the Native groups. Given the incompatibility of worldviews between indigenous and European peoples, alienation between the two became inevitable.

How relevant is the view of bounded space for today's world? If one looks at a map of the world and traces the expansion of European peoples and their descendants, one sees a tremendous disruption of "natural boundaries." The "Age of Discovery" ends with the populations of Europe in control of three entire continents—North and South America and Australia. There are serious inroads into other continents as well. No other population has equaled the movement of the Europeans. We are taught that the "swarm" of peoples is a simple matter of "might makes right." We are told also that it is "natural" for a people to scour the planet in search of needed resources—so long, that is, as the people doing the scouring are ourselves. The inhabitants of the "developed" world have a "right" to go where they please, regardless of the desires of the inhabitants of other occupied areas. The entirety of the planet's resources goes "naturally" to those with the desire and capacity to mine the surface and depths of the Earth. The actions toward others are justified under the guise of "bringing democracy" and "modernity" to the world's peoples. We ignore the fact that once self-sufficient groups, anywhere from two-thirds to three-quarters of the world's people, now suffer from malnutrition and disruption because of the elimination of ancient means of adapting to specific areas.

The relevance of the Native American perspective of seeing humans as "made for" specific areas is as important today as it ever was. There has always been trade among peoples. On the North American continent, the trade routes of Native peoples can be traced through objects found in ancient sites: coral in the southwestern United States; turquoise where none is native to the area; copper beads from the Great Lakes region are found in areas far from the waters; agricultural products, corn, beans, and squash, are found throughout the region and none of them are "natural" products gathered from the Earth. No traces can be found of populations harnessed by others for the sake of producing "goods" for the needs of others. Surplus in one area becomes the tradestuff in others. North American peoples seem not to have been "contaminated" with the germ of thinking themselves "owners" of the world. One of the highest values held by North American native groups is respect for the other *as other*, with all of the rights and privileges one holds for one's own.

There is something lacking in a people who do not recognize boundaries: there is no intimacy developed between a people and their homeland. There is, instead, an obsession over ownership that is easily given up in the name of profit or a better deal elsewhere. There is no need to consider the effect of too many people in a specific area, no need to consider the "carrying capacity" of a particular land base. There is no need to consider the biological ties between a people and their land base; "natural" immunities to a place can be acquired through medical technology. The movement of individuals from one area to another is seen as "natural" —an idea that is prevalent in a people who all came from someplace else.

Yet there is a sense of place in the hearts of immigrant "Americans," though some would argue that it is less the place that holds their hearts than the ideals that they share, one of them being the ideal of unrestricted movement and occupation. But, overall, the place that is called "America" is viewed largely as an "open space"—available to all.

This idea was brought home to me in a rather strange manner: I worked for a program to help youth avoid becoming gang members in a city. An important part of the program was teaching the youth the consequences of their actions on their own neighborhoods, teaching them that there was a responsibility that accompanied occupation of a place. Most of the youth were immigrants. They balked at the talk of responsibility to a place. "This is a *free* country," one of them reminded me. "Anyone can come here and do as they please." One need only "pay taxes" and avoid breaking the laws. "That's what everyone else did—they all came here from someplace else to do what they wanted." "It's a *free country*," which sounded oddly enough like "free pizza." Boundaries and borders were minor irrelevancies. That, in their estimation, was the attitude of the other "Americans" who came here from throughout the world. These youths were simply the latest arrivals in a long exodus from overpopulated and wasted lands—they had as much "right" to be here as anyone else. America as the world's "commons": *Free Pizza! Free* Country!

"We can go anywhere we like," chimed one student. "Except," said another, "for the Indians." They all agreed that the Indians, as original inhabitants, had a particular claim to the land. "It was theirs." "We can't go to the places where they live." Can I go to Vietnam, I asked? Or Mexico, or China? Places where they had come from? "Yeah, you can *go* there," they agreed, "but not to *live* there." Those places *belonged* to someone else.

The sacredness of their own "four directions" was inviolable. To be an "American" was to give up the sense of belonging and being *of a place*. Was their membership in a gang, specifically a gang defined by ethnicity, a substitute for being-of-a-place, I asked? "Yeah, man," they agreed, "we're *brothers.*" "*We have to take care of one another.*" How much more strongly could I have put it? To feel the sense of place, of a bounded and definite space, involves a sense of *relationship* with that place, of a very specific *responsibility* toward that place, as a unified whole—people and place together.

Without a sense of bounded space, there is no sacredness accorded to one's own space or place; one is not standing "in the center of the universe" looking out onto definite boundaries that define who and what one becomes. And if one grants no sacredness to one's own space and place, there is certainly no recognition of the sacredness of other peoples' places. The "modern" perspective has no sense of bounded space. This view, like that of the potential gang members in an American city, is a perspective of a "free" *planet.* 'Free' for the taking. No responsibilities attached.

## II. A Sense of Place

When the language that once was familiar is gone, when the rituals that created meaning and continuity are no longer practiced, what is left? These are the questions that plague me after reading yet one more plaintive wail that passes as poetry or literature offered under the label "Native American."

I know that not all such literary attempts fit in the category I have reserved for them. My friends and I used to discuss the state of Native American literature: "It's all about, 'I got drunk—rolled over my baby and it died—and I'm just miserable—'cuz I'm Indian,' kind of stuff," said my friend Eddie. If it was that bad being "Indian," who would still be around to want to be "Indian"? We decided that there was more to being Indian than what we called "Dead Baby poetry." What that "more" was, wasn't easy to focus on.

Most of what is written by and about Native Americans is all too real. We do suffer from a low life expectancy, a high suicide rate, and an equally high rate of poverty. Most Native Americans also are too easily identifiable, physically, to deny their heritage in order to assimilate into the mainstream. On the other hand, there weren't that many Native Americans we knew who would deny that they were Native American. Why was that? we asked. Why do we persist in an identity that has endured despite hundreds of years of enforced assimilation? Is there something good about who we are?

"There must be!" laughed another friend. "Look at all 'em white folks tryin' to be Indian!" Why would these various people *want to be Indian*? I thought of signs that I encountered when I was a teenager: "No Mexicans —No Dogs—No Indians." I thought of John Wayne when he went after all those "injuns" who impeded the way across the West of all those fine and upstanding white settlers. I thought of those carved and painted wooden Indian statues that still are displayed in "Western" shops. If that was the image of the Indian that the White World gave me as I was growing up, what was there about being Indian that the "wannabees" wanted so desperately?

On the surface, that question turned out not to be so difficult to answer. "You people are so mystical-spiritual-etc." Every White person *knows* about how Indians believe in "the brotherhood of all things" and in "balance" and "harmony" and all that good stuff that White folks profess to be after. They all thought we still had something left that they hadn't gotten from us yet. Maybe we did.

But if we did, it wasn't what they were after—except, perhaps, as a means to use in eradicating us from the face of the earth. Think how much easier it would be for "Indian experts" to say definitively what we were all about if no real indigenous persons existed to raise uncomfortable objections to white portrayals of indigenous groups: look at the mileage (and research grants) milked from "the mystery of the Anasazi."

What was left, after many indigenous persons had lost their native languages and no longer adhered to ritual in daily life, was a set of values instilled in childhood and reinforced by the Native communities. They served to ward off the assimilation attempts of educators, government officials, and missionaries. It seems, in talking with Native persons throughout North America, that there is something "pan-Indian" that has escaped the efforts of White America to rub out the final evidence of the real "winning" of the West.

There is, from the farthest north of Alaska to the tip of South America, a sense Native people have of belonging to the Earth—that, unlike the new, European Americans, they are made for the Earth; the Earth is not made for them. This view is expressed by the idea of the "Mother Earth," but the

Euro-American tends to misunderstand this in an anthropomorphic sense, thinking that there is a "goddess" that all Native Americans worship. The term 'Mother Earth' doesn't refer to a goddess. It refers to the Earth, the planet, with all of its rocks, volcanoes, streams, and oceans. It is a term laden with recognition of human dependence on the planet's many gifts. It is laden also with a sense of the fragility of the circumstances that make humans possible. There are personifications of the Earth as Mother— many indigenous groups have equivalents of "White Buffalo Woman," an anthropomorphic "spirit" who brings the people knowledge or foodstuff. White Buffalo Woman, however, lies in the realm of myth, legend, or religion. The idea, or definition, of the Earth as the producer of life and the conditions for life's existence lies in the realm of what is real to Native people. Offerings may be made to the idea of White Buffalo Woman, but Native existence for thousands of years depended on knowing common practices that allowed groups to survive in specific areas within the boundaries of resource availability.

Most North American indigenous groups are mistakenly described as nomadic. We are led to believe that the various groups simply wandered about the countryside picking what they needed, as did Adam and Eve in the Garden of Eden. If any groups did not fit the "wandering" mold, it was explained that they had "discovered" agriculture and had, therefore, to "give up" the nomadic lifestyle. The truth of the matter is that all indigenous peoples have a very strong sense of identity and that identity includes a sense of belonging in a very specific space. They had, and do have, a very strong sense of *bounded* space. "I," in the sense of myself as a specific kind of person, do not extend beyond certain boundaries.

Thus, not only do indigenous groups have a sense of belonging to the Earth, but a sense that they belong in a very small part of that whole Earth. Beyond their boundaries exist other groups who are equally endowed with a sense of themselves as being in bounded space. The fact that many groups did move seems rare enough to be granted the status of legend. The "journey" usually took place "in another world—before we emerged into this one." The lost bounded space is recreated within other bounded spaces.

The concept of existing within very definite boundaries has been given very little attention by researchers—yet this notion gives sense to the idea that indigenous peoples were "conservationists." If a group must exist with certain boundaries, then there is an incentive to use its resources with care, to maintain a sustainable population. It is no wonder that a sense of balance and harmony were important to Native groups. An anecdote concerning this notion of a sustainable use of resources was related to me by a friend at the Taos Pueblo. She said that the government had sent a troupe of agricultural experts to her village to teach them how to get better crops from their land. Taos is one of the oldest of the Rio Grande pueblos and may date back to AD 900. The village officials informed the experts that the people had farmed that ground for all of that time. "How long," they asked the officials, "have you been farming your land?" "Maybe," the villagers informed the experts, "you better send your farmers here so that we can teach them how we did it."

A people that has no sense of bounded spaces can scarcely be expected to "discover" the notion of boundaries. I have never read any research done on this topic, nor are there any papers being written on the effects of having such a "value" and how it affects cultural practices. The fact that a sense of bounded space can be destroyed by an excess of population is certainly a source of values that affect child-rearing practices. Young persons were encouraged to be physically active—to "not get too fat too soon." The idea was that body fat had something to do with early puberty, which, of course, had something to do with population growth within the group. "If you let your daughter get fat, she'll hit puberty before she can deal with it—you'll have problems with that girl." Recent gynecological research bears this out, as well as the notion that early puberty leads to later onset of menopause. No indigenous group could afford to deal with extended breeding times. There were other "values" of the community that conveyed disapproval of late pregnancies: "She thinks she's a young girl," was said derisively of a pregnant woman in her early thirties. Large numbers of children were not common among Native peoples. Those couples who did seem unusually fertile were either ridiculed or ended up "sharing" their offspring with other members of the community who were less fortunate. The children were not "given away" but ended up with two sets of parents: the birth parents, who were known to all, and the "raising parents" who were "mother" and "father." The shared offspring created even more bonds within a community.

The sense of community in a Native setting is not clearly understood by non-Native researchers. A community, as usually seen by a researcher, consists of either a "tribe" or a "clan." Focus is, in other words, on the persons in a group; it seldom takes into account the land area that the community occupies. Within, for example, the land area of a particular related group of people there will be specific areas that specific "clans" will see—not as their property—but as *themselves*. My father's family, for example, had come to identify themselves with a specific area that surrounded a natural spring and creek: Romero Spring and Romero Creek in the border area of eastern Colorado and New Mexico. The people identified themselves with the area they occupied and marked its proximity to other "safe" havens: the Picuris and Taos pueblos to the south and southeast with whom the people had ties owing to trading practices and marriage ties.

The "Romeros" were Apaches and, in the eyes of the church-dominated Spanish village system, defined as "nomads." Their lifestyle of combined farming in specific areas and the hunting of the buffalo that had been accessible in the eastern portions of their land base led to accompanying practices of trade: buffalo products for the pottery and products of the less "nomadic" pueblos of Taos and Picuris. The "nomads," however, had a sense of very definite boundaries beyond which "they ceased to be." They certainly had a sense of the area that was "home."

Euro-Americans also have a sense of place. Their homes are spaces that cannot be violated. If I walk in front of someone's home I make the proprietor uncomfortable; if I walk onto his yard, he comes out to confront me; but if I walk up onto his porch and make myself comfortable, I have become a definite threat. The sense of having personal space violated is very strong among most life forms. How that personal space is defined varies from group to group.

For the Native American the boundary of his home is simply larger than that of the Euro-American. Correspondingly, the sense of *personal* space is very different. A joke told to me by a Pueblo friend may not carry very well among those with a different sense of personal space, but I recount it just the same to make my point: some Pueblo people, driving through the Navajo reservation, are awed by the sparseness of the area. Then they spot two hoghans within a few miles of each other. "Must be a mother and a daughter," says one Pueblo to another and they laugh. The "joke" lies in the fact that the "sparseness" that overwhelms the Pueblo people is in relation to habitations and not the appearance of the landscape; they, after all, are peoples who represent at least two dozen different groups strung about the banks of the Rio Grande all within an area of about 150 miles from north to south. Their own numbers do not exceed those of the Navajo, but they tend to live in small villages occupied by many related peoples. The punch line of the joke is based on a characteristic of many southwestern Native people—they tend to be matrilineal. The closest possible relationship in this system is between a mother and her daughters. The Pueblos recognize the different sense of personal space between themselves and the Navajo while at the same time granting recognition of shared values between the peoples. Which is why their comments are a "joke" rather than an act of derision.

While the recognition of the importance of having "a sense of place" is now common among those Americans trying to create what they call 'environmental ethics,' the use of supposed Native American perspectives to strengthen this argument is based on a lack of understanding of the true sense that Native Americans have of "place." In comparison to the Native American perspective on "place," the Euro-American's view seems somewhat *amorphous*. It is not only Native Americans that have a sense of place that is very specific; most indigenous peoples have a similar concept of bounded space. Their "place" is the foundation of cultural mooring and values; it is not simply "the environment" that they accidentally "occupy" —they are the children of that place. There is no such artificial distinction between themselves and some alien "other" that is termed "nature." The lack of a sense of boundaries is what makes the Euro-American sense of place "amorphous" and unique.

Recognition of a people's own boundaries is an equal recognition of the bounded spaces of other peoples. The Euro-American lacks this sense of bounded space. He can tomorrow—given the resources—buy himself a ticket to any part of the planet and suddenly appear in the "yard" of other persons. He has a "right" to go anywhere he pleases because he is "free." This "freedom" is interpreted by the indigenous person, who has a different sense of space, as merely "lack of attachment." A people without a sense of boundaries for themselves can certainly not recognize the sense of boundaries of others.

The entire concept of "international law" as it developed in the European sensibility was a direct means of justifying the intrusion of Europeans into the bounded spaces of people unlike themselves. The Spaniards and the Catholic Church had to confront this issue shortly after their intrusion into occupied territories of the American continents. Their justification was that they had a "duty" to spread the word of Christianity—throughout the entire planet—and having spread that word they then had the "right" to "protect" the converts to Christianity in what otherwise might be seen as "foreign" lands. On the part of the Europeans, they were engaging in acts of "discovery" fueled by the notion that their god had given them the entire planet. They fought wars with China and Japan over their "right" to enter those countries.

When those in search of a new relationship with the land turn to Native Americans, there is a failure to take into account the sense of bounded space. What follows from this incomplete understanding is a rejection of Native American notions based on the claim that they were not "conservationists"—that they merely used up the land and resources and then moved on. This dismissal is, after all, consistent with the view of the Native American as a homeless nomad. The nomad status allows the justification of "taking" land—it didn't "belong" to anyone in the usual European sense of proprietorship.

There is no denying that moves did occur among indigenous people. Their histories and legends are full of stories of migrations. The migrations were few enough, however, to merit retelling. The Pueblo people have legends of having come from an area farther north than their present occupations. In their own versions there is no "mystery of the Anasazi"—they simply moved south. The reasons given range from an attempt to seek more fertile grounds to the idea that the population grew too great in one area and the people began to fight among themselves, so they decided to disperse and live from then on in smaller, more manageable communities. We have to remember that these moves took place over at least a hundred years and happened perhaps a thousand years before the current telling of the stories. They were not moves undertaken simply because the game moved away one year. They were moves of tremendous import and trauma.

Another ramification of the need for indigenous peoples to "ground" themselves in specific places is the creation of "emergence" myths that relocate the people into their present situations. I grew up believing that the Apache of northeastern New Mexico and eastern Colorado "emerged" from the Mother out of the lake atop Taos Mountain. There were no stories of having come to the area from someplace else. There was a good explanation for the fact that they no longer occupied the area around Folsom and Raton, New Mexico: the White men came. A retreat to the hills was a logical act, but the move was still within their historical boundaries of what the Spaniards labeled "Apacheria" on their maps of the area northeast of Taos and Santa Fe. The need to identify with a specific area is very strong among indigenous groups. Even today, when Indians displaced from the southeastern United States to "Indian" territory in Oklahoma visit their original homelands, they begin by pointing to the known place markers. The visits, as well as the pointing out of known boundaries, are a means of reasserting—not ownership—but identity. It is the hills or lack of them that grant identity to a people. The people of the deeply wooded forests will not be the "same" people as those of the broad expanses of southern Wyoming.

Bounded space has ramifications that cannot fully be brought out by any but the indigenous person who is brought up with that sense of space. As a child I had never visited the Taos pueblo village. I knew no one there. I had no "right" simply to show up on their doorstep. My father had spent part of his childhood on the Taos grounds and pointed out the cottonwoods that he had planted with his father to serve as windbreaks, but the government bought out the non-Taos Natives with offers of land across the river on the "Spanish" side and my father's family moved there. Now there was a fence between my father and the home he knew as a child. We didn't even approach the fence. We no longer had a right to be there.

The sense of the extended personal space that protects identity is well practiced by the indigenous and mixed-breed populations in northern New Mexico to this day. There are well-delineated lines of where the "Hispanics" live and what is "Indian" territory. Even with the many intermarriages among the two peoples, the sense of "what is what" is clearly recognized. My cousin who married a man from Nambe (a pueblo south of Taos) has become Nambe; her children are Nambe even though part of her family maintains a "Hispanic" identity. The two peoples have lived side by side for centuries. During that time many intermarriages have taken place, yet, there are still in existence two very distinct peoples in the Taos area. There is no sense here of the "melting pot theory." There is, however, a tremendous respect between the people.

Into this clearly delineated social arrangement, the Anglo-American has made an appearance. He has no sense of place to match that of the previous residents, but he does have a sense of needing to belong. He decorates himself with Indian jewelry and salts his speech with hispanicisms of the area: "Nice day, no?" and "Bueno'bye" (for goodbye). He fails to catch an inkling that it is *place* that is missing from his attempts to fit in—this, despite the fact that the Anglo owns most of the property surrounding the federally protected Indian ground. He may *like* his new place better than any other place on earth, but he is just as comfortable in San Francisco or New York City because he carries his identity with him. The others suffer from a permanent case of homesickness when they leave the area. Homesickness is accompanied by an insecurity about identity that only trips home can alleviate. The sense of home is not the culture, not the food, not even the many relatives. It is the place: the look of early morning; the smell of the juniper; the particular expected temperature for the kind of day it is, for the time of year it is; the mountains being in the right place. There is an assurance of being in the right place and being recognized by others as "not a stranger" even if they do not know who you are.

The sense of one's self as a being of a particular place is what goes into being a Native American. It is part of the person and the culture that escapes notice by the researchers eager to depict the Native American. At the same time, these values are comforting factors in being who we are. It is more rational to recognize that we are part of a whole and that we are dependent upon the Earth for our continued existence. We are not "stewards" of the Earth and certainly not "overlords"—we are dependent, perhaps chance creatures on a living planet. We are not separate from her—there is no such thing as an alien 'nature' existing outside ourselves that must be conquered or tamed. We, as human creatures—I, as an individual —are part of the Earth, of the Mother.

Beyond the loss of language, the loss of daily ritual practice, and beyond "Dead Baby poetry," what the Native American has not lost is a sense of place.

# Biodiversity: The Human Factor

Biodiversity is a term drawn from the sciences to indicate a recently acknowledged phenomenon: a healthy ecosystem is one that exhibits a high degree of diversity. A wheat field extending for hundreds of acres, for example, is not biodiverse. A local, intact, wooded area with a variety of creatures as well as a variety of vegetation would be an example of a biologically diverse and healthy ecosystem.

The term applied to a system that lacks this diversity is *monocultural*. A monocultural system like the wheat field excludes all other types of life forms. This type of a system is also subject to the vagaries of whatever invasive life form might seek to compete with the wheat field. In a healthy ecosystem that displays a great degree of diversity, an invasive life form, say a virus or fungus, is unlikely to be able to destroy the entire system. Only some of a healthy system's many life forms will be attacked: the others will survive. This survival allows that the conditions, which were conducive to the appearance of the now decimated life form, can continue and may provide for the future reappearance of the destroyed form.

A biologically diverse system displays another factor that is missing from the monocultural system: the various life forms eventually reach a dynamic, life-enhancing interrelation within their ecosystem.

There are few scientists today who will deny the significance of biodiversity: there are, however, few that have thus far made the analogy between human social groupings and the part such groups play in maintaining the health of an ecosystem. The fact that such an analogy has not been drawn is the result of some very basic assumptions about the nature of human beings.

## Human Adaptability

One such assumption is that humans are not really part of "nature." Humans are accepted as having evolved from nature, but, because of their supposed uniqueness as self-aware creatures, they are seen to be something over and above nature. Humans, then, by virtue of their superior status, are not taken into consideration as one of the many species that go into the creation of a healthy and diverse ecosystem. Human beings are also assumed to be made up of a singular species. This view is depicted in such concepts as "mankind" or simply "man." We have grown accustomed to speaking of the species in the singular.

Although subdividing human beings into subspecies has its own detrimental effects, thinking of people as all alike has led to some particularly destructive mistakes. One is the assumption that, if human beings are only one singular species, then any deviation from a norm can only imply a distorted form of the original. Another assumption is that if human diversity exists, it is because some humans have failed to evolve at a rate equal to that of others. These two assumptions have led to horrible consequences for human groups that are unlike a more powerful group. Rather than accepting diversity as a natural phenomenon, human beings are labeled according to the singularity notion as "developed," "developing," or "undeveloped." The terms are an attempt to escape from equally devastating terminology, that is, "primitive" and "stone age." The concept of singularity has led to the idea that only one right form of existence is "normal" for human beings; all other forms are either outright "wrong" or examples of the evolutionary path that the "right" group traveled in order to reach its "correctness." The characteristics of the truly "other" are thus abrogated. The other becomes a living fossil for the delight and examination of the group that has laid claim for itself the right to be representative of the whole. The inability to move beyond the assumption of singularity is one of the main factors that prevent scientists from properly placing human beings within an ecosystem.

Adaptability, however, is the hallmark of a successful species, and no species has shown the tremendous adaptive capacity of human beings. Humans are found in the harsh environments of the Arctic north, in the heat of equatorial regions, and at elevations beyond which some humans can tolerate. At each of these locations we find human beings who have managed not only to survive but to thrive. There are those who would argue that their survival was dependent on a human ability to adapt surroundings to human needs. This is an erroneous argument. The survival of human beings in a large variety of environments is dependent on the human capacity to adapt to those environments.

A great part of that adaptability lies in the fact that humans, unlike other life forms, have the capacity to invent myths that justify their existence in whatever specific area they find themselves. From an early childhood, the group provides a child an identity that includes not only language and lifestyle but also a description of the geographical location together with a justification for why the group is there and not anywhere else. These descriptions and justifications serve as the matrix of explanation for all future circumstances that the group encounters.

The adaptive success of the human species lies precisely in the ability to invent what we usually call "creation myths." Creation myths are as diverse as are the people and the locations that elicited them. Yet this example of diversity is again dismissed by the assumptions of human singularity and the idea that humans are beyond nature. Instead, it is commonly believed that human beings, because of their singular quality, all share some common notions. This is the origin of such concepts as that of the "archetype" or the idea that all human "explanations" (myths) are but variations of a theme.

When human beings do share mythological notions, they are more likely to be the result of being human than that they are the result of labors to elaborate a singular but forgotten origin myth. All human beings exist in groups, have families, and have commonalities in physical characteristics (vision, hearing, bipedalism). How those groups are formed and what constitutes a family is "culture specific." Shared physical characteristics guarantee only that humans see, hear, think, and walk upright. These characteristics do not guarantee any singularity in what a group chooses to focus on, or what they hear as relevant, or even what they think.

This is not to deny that there are some common themes to be found among peoples. But the diversity of explanations or interpretations of those themes will be dependent on the particular group's needs. The closer the ties, both through bloodlines and geographical proximity, the more likely there will be themes that seem to have something in common. But the more basic fact is that themes undergo variation, and those variations, however subtle they may appear to an outsider, bear tremendous meaning to adherents.

We have not yet understood human thought inventions as signals of diversity and of the capacity of human beings to be highly malleable. We tend, rather, to see such diversity as a threat to the validity of our own invented explanations. We fail, also, to see that human beings living in very different ways in very different places might be adaptations to particular locales. We are certainly not prepared to see these adaptations as the means of existing in some sort of mutually sustaining relationship with a particular ecosystem.

We are prepared to accept the fact that certain animals seem to be uniquely adapted to unique circumstances and that the adaptations seem to provide a niche for that animal in a specific environment. We celebrate the discovery of ecosystems—those interdependent and seemingly self-sustaining locales. We recognize the necessity of biodiversity for the maintenance of that system. What we cannot yet accept is that humans also are capable of developing ways of becoming part of a healthy ecosystem.

## Monoculturalism and Human Diversity

The shelves of our bookstores are filled with titles exclaiming the plight of the planet. We read about the death of the planet Earth. There are appeals for us to "save the Earth" and for contributions to save the rain forests and endangered species. Seldom do we see books exclaiming the potential for the demise of the species. Yet we are becoming, like the wheat field, a perfect example of monoculturalism. And like the monocultural field, we risk extinction through our inability to accept human diversity.

We do not expect that spotted owls will simply move into city parks should their habitats be destroyed. We know that the spotted owl will not survive transplantation. We do not, however, feel any qualms about displacing a population when we need their resources. We like to think of such an action as a good intention—we are assisting in their development. We send in the missionaries to destroy indigenous belief systems that enabled humans to exist in an environment in which the missionaries themselves could not exist without their "life-support" systems.

The loss of the lore of a group is also the loss of the justification for their lifestyle. Many indigenous groups tend to cling to what they call "traditional" lifestyles while praying to new and alien gods, without ever realizing that in giving up their ancient gods they give up also the meaning that lay embedded in their "traditions." We think we do peoples a favor by teaching them new lifestyles and giving them new work habits, even while we bemoan the fact that they nevertheless seem incapable of living the way that we do. Because we fail to understand that at the root of our explanations lie assumptions that we take for granted, we fail to give the newly developed nations the rationale for the change of lifestyle.

And what are those assumptions? The particular matrix that supports the theories of singularity and the human's elevation out of nature has its roots in Christianity. Scientists, despite their escape from the more superficial aspects of dogma, are deeply indebted to the Christian matrix. The Big Bang is a secular version of Creation: in both instances something is caused to arise from "nothing." The evolution of the species, which could be an explanation of how different species and subspecies arise to fill ecological niches, becomes instead a theory by which humans are portrayed—not simply as one of the many diverse life forms—but as the culmination of a progressive process striving to create a particular type of human being.

The hunter-gatherer lifestyle still practiced by many peoples is interpreted through this matrix as a "vestige" of modern man's own past. Modern man does not see the other as an example of a truly viable relationship with the Earth but as a mere living fossil. He cannot truly see or understand the other, because he sees in the other only himself in his imagined past manifestations. The other becomes merely an anachronism doomed to extinction.

Benevolently, modern man offers to assist what he sees as his retarded or regressive brother to become "modern" by destroying the brother's habitat. No one notices that the indigenous citizen of a rain forest may be a fully evolved and developed life form occupying a specific niche in ways that guarantee the health of a particular geographical environment. That such groups are just as much a product of an evolutionary process as "modern" man is overlooked, because this would require viewing them as equals.

It may have taken thousands of years for the Tibetan to adapt to his high-altitude home, both psychologically and physiologically. Certainly the lifestyle that evolved in a group living with its environment for thousands of years, with the prospect of many thousands more, should be recognized as valid. Examples of such people continue to exist. A failure to recognize their value destroys a healthy planetary system.

How long, for example, did it take the people of Africa to develop healthy relationships with their environment? When modern man arrived on that continent, the diversity of life forms was enticing. Modernization destroyed that diversity, including the traditional lifestyles of those adapted to the unique ecosystems.

The transformation of nations from underdeveloped to developed status seldom benefits the people of the area. There is left, in the wake of modernization, an unstable social system made up of conflict between the powerful and the powerless. Former "natural" boundaries are destroyed as boundaries are redrawn based on the needs of modern civilization. The subsequent displacement of indigenous groups leads to the destruction of a lifestyle that was once geared to a specific location. The result of modernization attempts is not the elevation of "backward" people onto a higher notch on the scale of evolutionary progress. The result is an incomplete and perhaps impossible attempt to create a monoculture.

Yet, no scientist or politician argues, with any seriousness, for the preservation of the indigenous people in the Amazon rain forest on the premise that those people may be necessary for a healthy ecosystem. They envision a preserved tropical ecosystem empty of humans save for the few modern experts ("stewards") necessary to maintain the system. The rain forest becomes nothing more than a zoo specimen, and the specially adapted cultures are destroyed by modern-day missionaries who come under various guises to assist with "educational," "medical," or "developmental" projects.

The responsibility for maintaining the diversity of life falls on the shoulders of modern man. It is his attitude toward the Earth and its varieties of humans that most threatens the demise of the very diversity he celebrates as essential to the health of a planet. Edward O. Wilson, in his highly acclaimed work *The Diversity of Life*, calls biological diversity "the key to the maintenance of the world as we know it." "It holds the world steady," he says. "Every habitat, from Brazilian rain forest to Antarctic bay to thermal vent, harbors a unique combination of plants and animals. Each kind of plant and animal living there is linked in the food web to only a small part of the other species. Eliminate one species and another increases in number to take its place. Eliminate a great many species and the local ecosystem starts to decay visibly . . . [leading to] . . . an eroding ecosystem."[1]

The ecosystem of which he speaks so eloquently is made up of interacting and interdependent communities. It is time to see that humans are a part of the ecological web and that they too play a vital role—not as stewards over an inferior and mindless nature—but as a necessary part of a healthy and diverse system of life.

# A New Reverence

This generation of humans has had to learn the consequences of humanity's overall effect on the planet. We now know about holes in the ozone layer, the greenhouse effect, nuclear winter, acid rain, global warming, and the effects of pesticides and chemical residues on human and animal life. We are aware of the effects of these various pending and actual disasters: an increased incidence of skin cancer, a slow suffocation through an increase of carbon dioxide, a freezing drought brought about by the release of nuclear contaminants, the death of forests and lakes through the increased acidity of rainfall, who knows what consequences from global warming, and an increasing incidence of infant malformations or miscarriages. Our reactions to this newly presented knowledge are twofold: we either experience "psychic numbing" and choose to ignore the portents surrounding us, or we demand that our scientists and technicians do "something" about it. We have, in the first case, lost hope. In the second case, we rest our hope on the belief that human ingenuity will quite simply "come up with a solution." In either case, we, as individuals, avoid responsibility.

We consider ourselves "scientific" man, "technological" man, and hold ourselves as the acme of an evolutionary progression that began with the single amoeba and has culminated with humans circling the globe in space stations. We imagine our future filled with voyages to distant stars, labor-saving devices that eliminate the old curse of "earning our bread by the sweat of our brow"—but we cannot imagine environmental disaster on a planetary scale. And if, in moments of fleeting duration, we stop to consider the price we have had to pay for our present and future achievements, there are few of us who would regret that price. We can rise in indignation should a new and potentially polluting project be proposed for our community—"build it elsewhere," we can say. What we cannot say is, "Why build it at all?"

The roots of our present ecological disaster have been plumbed many times by various thinkers. Lynn White Jr., in a 1967 article, "The Historical Roots of our Ecological Crisis," cites the "orthodox Christian arrogance toward nature" as an important root.[1] White brings his focus to the new definition of human that results from the Judeo-Christian philosophy. Humans are created by a god in the image of god. The Earth is created by the deity for our use: People are to "subdue, dominate, and name the things of the Earth." The root cause of the state we now find ourselves in, according to White, can be traced to these new definitions of humans and the world. The roots are of a religious nature.[2]

What Lynn White did not do in his pivotal work was to explore how those initial ideas of Christianity managed to endure the many changes that the West has undergone since the church fathers firmed up the "Christian" view. The roots of present attitudes about humanity's relationship with the Earth have undergone secularization: they have become "philosophical" concepts and ideas. As deeply rooted philosophical concepts, the attitudes that White perceived as originating in the Judeo-Christian tradition have been given new focus.

White makes no distinction between the Judaic and Christian portions of the religious roots. He traces a certain alienation from the Earth among human beings to the charge to subdue and dominate the Earth. But he does not take into account the fact that Christianity differs in this view from early Judaism. The original Judaic myth has the deity oust his previously perfectly created humans from an equally perfect "Eden" or "home." The deity sees this ouster as temporary and promises to lead his people back into an appropriate home eventually. That home is presumed to be on this planet. Christianity, building upon this initial promise, has the deity offer his own son to the descendants of Adam and Eve as a leader who will guide the people to a new and rightful home. The son, however, offers a different conception of "home." He says, "My kingdom is not of this world." Whatever degree of alienation from the Earth is caused by the Judeo-Christian account in Genesis, it is enhanced in the Christian postulation of "another world" as the true home of mankind.

A further alienation of humans from the world comes about through an early and very influential patristic thinker, Augustine. Saint Augustine incorporates Plato's dualistic view of the human into Christianity. The dualism of mind and body allows that there will be some connection between "another world" and its otherwise "earthly" occupants. Plato postulates an immortal soul trapped in a very mortal body that survives extinction through the transmigration of the soul. The new definition of the concept of the soul by Augustine goes beyond Plato's distinction between body and soul. For Augustine, the immortal soul casts humans nearer to the image of God, and the world, which for Plato was a god, becomes a mere artifact.

Dualism, the idea of an immortal soul that is separate and different from the body, has had a long history and significant effects on Western thought. The idea put forth by Augustine is perpetuated throughout the history of Western thought. In the work of Descartes, talk about the soul becomes talk about the "mind." In the latter part of the twentieth century the mind/soul concept becomes a concept of "consciousness." Despite the change in terminology the dualistic view of the human is maintained: mind/soul/consciousness is superior to and separate from "a body." All three concepts serve as a mark to distinguish humans from "animals." The concept of humans as unique in the world is maintained: human beings are superior to other forms of life and as such occupy a place on the planet that elevates them from their planet.

As modern and contemporary humans, we fail to credit our present theories of "man and the world" to religious origins. We imagine ourselves to have escaped from religious dogma, claiming to be the rightful descendants of the inquisitive and ancient Greeks. Lynn White shows that this is not so. A further analysis of the roots of modern concepts also shows that the modern concepts are less of Greek origin than they are remnants of early Christianity. Nor has the influence of philosophy brought about much change in the basic paradigms that can be drawn out of Christian concepts.

As long as the notion persists—in science and philosophy, as in religion—that humans are somehow superior to the Earth itself, that humans are separate and apart from all else, no new definition of humans and the world is forthcoming. Without a reevaluation of human nature and the human dependence on the environment, there can be no "new" environmental ethic. And without a new ethic regarding this dependence and relationship, there is nothing to guide humans to behavior more conducive to survival in the very narrow range of conditions that allow humans to survive as a species on this planet.

Human beings can imagine the "death" of the planet. But what is missing from all of these scenarios is the full force of the fact that we cannot survive the death of our environment. The planet could well survive the greenhouse effect or even a nuclear winter—humans could not. We fail to see ourselves as a dependent (at most symbiotic) life form that exists only through various interdependencies and interrelationships between man and tree, man and water, man and animals, and so on. Human life exists in a very small range of specific planetary circumstances. We persist in seeing ourselves as a superior life form—as some ethereal creature of pure thought—mind versus matter. We persist in seeing ourselves as "caretakers" of the Earth—a position, regardless of the good intentions involved, that blocks the real situation: Human beings are merely one sort of creature, among many other creatures, that the Earth in all of her diversity was capable of producing. We are not unique except as all other things on Earth are unique. We are not superior creatures—not so long as we eat, breathe, sleep, and walk about. We are not an important facet of the planet (except, perhaps, as a potential destructive force). The planet survived long before us and will survive long after we are gone. Is it possible that the dinosaurs—had they been thinking beings—once imagined themselves to be the reason for which the Earth came into existence?[3]

There is a possible solution to all of this. We can try to get out of a conceptual framework that has allowed the present situation by looking at another. The Earth has produced humans in such a fashion that they have a certain flexibility in their thought patterns. There is not one language, but many. There is not one way to describe the workings of the planet, but many. And there is more than one set of explanations for the relationship between humans and the Earth.

What, for instance, would a culture be like if it had a conceptual framework different from that of the Western tradition? What if there existed a culture that described the planet as a whole, living organism, itself teeming with numerous life forms, rather than as an inanimate object that exists merely as raw material for human use? Would such a perspective entail from that culture a different set of actions? If humans were to see themselves as part of a natural and ongoing process along with plants, rocks, animals, stars, would this view influence their actions? Would there be different expectations of themselves and their fellows? Of their ethics?

Because I am familiar with the worldview of the Native American, as a

Jicarilla Apache woman; and because I am familiar with the worldview of the West, as a philosophy professor, I can offer a glimpse of another conceptual framework.

Imagine a universe with no beginning—absolutely infinite. Imagine this also as a living thing that exhibits its life as motion. The motion displays diversity. Motions encountering motions create new motions. You might call these motions "things." I would call them "events," "happenings." There is no dichotomy of matter and energy—but rather one "event" manifesting itself as something temporarily distinct from its surroundings. Within this distinct event are other events, multiple "evolutions," if you like. The "evolutions" are necessary events given the circumstances in which they come into existence. This circumstantial, but necessary, quality gives to each of the events a sense of place.

All human groups give an account of their existential circumstances in their mythologies: they explain why they are where they are and not in some other place. Each Native American group has a creation story—not necessarily for the "Beginning" of the universe—but for their own unique beginning. The story describes not only the appearance of humans but of humans in a very specific place. They are, in effect, that place and no other. They have boundaries beyond which their identities do not carry.

No Native American is a thing separate from his or her surroundings. The universe operates in an orderly fashion; things have their rightful places. If there is change, it is to be expected. The universe is not a still and static place, but rather tends to recreate its own harmonious order.

Human beings are not meaningless things in this universe. Their every act affects the universe. There are repercussions and consequences to each action. Humans, perhaps unlike other life forms, have a greater capacity for memory. They can remember the consequences of their former actions. This capacity does not make of the human something "superior" to the other events in the universe. It makes humans more responsible. They alone can know and understand the consequences of their actions. Wisdom consists of the ability to foresee the consequences, both potential and actual, of each human act.

Human beings, in this conception, live in a good universe—in a fertile and generous world that is, as is the human, exactly what it is meant to be. Humans sustain their being by acting in a manner that is balanced with the rest of the environment. They exist best in harmony with the land.

Their ethical principles are drawn from the universe at large: balance, harmony, beauty, rightness.

If a people actually believe that the Earth is a good place, that it is a whole, that it is what it is meant to be, where would the incentive to change it come from? If people believe that they are themselves an important part of a greater whole, where would the incentive to transform themselves come from? And if they seriously believed that their every action could trigger many and unforeseen reactions, wouldn't their actions require much thought?

The image of the Native American that is prevalent in the United States is a product of someone other than the Native American. The Native American's own image was one that allowed him not only to survive but thrive on this continent for thousands of years. When Europeans first arrived on these shores they described a paradise. Five hundred years later the land suffers almost three hundred million people. The air, even on the mountaintops, is dirty, and you can no longer safely drink the water in even the most isolated of streams.

One of the false images of the Native American is that of some quasimystical being who spoke to trees and birds and received all knowledge— not through efforts as a human being, but through a "spirit guide." If the American aboriginal peoples were truly of such a nature, they would never have survived. Embedded in the mythology, the legends and traditions, is a pragmatic core to Native American belief systems. This pragmatism was and is based on acute observation of the environment. The American aboriginal peoples have no such thing as an environmental ethic; the environment is not something separate from themselves. The Earth, being their producer and sustainer, their Mother, is a part of a greater whole to which the Native American must extend a sense of responsibility.

It is unrealistic to expect that residents of the United States will give up their time-honored view of themselves as superior beings trapped in mundane bodies in a "hostile" environment. Or that the view of themselves as being the product of very specific circumstances in a very specific environment might prevail. The people remain, after five hundred years, sojourners, ghostly beings residing in decadent "bodies," on inanimate and alien ground.

The conceptual definitions of ourselves as humans are difficult to overcome once they have been established. However, when there comes a time that our definitions do not match our circumstance, humans seem to be flexible enough to change their concepts. This change, however, is not a simple task. At one time Western history seemed to suffer from a gap that was called the "Dark Ages." It was an era that was glossed over in most history classes. One got the impression that during those nearly one thousand years absolutely nothing happened. But it is possible that those many years provided the time necessary to eradicate the concepts of human nature and the universe that had truly been of Greek origin. Western man came out of the Dark Ages with an almost unquestioned belief concerning human nature and the place of the human in the world. The new definition of human beings brought about as a result of Darwin's research has not prevailed even today.

It might not, perhaps, be so unrealistic to expect that sometime soon the residents of the many states, "united" though they may think of themselves in an abstract sense, might develop a sense of themselves as being a part of the land and the land as a part of themselves. They might even develop a sense of identity as a people. The development of a sense of place might be a first step in the development of a new attitude, a new relationship, between Western man and his environment.

I am not making an appeal to all of us to "return" to simpler times as we imagine the early Indian to have existed in. The Native American foundational belief system, however, appears to be a moral realistic view of our position on the Earth, and suggests what might be required in order for change in our thinking to occur. White calls for a new religious view ("whether we call it that or not"). We might call it a "new reverence."[4]

# Preparing for the Seventh Generation

Discussion of the need for a new environmental perspective is largely led by scientists and legal experts. They talk about the human relationship to the environment from a forum based on the latest findings from numerous scientific disciplines and the dilemmas posed in a legal context of individual desires and community needs. Notably absent from these discussions are representatives from the theological and philosophical communities.

The scientist, armed with an arsenal of modern scientific findings, proposes to convince a *rational* audience of nonscientists that a new attitude about human and environment is necessary in order to forestall dire environmental consequences. The legal expert, usually under the newly acquired title of "ethicist," proposes to use the letter of the law to convert a society given to slogans such as "Each man works so as to enhance his own self-interest" to some sort of altruistic behavior predicated on seeing the environment and human use of that environment as something to "save" for a rainy day. This, on the assumption that cautious use today means extended usage into tomorrow.

The excluded theologians, if they have an opinion at all on such issues, seem mired in discussion about "free will" and "determinism," "God's will," and the "afterlife." The philosopher is too caught up in analyzing language and its usage to address issues as mundane as human and environment. This is unfortunate, because the theologian and the philosopher are largely to blame for the present view of humans and their environment. It is their fields that have provided the conceptual underpinnings that allow the present state of environmental degradation to exist. The theologians, bound as they are by dogma, cannot afford to reevaluate the identity and role of the human without jeopardizing the very roots of their belief systems. The philosophers are allowed by tradition to question all roots of any system; but through sheer conformity to modern disciplinary perspective, they have set aside crucial questions as "nonrelevant" or "metaphysical."

But it is in precisely that realm termed "metaphysical" that the foundations for a new environmental perspective must be sought. The term 'metaphysics' has come to represent many things to contemporary people —it might indicate astrology, a new guru, or even discussion of "New Age" crystal application. In its original usage, the term simply referred to those explanations offered by human inquirers for dilemmas, conditions, or causes for which there appeared to be no "empirical" explanation. *Meta*physics simply was that which went *beyond* the physical (and accessible) to what we might call the realm of the "hypothetical."

Unfortunately, once a hypothesis became accepted it was no longer seen to be hypothetical but became "real." The "reality" that we accept today was once a hypothetical solution to an irresolvable problem. One of these most crucial of "realities" is our definition of what it is to be human: a human is a being superior to all other life forms; he is superior by virtue of his reasoning abilities, his "self-consciousness," and even his ability to envision himself as something apart from, and superior to, his environment.

All "new" perspectives now being offered to reconcile humans with their environments are doomed to failure until this "reality" of identity is examined and compared to other possibilities. "Other" possibilities? There are other possible "definitions" and "descriptions" of what the human being might be. These definitions and descriptions may be sought in scientific explanation, or they may be sought in other cultural perspectives.

For example, somewhat over a hundred years ago Charles Darwin offered a new definition of the human animal—a definition consistent with the latest scientific findings of his day. Darwin's "definition" met with the usual reaction to new hypotheses, where the old are thoroughly entrenched: Man descended from APES? Ridiculous! A hundred years later, the war of hypotheses is still serious enough to cause textbook publishers to present evolution as a "possible" theory in as few nonoffensive pages as possible.

Old definitions, once accepted, become "realities" that only fools (and philosophers, if they are tending to their business) dare to question.

None of the "new" environmental perspectives propose to redefine humans as a preliminary step to reevaluating the human's relationship to the environment. We "know" that humans "are a superior species," a "thing" apart from and somehow beyond anything this Earth has known. Our "knowledge" about the human colors our acceptance of a new perspective. Notice how quickly present environmental crises are labeled problems of the *planet*, rather than of *humans*. We hear talk about "saving" the planet or predicting the "end" of the Earth. We completely set aside the reality of the issue: it is not *the planet* that is in immediate danger—it is *us*, the human animal. We tend, instead of acknowledging this dire fact, to envision ourselves as somehow capable of escaping a planet that is no longer habitable. The planet may die—but we, the human species, will survive. Even accepting the fact that our immediate conditions for survival are at risk, we tend to portray ourselves as "saviors" of the planet, of the spotted owl, the rain forest. Human superiority is salvaged through portrayal of ourselves as "caretakers" or "preservers" of an *object*.

As in Darwin's day, however, scientific findings about the state of the planet and humankind's dependence on that planet direct us to a definition of the human that is at odds with what we call "real" human nature. Humans, since the guarded acknowledgment of their development on *this* planet, are known to require very specific conditions in order to continue as a species. The temperature cannot be too high or too low for any period of time without severe consequences. The atmospheric mixture offers us "breath" only within a very narrow range of circumstances. We are not only creatures of *this* planet but of very specific and fragile conditions on this planet.

Humans, from this perspective, are not creatures above and apart from "nature"—they are a part of nature.

But, we might argue, even if we aren't superior to our environment, we are still the only "intelligent" species. Modern man, guided by REASON, has accomplished more than any other species or earth form.

Intelligence, unfortunately, has conditions that seem to exclude the human species from its realm. Intelligence involves the capacity to foresee the consequences of our actions. Obviously this species is woefully lacking in foresight. If we really "knew" that radioactive elements couldn't be properly stored or eliminated, would we have created nuclear reactors or bombs? Or take a simpler case: if we really "knew" that private cars were more destructive to our survival than mass transportation, would we have opted for interstate highways instead of an efficient mass transit system? The human can properly be credited with a superbly active power of imagination. But true intelligence harnesses imagination to disciplined and even pragmatic actions. The human *approaches* intelligence—he rarely *displays* it.

"Ahhh, but," you say, humans are "self-conscious." We have an advantage over the less intelligent creatures. We can be aware of *ourselves*. Again, this isn't much of an advantage if that "self-awareness" allows us to portray ourselves as separated from the very conditions that allow our existence.

We *are unable to*, despite the findings of science in the latter part of the twentieth century, see ourselves as *merely* one life form among many. We cannot really accept ourselves as products of very narrow planetary conditions. All of the gains brought about through human action are irrelevant if we persist in tacking on those new developments to old perspectives.

The problem is that all information about the environment and humanity's "new" condition in regard to the present "state of the Earth" is being offered to "unbelievers." The consequence is that we accept the information, but have no incentive to change ourselves because we don't know what we can change *into*. And even knowing that there are alternative descriptions for the human animal, we will not change if it requires giving up the old paradigms. Consider ourselves in the position of the Catholic cleric confronting the Copernican theories that supplanted geocentricism.

The problem, then, of educating a populace to environmental crises is not to shove more and more facts about ozone holes, erosion, and greenhouse effects into the arms of the populace, but to discover ways to convince humans that their definitions of themselves must change. These definitions must be in accord with new findings about humans and our position on and in this planet.

The problem is an extremely difficult one. Imagine yourself trying to "deprogram" a devout Christian: what happens to Christians deprived of their belief in a God, a cosmic plan that is built around the human, a soul, an afterlife? We leave them adrift. As Dostoyevsky said, confronting atheism, "Without God, all things are possible." If a belief in god and ultimate rewards and punishments are all that prevents our reversion to "savagery," then it is to savagery we turn when deprived of our old beliefs. It is not enough to deprive the old believer of outdated and perhaps harmful beliefs. One must also provide new beliefs.

If it is "human" to need a definition of ourselves in order to justify our behavior toward one another and our planet, then new definitions must be found. And new definitions are sometimes reached only by comparing the old and the new.

What if, for example, we begin to question every facet of the old definitions? Based on the latest research into the workings of the brain and neurological system, where does the "old" concept of "mind" as something apart from the body fit? What if there were no such thing as "mind"? Would we lose some sort of status in respect to other animals, if we thought that we did not have any more brains than they? Would we accomplish less if we believed that *thinking* was an action of a person rather than a process of a disembodied "mind"?

Would we be less responsible if we thought that we had only this life to live?

Would we be less "unique" or "individual" if we found that most of our "individuality" was a product that the group shared? That our thoughts, ideas, goals, were a "program" we received from our parents, our culture?

What if we saw ourselves as creatures not *independent from* but *dependent upon* the planet and very specific and narrow planetary conditions? Would we care less for our environment if we thought we were dependent on it?

And if it is "human" to worship the sacred, would we be less if we began to credit the planet as "the sacred"? Or, since to credit the planet with sacredness serves to separate ourselves from it, to see ourselves as "sacred"?

These are the questions that "environmentalists" and "ethicists" fail to address. Yet these are the questions—the metaphysical questions—that must be considered and examined very carefully if we are to change our current conditions, if we are continue the existence of the human species.

We must reexamine the old issues that led to the present definitions of humanity, and this is the realm of philosophy: What is it to be human? What is it to be on this planet? What is humanity's role? These are not the questions that scientists and legalists pose for their listeners. These are questions routinely posed by theologians and philosophers. Unfortunately, theologians long ago prepared the answers to those questions; to reopen the questions would be to undermine their own credibility. We need, perhaps, a Socrates who instead of asking the old questions about truth, virtue, and justice would ask us about "progress" and "mind" and "human superiority."

It is, of course, possible that human beings are mere aberrations—a fluke coughed up by a planet practicing infinite creativity and diversity.

We may be only the latest species of "dinosaur." If that is the case, then we should be satisfied with using our many talents to record the demise of the human species as we now record and number the many nonhuman and human "primitives" that we watch waste slowly away under the onslaught of "progress." But this is precisely not the case. A true display of intelligence involves foresight—the ability to imagine our own species a thousand years from now. Or, as the American "savage" would say: "We must act as though we were preparing for the seventh generation. They are below us now and in the ground, waiting for their turn."

# Native Americans in the New Millennium

Wade Davis, an anthropologist, has coined a new term, 'ethnosphere.' He means, by this term, to indicate the importance of the survival of the diverse groups of human beings around the world. He recognizes that each of the groups represents a specific adaptation to a specific region of the Earth.

As a Native American, I find this insight valuable. Not only do the diverse groups represent a specific adaptation, they also represent the impressive range of human thought. Why is this important? We have become accustomed in the normal academic environment to hearing vast generalizations made about human beings, those propositions that begin with "All men are . . ." The list of what it is that composes the essence of being human is very narrow. Humans, for example, are said to be "individuals"—essentially independent, autonomous, singular individuals. They are driven, it is said, solely by self-interest. It may be argued that there are other definitions of what it is to be human, but the offered definition/description is that which is dominant in the American context.

But what if this theory is merely one among many other theories about what it is to be human? We can make generalizations only when we believe that we have taken into account all of the facts about that which we would generalize. Can a universal statement about human beings be made without taking into account *all* of the observations about human existence? Wade Davis encourages us to seek out these other accounts when he makes a plea for the continued existence of other cultures.

The Native American is one of those cultures on the verge of extinction through being overwhelmed by the newly dominant "civilization" that has become "The United States of America." Not only are the languages being swept away, but the concepts that were engrained in those languages that gave meaning to the various lifestyles of diverse groups of Native Americans are also undergoing subtle changes.

Consider for a moment the reality that is overlooked in the contemporary portrayals of Native America. There were over five hundred languages spoken when the Europeans first came to this continent. Several hundred no longer exist. English has become the lingua franca of most Native peoples in North America. There were also many diverse lifestyles that were overwhelmed by the arrival of the Europeans. We are accustomed to hearing of the "vicious" behaviors that existed between Native groups. We are not told that much of that behavior, if it truly was as extensive as it is portrayed, was a result of the European wave of population that displaced Native peoples from their original homelands. As the Europeans take over a homeland, the displaced people move into the territories of other Native peoples, causing a friction that did not formerly exist in a land that was vast and fertile and fully occupied.

There are aspects of Native behavior and accommodations to the land that are not explored, because the concepts behind them are so alien to the European researcher who would "explain" the Native American. The homeland notion comes with a conceptual background that involves the idea of boundaries. All Native peoples, regardless of their present circumstances, know the former boundaries of their original homes. There was no individualized concept of ownership of property. The people saw themselves as "a people" occupying a place to which they had adapted over centuries, perhaps thousands of years, of occupation. They identified themselves as being of that place and adapted to no other place—they were *born for that place*. Contrast this idea of place and boundaries to that of the Europeans who come equipped with a conceptual notion of themselves as the rightful owners, not of a specific place, but of a world that their mythology encourages them to "subdue and dominate."

The idea of bounded places is perhaps a natural concept born out of the fact that human beings are beings of the flock or the herd—they do not exist as singular beings wandering about the countryside in the manner of Hobbes's view of the "state of nature." Witness, for example, how "territorial" Europeans become once they have settled into a specific place: France is not Germany and would expel the intruders. Of course, they do at the same time demand the "right" to go into the nations that are not part of their own encompassing idea of civilization. The "natives" of other places are mere obstacles when the European decides to expand his idea of homeland. It is not until the middle of the twentieth century that the notion occurs to the European that other peoples might also have a sense of "home" connected to place. Colonialism ends when this notion is accepted.

A sense of humans occupying a specific bounded space cannot be isolated from a sense of what it is to be human. Humans, in a Native American context, are not naturally autonomous individuals; they exist as *groups*, and the group is held together by a specific language held in common. It is not only the occupation of a specific place that identifies a specific group to other groups; different languages, even if they are only dialects of a larger language family, also serve as identifying markers of specific groups. No other life forms seem to have such a strong bonding "mechanism" as language has proven to be. A common language guarantees that the group, as a whole, is "on the same wavelength"—they share common understandings that need not be explicit frames of reference every time they communicate. That the European conquerors of America were aware of this fact was the reason behind the concerted efforts to eradicate the use of Native languages.

Native Americans are usually portrayed as "nomadic" groups that existed in a continual state of war with one another. This is absolutely not the case. There was an extensive trading system of goods between the diverse groups. One of those items of trade was marriageable youths. All groups practiced exogamy to a large extent. The "in-comer," one married to someone of another group, created a bond between groups in that each group had at least one member that could speak the language of some other group. The "in-comer" gave up an identity as a member of one group and took on the identity of the group into which he or she married. This giving up of an identity ensured the continued existence of a specific group—even though the bloodlines had been mingled. This practice is very visible in the southwestern United States where intermarriage between "Hispanics" and "Indians" is not uncommon. "In-comers" take on the identity of the group into which they marry. A conscious choice is made to do so and comes to account for the lack of corruption of each group's identity. After several hundreds of years of intermarriage between the two southwestern groups, there has been no extinction of either the Hispanic or Indian identity.

The practice of exogamy signals another aspect of what it is to be human that is absent from the sensibility of the European: a toleration and acceptance of the other as *other*. Even now it is visibly noticeable that the diverse Native American groups who often come together in regional "powwows" do not waste time arguing over whose myth of origin is the "correct" myth. It is understood that each group has its own origin story that pertains only to its group and that all other groups will have their own unique stories or "explanations" that account for their existence in a specific place with a specific identity. The practice of non-Native ethnographers of trying to pinpoint an "original" creation story out of a maelstrom of diverse accounts is foiled even within groups that have language and place in common: the Navajo creation myth, which is presumed to be a singular story, is "told" in different ways according to the area that a group within the group occupies. In the eyes of a Native American, this is not an "aberration" but a natural process of *grounding* one's family or clan in a specific area. Each telling, or variation, of a common story is "correct" in that it explains the existence and validity of a specific family or clan within the larger group.

The European imagines a coming universalization of what it calls, beforehand, "mankind." The singular term (*man*kind) defies even the accounts of its own mythology, that is, the Biblical account of the "tower of Babel," in which the people, who all share a common language, strive to build a tower that will reach into the heavens; God strikes down the tower and disperses the people from their common goal by creating various and diverse tongues (babble). But mythology, especially a mythology that is no longer a living myth, has a tendency to overlook inconsistencies: the duty to "multiply" and "dominate" is not seen as inconsistent with the gods' actions in destroying the tower of Babel.

Tolerance is not a "built-in" concept for the European—there is always the enemy *other* who exists as competitor in a barren land with scarce resources (the Earth, outside the Garden of Eden, as depicted in the Old Testament). The *other* represents an enemy also in the sense that he would challenge the "truths" held by one group over the *truth* as held by another. Competing paradigms, in other words, are not allowed within the European conceptual framework: "One World, One People" signals more than just a vision of peaceful existence of diverse peoples—it signals the eventuality of no diversity at all. Monoculturalism is seen as a naturally occurring event in the teleological progressivism that rules the views of the European.

'Nationalism,' the notion that diversity is natural, that bounded spaces with specific identities within those boundaries are 'natural,' is dismissed as an archaic and primitive notion, despite the fact that the never-ending conflicts between identifiable diverse peoples constitute the source of most wars presently conducted even within the European sphere of influence. Witness the "balkanization" of the former Yugoslavia, or the USSR or Northern Ireland. "Ethnic cleansing" is not a new form of warfare that suddenly developed with the breakup of the former "communist" world. It has been a common practice since the Biblical injunction to the Hebrews to "go down into the land of Canaan and slay every man, woman, and child, and of those who are left, make them your slaves." Most colonial enterprises, in America, India, Africa, followed this same trend of events.

Another aspect of Native American thought that is dismissed or seen as merely "spiritual" (read here *impractical*) is the view of the Earth as a natural home, or "mother," to the human species. European peoples[1] see themselves as special creations, or special evolutions, that set them apart from other life forms and other peoples. They are an exception on a very small planet. The Earth is almost an "accidental" home, a temporary home, that they must overcome or outgrow. The Earth is a lifeless ball of matter that serves to provide the raw material for the imaginary creations of beings, themselves created "in the image of God," who would remake the Earth into their own image of a "more perfect world."

Despite the discovery of knowledge about the human's dependence on and effect on the Earth, the primal myth of humans as special and unique and with a god-ordained mission to subdue and dominate still drives the imagination of Europeans and their various manifestations as other identities (Australian, Canadian, American, etc.). They have not, despite all of their accumulated knowledge about the workings of the Earth, accepted the fact that they are dependent on a very narrow set of circumstances (the existence of oxygen, water, etc.) for their continued survival. They imagine that, having exhausted the Earth as resource, they will simply move on to other planets. There is precedent for this view: when the resources of Europe faltered, the European "discovered" other resources on other continents. Conquering the stars could not be more difficult than conquering the continents; there must, it is thought, be millions of Earth-like planets in the universe just waiting to be "discovered."

The "world," as interpreted by the Native American, offers a more realistic portrayal of the facts of human existence. Human beings are not solitary creatures forcibly and reluctantly held together simply on the basis of authority exercised either by a lone individual or a code of laws. That humans are social creatures *naturally* is not a social fiction. "Individuals" are an equally natural occurrence, but it is the group that turns each into a human being; that is, people become human when they learn the language, the cultural structure, the rules of the group. There has been enough evidence gathered to prove that a human being who fails to learn language before the age of puberty fails to learn to speak at all; that the human infant needs the ministrations of others in order to survive; and most importantly that the truly isolated, autonomous individual is always an anomaly: a hermit, a loner, antisocial.

The very existence of diverse groups of humans complete with their unique languages and lifestyles is proof of the success of a species: the human has shown how very effective is its ability to adapt to various ecological niches. Humans have survived and thrived in all such niches, from the high mountain regions to deserts and Arctic cold. The inability to accept this very fact about human beings, an inability illustrated by the need to turn Arctic dwellers into replicas of a European, denies the very trait that has allowed humans to exist as a species. The proliferation of cultures and language is a form of adaptation to the environments offered by the Earth.

The European, armed with a different definition of what it is to be human, seeks not to adapt to the conditions of the Earth, but to adapt the Earth to a vision of what human beings should be. This need leads to another aspect of the European perspective on what it is to be human: monoculturalism, "one world, one people," becomes an overriding concern. There can be no tolerance, within this framework, for the existence of different lifestyles and all that pertains to maintaining that difference. The Amazonian must wear T-shirts and blue jeans, pray to a monotheistic, extraterrestrial god, and "get a job." The European masks this attempt to create a monocultural world under the guise of "bringing people into modernity"—'modernity' meaning simply an adoption of the European lifestyle and conceptual framework.

Someone pointed out to me that the "Indians," in all of their thousands of years of existence, "failed" to produce the trappings of a modern society. Maybe so. But on the other hand, they also did not create worldwide pollution, nuclear bombs, and overpopulation.

The very sense of a bounded space as homeland requires that the population numbers fit the space available; there are few Native populations that have failed to develop either social constraints against overbreeding or actual herbal medicines that could be used to keep the population in check. Humans have not all been guided by the dictum to "multiply" and "dominate." At the end of one's bounded space there is the beginning of the boundary of another people who have as much "right" to survive. Wars, or what might be interpreted as such, did occur. But they were usually highly ritualistic and limited. Wars of total annihilation are a product of European predilections.

The Native American has more to offer the world than does the European: a sense of bounded space; a sense of our utter dependence on some very specific planetary conditions for our survival; a sense of humans as group beings, each representing a "correct" method of living on the planet, that is, tolerance for the existence of the other as other.

Today, Native Americans exist as a subject population that must be brought into the European sphere. They serve only two purposes: either they are living fossils of a European's imagined past, or they are a living experimental laboratory upon which the practice and skills of destroying other cultural perspectives might be honed. In either of these manifestations, the Native American is doomed to extinction despite the purity of bloodline. But there is more than this that is available to the Native American: to maintain an identity, a culture, a language, and most of all, the obligation to speak—to say, "I am not that," and to stand as an alternative way of seeing, interpreting, and explaining the world.

# The Dream

*"I'm on my way home," Viola Cordova writes, "I'm always on my way home." In many ways, this is her answer to the question raised in this section: What is the role of humans in the world? In this short dream sequence, which takes place in the mining town of Superior, Wyoming, Cordova shows how the particulars of a home—the dog barking and the rise of the hill—provide a deep-rooted sense of the comfort and certainties that come from belonging to a place.*

It is late at night. I am walking alone in no hurry. Even in winter when there are snowdrifts across the road and path, I am not uncomfortable. I am always on my way home from somewhere. Occasionally on my walk I look behind me, up the road. I seem to look merely out of curiosity, as I am not expecting anyone, nor am I afraid of being alone. I look for approaching vehicles and sometimes there are dim headlights far away. They apparently turn off the road and never pass me.

After I have crossed the bridge, on the curve of the path, I hear either a horse whinny or a dog bark. They make this sound only once, sort of as a last-minute greeting before settling down, perhaps in acknowledgment of my presence. After hearing their sound, I hesitate and look around. There are no people here. Though I am aware of people sleeping in the house, they are not aware of me. The dog does not even mind that I am out and looking toward "his" house. He goes back to sleep. The road behind me stretches on endlessly, up a slight rise and far away. There are people at the end of that road. I have been there and I seem to go there often, but when I leave there, I always walk home. Alone.

The only variation in the dream is the weather, and sometimes a dry gulch is full of water and there are juniper trees along the bank. Otherwise there is only sagebrush. The horse appears in the full-water scene, whereas the dog appears in the snowy scene. At other times I hear, or am aware of, both of them being there.

I meet no one and there are no lights except the moonlight and the lights twinkling from home, which appear very comfortable. The dream ends with my knowing that I'm on my way home.

# Coda: Living in a Sacred Universe

"It is difficult to explain," a friend of mine says. He is speaking of the idea that it is the Universe itself that many Native Americans hold as sacred. How does one go about explaining that there are no other dimensions in which sacredness dwells because we can know only one dimension?

The late Tewa anthropologist Alfonso Ortiz claimed that all religious concepts were embraced by Native Americans, on the grounds that "the more religion the better." The alien religious concepts are seen as additions to Native beliefs and not as explanations, nor even equivalents, of Native beliefs. The various beliefs are welcome so long as they offer avenues to celebration of what is seen as sacred.

We must take note here that Ortiz is a "Pueblo" Indian, and that all Pueblos seem to have in common a concept of the *kachina*. Kachinas are personifications of the animating "something" that causes a "thing" to exist as itself. Jesus and his mother, Mary, can be incorporated, by those inclined to do so, into the realm of kachinas, which includes also personifications of butterflies, sun, wind, trees, and a multitude of other things. The personification, if one is familiar at least with the carved kachinas that make it into the tourist market, is a humanlike figure with an inhuman head. During "sacred" ceremonies, humans take on the guise of a kachina in celebration of and thanksgiving to the particular entity that they represent. The idea of representing the animating "spirit" of the various forms that contribute to the well-being of a people is widespread in the Southwest; the Apache and the Navajo also share this idea of representation, perhaps as an influence from their Pueblo neighbors. The complication in explanation that arises here is that the kachinas, even as "spirits," are not from another dimension. They are part of *this* world. They serve to remind us that this world is sacred; this world is worthy of our reverence, awe, attention, and care. They represent those things on which we depend for our continued survival. The butterfly is given a special consideration, for example, because it pollinates the corn that feeds the people. It is not more, but also not less, a sacred being than the corn itself.

I have heard, from those familiar with the concept, that Einstein's idea of matter and energy as interchangeable states might serve as an explanation for what is actually "in attention" during a celebration of the sacred. A Native American would use the term, however, not as describing two distinct states but rather as one singular state with two facets: *matter-energy* rather than matter *and* energy.

Our daily life requires focus on particular *aspects* of things—the *process* of growing corn, for example. Our ritual life, on the other hand, reminds us that an aspect is a part of a greater whole: the water that gives the corn life, the Earth that sustains the plant, the Sun that provides energy, the Universe because it is *as it is*. Everything *that is* becomes a part of a whole that we deem "sacred." We live, in other words, in a Sacred Universe. And it is this "form of life" that my friend states is "difficult to explain."

Where *does* the human being fit into the sacred universe, and how? We are all familiar with the statement credited to Native Americans, that we believe that "all things are related." We seldom hear about what that "relatedness" entails. I suppose one could use the analogy of a stone thrown into a pond. Each "thing"—stone, air molecule, plant, animal, or vegetable—causes a ripple to form in the pond. The singular, particular being is not merely itself tossed into the pond. It is also the ripple, the wave, that is formed by the action. Our "waves" overlap and extend beyond what we can foresee. Wisdom is knowing the effects of those "overlaps." This is how "relatedness" enters the picture: a statement that "all things are related" reminds us that we are not separate from all other things and that our actions have far-reaching consequences.

This view, of a stone tossed into a pond, is very far removed from the notion of a human being as "a bit of cosmic dust" floating in "empty" space. Human beings may have the broadest range of connections to the Universe of any being that exists. We might believe that our skin closes us off from the rest of the world, but it is in actuality a very permeable surface. Aside from absorbing the world through skin and lungs, we also see and hear and taste. Our senses connect us to the world. We have a broad range of emotional reactions; these, too, connect us to the world. And we have memory. Our extensive memory may be that which distinguishes us from other animals. Just as the bear can be distinguished from the cougar through his characteristics, lifestyle, body type, geographical range, we have our tremendous capacity to remember. Knowledge, in a Native American sense, is derived from the connections we make between all of the facets of our sensate experience and the memory of the consequences attendant upon all of those experiences. And, of course, all of our actions have consequences. We are not "meaningless" beings, because all of our actions bear a "meaning" for something else.

Throughout North America, indigenous peoples have the notion that they are cocreators of their world. We can bring things into existence that did not exist before. There are various versions of a mythic tale told in the Southwest about the Monster-Slayer. He, or they, as they are often twin sons of the Sun and the Earth, come to the people to rescue them from monsters ranging the Earth. Some monsters are slain, but not all of them. Some give good arguments for why they should remain. Death, for example, is allowed to remain, for without dying, Death claims, there could be no new people born, for the Earth would soon become overpopulated. Hunger is allowed to exist, because it maintains the industrious of the people. Lice are left behind because they force the people to keep themselves and their environs clean. One monster that *is* slain is Fear. For all else the people must accommodate themselves. Those monsters not so specifically named that happen to arise are the responsibility of the people themselves; no hero will assist in those circumstances. One example of a human-created monster is War. Humans alone are responsible for the creation and the ousting of this "monster."

What the story "tells" is that humans, because they are cocreators, can bring into existence all sorts of things. It is better, in this sense, to bring into the world only what is harmonious with the whole. 'Beauty' is the usual translation of the idea of a harmonious whole. As in many Navajo poems, one is encouraged to "walk in beauty," to bring "beauty" into being.

The greatest "duty," if it can be so called, of a human being is to cause no disruption to the greater, and "beautiful," whole of whatever it is that is. Humans, too, are responsible for dealing with the "monsters" that continue to plague mankind—war, hunger, poverty, disease—particularly if they have, themselves, brought them into being.

All of the "descriptions" I have mentioned, of the Universe, of the Sacred, of human beings, have relevance in our daily lives. The Native American is admonished to maintain the sacredness of the entire whole. It is difficult to explain that the mundane is actually the sacred. But it is even more difficult to explain how it is that Native Americans, despite the many and continuing attempts to eradicate their belief and value systems, persist in thinking, *knowing*, that their descriptions are the *right* ones—for *this* "world."

# NOTES

### Editors' Introduction

1. V. F. Cordova, "Oh father, holy sun . . ." fragment, n.d., archives, Department of Philosophy, Oregon State University.

### Author's Introduction: Why *Native American* Philosophy?

Source: "Why *Native American* Philosophy?" unpublished manuscript, n.d., archives, Department of Philosophy, Oregon State University.

1. José Ortega y Gasset, *The Revolt of the Masses* (New York: W. W. Norton, 1993).

2. V. F. Cordova, "Coming to America," unpublished manuscript, n.d., archives, Department of Philosophy, Oregon State University, 20.

3. Preceding paragraph added (the editors).

### The Bridge over Romero Creek

Source: "The Bridge," unpublished manuscript, n.d., V. Cordova Papers, box 4, folder 9, Center for Southwest Research, University of New Mexico.

1. From this point to the end of the chapter, from "Bridges," unpublished manuscript, n.d., archives, Department of Philosophy, Oregon State University.

2. The editors moved the story of Nasaria and Faustin's walk from Romero Creek to Taos from this point to the end of the chapter.

3. The editors found no reference to the source of this story.

### Taos Bridge

In Cordova's papers, the chapter heading "Taos Bridge" follows the "Bridges" essay, but has no text. Readers will notice that Dr. Cordova's usage slides easily among "Native American," "indigenous," and "Indian," all of which, she recognizes, are shadows of her real self, a Jicarilla Apache person.

1. From "Savage Thoughts: Reflections on Post-Columbian America," unpublished manuscript, n.d., V. Cordova Papers, box 3, folder 2, Center for Southwest Research, University of New Mexico.

2. From "The Collector," unpublished manuscript, May 2001, V. Cordova Papers, box 4, folder 4, Center for Southwest Research, University of New Mexico.

3. Part II is from "And with the Shoes . . . ," unpublished manuscript, June 2001, V. Cordova Papers, box 4, folder 4, Center for Southwest Research, University of New Mexico.

4. Part III is from an untitled, unpublished manuscript, n.d., V. Cordova Papers, box 4, folder 6, Center for Southwest Research, University of New Mexico.

5. Part IV is from "Knowing Who You Are," unpublished manuscript, n.d., V. Cordova Papers, box 2, folder 2, Center for Southwest Research, University of New Mexico.

## The Bridge to America

Source: "Savage Thoughts."

## America

Source: "Savage Thoughts."

1. The editors decided not to change Dr. Cordova's use of the generic "he" and "man." She was not a careless writer, nor was she unaware of the way that word choice can exclude people and shape exclusionary ideas.

## Windows on Academics

Source: "Savage Thoughts."

1. Here to end, from "Philosophy and the Native American," unpublished manuscript, n.d., V. Cordova Papers, box 3, folder 4, Center for Southwest Research, University of New Mexico.

## Windows on Native American Philosophy

Source: "Approaches to Native American Philosophy," unpublished manuscript, n.d., archives, Department of Philosophy, Oregon State University.

1. Gerardo Reichel-Dolmatoff, "Cosmology as Ecological Analysis: A View from the Rain Forest," *Man*, n.s., 11, no. 3 (Sept. 1976): 307.

2. From "It's the Concepts," unpublished manuscript, n.d., archives, Department of Philosophy, Oregon State University.

3. Wittgenstein, *Philosophical Investigations*, trans. G.E.M. Anscombe, 3rd ed. (New York: Macmillan, 1968), 103e.

4. Lem, *Solaris* (New York: Harvest Books, 2002).

## Matrix: A Context for Thought

Source: "Matrix," unpublished manuscript, n.d., archives, Department of Philosophy, Oregon State University.

1. A matrix is defined as something within which something else originates and takes its form.

2. Wittgenstein, *On Certainty*, ed. G.E.M. Anscombe and G. H. von Wright (New York: Harper and Row, 1969), 94, 95.

3. Wittgenstein, *On Certainty*, 88.

4. Wittgenstein, *Philosophical Investigations*, 223e.

5. Wittgenstein, *On Certainty*, 611.

6. Whorf, *Language, Thought, and Reality* (Boston: MIT Press, 1964).

## Method: A Search for Fundamental Concepts

Source: "Philosophy as Method," unpublished manuscript, n.d., archives, Department of Philosophy, Oregon State University.

1. Durkheim, "Religion and Ritual," in *Selected Writings* (Cambridge: Cambridge University Press, 1972).

2. *Weltanschauung* is the German word indicating a worldview or cosmology, a conception of the whole.

## "They Have a Different Idea about That ... "

Source: "The Perspectival Approach," unpublished manuscript, 1997, archives, Department of Philosophy, Oregon State University.

1. Cordova, "The Context of Western Thought," unpublished manuscript, n.d., archives, Department of Philosophy, Oregon State University.

2. Wittgenstein, *Philosophical Investigations*.

## Language as Window

Source: "A Linguistic Perspective," unpublished manuscript, n.d., archives, Department of Philosophy, Oregon State University.

1. See Whorf, *Language, Thought, and Reality*.

2. Whorf, *Language, Thought, and Reality*, 252.

3. Chase, foreword to Whorf, *Language, Thought, and Reality*, iv.

4. Chase, foreword, vii.

## The Philosophical Questions

Source: "The Philosophical Questions," unpublished manuscript, n.d., archives, Department of Philosophy, Oregon State University.

1. Wittgenstein, *On Certainty*, 29.

## How It Is: A Native American Creation Story

Published as a chapbook under the auspices of the Center for Applied Studies in American Ethnicity at Colorado State University as part of its program in Native American Studies Curriculum materials and development. Copyright © by Viola Cordova 1994. Used with permission.

## What Is the World?

Source: "What Is the World?" unpublished manuscript, n.d., archives, Department of Philosophy, Oregon State University.

1. Whorf, *Language, Thought, and Reality*.
2. Preceding two paragraphs, Cordova, "What Is the World?"
3. Lao Tzu, *Tao Te Ching*, trans. John Wu (New York: Shambhala, 1989).
4. Preceding six paragraphs, Cordova, "What Is the World?" 1–4.
5. Preceding two paragraphs, Cordova, "What Is the World?" 4–5.

## *Usen*: The Unidentifiable *Is*

Source: "*Usen*," unpublished manuscript, n.d., V. Cordova Papers, unprocessed, Center for Southwest Research, University of New Mexico.

1. Johnston, *The Manitous: The Spiritual World of the Ojibway* (St. Paul: Minnesota Historical Society Press, 2001).
2. Harrod, *Renewing the World: Plains Indian Religion and Morality* (Tucson: University of Arizona Press, 1992).
3. Whorf, *Language, Thought, and Reality*.
4. See the work of F. M. Cornford, *From Religion to Philosophy: A Study in the Origins of Western Speculation* (Princeton, NJ: Princeton University Press, 1991).

## Mother Earth

Source: "MOTHER EARTH: The Implications of a Belief," unpublished manuscript, n.d., archives, Department of Philosophy, Oregon State University.

1. Lovelock, *Gaia: A New Look at Life on Earth* (New York: Oxford University Press, 1979).

## Time and the Universe

Source: mainly, "Some Conceptual Differences," unpublished manuscript, n.d., archives, Department of Philosophy, Oregon State University.

1. Preceding paragraph from Cordova, "The Concept of Monism in Navaho Thought" (PhD diss., University of New Mexico, 1992).

2. Preceding paragraph from Cordova, "The Concept of Monism in Navaho Thought."

## What Is Reality?

Source: "Insanity and the Native American," unpublished manuscript, 1980, V. Cordova Papers, box 3, folder 1, Center for Southwest Research, University of New Mexico.

1. Kesey, *One Flew Over the Cuckoo's Nest* (New York: Penguin Books, 2002).
2. Silko, *Ceremony* (New York: Penguin Books, 1986).

## Artesian Spring: A Poem

Source: "Artesian Spring," unpublished manuscript, n.d., V. Cordova Papers, box 1, folder 1, Center for Southwest Research, University of New Mexico.

## Who We Are: An Exploration of Identity

Source: *Who We Are: An Exploration of Identity*. Published under the auspices of the Center for Applied Studies in American Ethnicity at Colorado State University as part of its program in Native American Studies Curriculum materials development. Copyright © Viola Cordova, 1994. Used by permission.

## What Is It to Be Human in a Native American Worldview?

Source: "What Is It to Be Human in a Native American Worldview?" unpublished manuscript, n.d., archives, Department of Philosophy, Oregon State University.

1. Dennis McPherson and J. Douglas Rabb, "Some Thoughts on Articulating a Native Philosophy," *Ayaangwaamizin* 1, no. 1 (spring 1997): 11–22.

## Credo: This I Believe

Source: "Credo" is composed of elements of three different lists, from the following: Cordova, "What Is It to Be Human in a Native American Worldview," 18–19; Cordova, "Some Conceptual Differences," 10–11; Cordova, "On Being Human," unpublished manuscript, n.d., archives, Department of Philosophy, Oregon State University, 2–3.

## Critiques. I. Against Individualism

Source: "Individualism," unpublished manuscript, n.d., V. Cordova Papers, unprocessed, Center for Southwest Research, University of New Mexico.

1. Preceding two paragraphs from Cordova, "Values" and "Place and Identity," unpublished manuscript, 1997, V. Cordova Papers, unprocessed, Center for Southwest Research, University of New Mexico, 10.

## Critiques. II. Against the Singularity of the Human Species

Source: "Mankind," unpublished manuscript, n.d., V. Cordova Papers, unprocessed, Center for Southwest Research, University of New Mexico.

1. Preceding paragraph from Cordova, "Values" and "Place and Identity," 14.

## Becoming Human

Source: "Spirit, Soul, and Self," unpublished manuscript, n.d., archives, Department of Philosophy, Oregon State University.

1. Bartolomé de las Casas, *In Defense of the Indians* (DeKalb: Northern Illinois University Press, 1992).

## Time, Culture, and Self

Source: "Time, Culture, and Self," unpublished manuscript, n.d., archives, Department of Philosophy, Oregon State University.

1. Bury, *The Idea of Progress: An Inquiry into Its Origin and Growth* (New York: Dover, 1987).

## Cowboys and Indians

Source: "Cowboys and Indians," unpublished manuscript, n.d., archives, Department of Philosophy, Oregon State University.

## What Is the Role of a Human Being?

Source: "What Is the Role of a Human Being?" unpublished manuscript, n.d., archives, Department of Philosophy, Oregon State University.

1. McPherson and Rabb, "Some Thoughts on Articulating a Native Philosophy."

## Bounded Space: The Four Directions

Source: "Bounded Space: The Four Directions," unpublished manuscript, n.d., archives, Department of Philosophy, Oregon State University.

## Bounded Space. II. A Sense of Place

Source: "Values" and "Place and Identity," 1–10, 14.

## Biodiversity: The Human Factor

Source: "Biodiversity: The Human Factor," paper presented at the NAES Conference, 1994, V. Cordova Papers, unprocessed, Center for Southwest Research, University of New Mexico.

1. Wilson, *The Diversity of Life* (New York: W. W. Norton, 1993), 15, 14.


## A New Reverence

Source: "The Philosophical Roots of Ecological Crisis," lecture delivered at the Colorado State University Colloquium sponsored by the Center for Applied Studies in American Ethnicity, n.d., V. Cordova Papers, unprocessed, Center for Southwest Research, University of New Mexico.

1. White, "The Historical Roots of the Ecological Crisis," *Science* 155 (1967): 1203–1207.

2. Preceding three paragraphs, "The Problem," V. Cordova Papers, box 3, folder 4, Center for Southwest Research, University of New Mexico, 1–2.

3. Preceding paragraph, from "The Problem," 8.

4. Preceding paragraph, from "The Problem," 17.


## Preparing for the Seventh Generation

Source: "Rethinking the Human Character: First Steps in Creating a New Environmental Awareness," unpublished manuscript, n.d., V. Cordova Papers, unprocessed, Center for Southwest Research, University of New Mexico.


## Native Americans in the New Millennium

Source: "Native Americans in the New Millennium," unpublished manuscript, n.d., archives, Department of Philosophy, Oregon State University.

1. Cordova: Here I must apologize to those Europeans who object to the broad use of the term 'European.' It is true that peoples descended from European lineages now inhabit different continents and profess to have different identities; they have not, however, overthrown the old conceptual framework that allows one to speak of "the West" or "Western tradition." They remain European in contrast to the Native populations of the colonized areas.


## The Dream

Source: "The Dream," unpublished, handwritten manuscript, n.d., archives, Department of Philosophy, Oregon State University.

## Coda: Living in a Sacred Universe

Source: "When the Sacred Is the Mundane," unpublished manuscript, n.d., archives, Department of Philosophy, Oregon State University.

# WORKS CITED

Augustine. *The Confessions*. Boston: Harvard University Press, 1912.

Bury, J. B. *The Idea of Progress: An Inquiry into Its Origin and Growth*. New York: Dover, 1987.

Casas, Bartolomé de las. *In Defense of the Indians*. DeKalb: Northern Illinois University Press, 1992.

Chase, Stuart. Foreword to *Language, Thought, and Reality*, by Benjamin Whorf. Boston: MIT Press, 1964.

Cornford, F. M. *From Religion to Philosophy: A Study in the Origins of Western Speculation*. Princeton, NJ: Princeton University Press, 1991.

Deloria Jr., Vine. *Spirit and Reason: The Vine Deloria Reader*. Edited by Barbara Deloria, Kristen Foehner, and Sam Scinta. Golden, CO: Fulcrum, 1999.

Durkheim, Emile. "Religion and Ritual." In *Selected Writings*. Edited by Anthony Giddens. Cambridge: Cambridge University Press, 1972.

Erdoes, Richard, and Alfonso Ortiz. *American Indian Myths and Legends*. New York: Pantheon Books, 1985.

Harrod, H. L. *Renewing the World: Plains Indian Religion and Morality*. Tucson: University of Arizona Press, 1992.

Johnston, Basil. *The Manitous: The Spiritual World of the Ojibway*. St. Paul: Minnesota Historical Society Press, 2001.

Kesey, Ken. *One Flew Over the Cuckoo's Nest*. New York: Penguin Books, 2002.

Lao Tzu. *Tao Te Ching*. Translated by John Wu. New York: Shambhala, 1989.

Lem, Stanislaw. *Solaris*. New York: Harvest Books, 2002.

Lovelock, James. *Gaia: A New Look at Life on Earth*. New York: Oxford University Press, 1979.

McPherson, Dennis, and J. Douglas Rabb. "Some Thoughts on Articulating a Native Philosophy." *Ayaangwaamizin* 1, no. 1 (spring 1997): 11–22.

Ortega y Gasset, José. 1932. *The Revolt of the Masses*. New York: W. W. Norton, 1993.

Reichel-Dolmatoff, Gerardo. "Cosmology as Ecological Analysis: A View from the Rain Forest." *Man*, n.s., 11, no. 3 (Sept. 1976): 307–18.

Silko, Leslie Marmon. *Ceremony*. New York: Penguin Books, 1986.

Wheelwright, Philip. *The Presocratics*. New York: Odyssey Press, 1966.

White Jr., Lynn. "The Historical Roots of our Ecological Crisis." *Science* 155 (1967): 1203-1207.

Whorf, Benjamin. "An American Indian Model of the Universe." *International Journal of American Linguistics* 16, no. 2 (April 1960): 67–72.

——. *Language, Thought, and Reality*. Boston: MIT Press, 1964.

Wilson, Edward O. *The Diversity of Life*. New York: W. W. Norton, 1993.

Wittgenstein, Ludwig. "Notes on Frazer's *Golden Bough*." In *Wittgenstein: Sources and Perspectives*. Edited by C. G. Luckhardt. Ithaca, NY: Cornell University Press, 1979.

——. *On Certainty*. Edited by G.E.M. Anscombe and G. H. von Wright. New York: Harper and Row, 1969.

——. *Philosophical Investigations*. Translated by G.E.M. Anscombe. 3rd ed. New York: Macmillan, 1968.

# SOURCES

Cordova, V. F. "And with the Shoes . . ." Unpublished manuscript, June 2001. University of New Mexico, Center for Southwest Research, V. Cordova Papers, box 4, folder 4.

———. "Approaches to Native American Philosophy." Unpublished manuscript, n.d. Archives, Department of Philosophy, Oregon State University.

———. "Artesian Spring." Unpublished manuscript, n.d. University of New Mexico, Center for Southwest Research, V. Cordova Papers, box 1, folder 1.

———. "Biodiversity: The Human Factor." Paper presented at the NAES Conference, 1994. University of New Mexico, Center for Southwest Research, V. Cordova Papers, unprocessed.

———. "Bounded Space." Unpublished manuscript, n.d. Archives, Department of Philosophy, Oregon State University.

———. "Bounded Space: The Four Directions." Unpublished manuscript, n.d. Archives, Department of Philosophy, Oregon State University.

———. "The Bridge." Unpublished manuscript, n.d. University of New Mexico, Center for Southwest Research, V. Cordova Papers, box 4, folder 9.

———. "Bridges." Unpublished manuscript, n.d. Archives, Department of Philosophy, Oregon State University.

———. "The Collector." Unpublished manuscript, May 2001. University of New Mexico, Center for Southwest Research, V. Cordova Papers, box 4, folder 4.

———. "The Concept of Monism in Navaho Thought." PhD diss., University of New Mexico, 1992.

———. "The Context of Western Thought." Unpublished manuscript, n.d. Archives, Department of Philosophy, Oregon State University.

———. "Cowboys and Indians." Unpublished manuscript, n.d. Archives, Department of Philosophy, Oregon State University.

———. "The Dream." Unpublished, handwritten manuscript, n.d. Archives, Department of Philosophy, Oregon State University.

———. "Ethics: The We and the I." Unpublished manuscript, n.d. Archives, Department of Philosophy, Oregon State University.

———. How It Is. Fort Collins, CO: Center for Applied Studies in American Ethnicity, Colorado State University, 1994.

———. "Individualism." Unpublished manuscript, n.d. University of New Mexico, Center for Southwest Research, V. Cordova Papers, unprocessed.

———. "Insanity and the Native American." Unpublished manuscript, 1980. University of New Mexico, Center for Southwest Research, V. Cordova Papers, box 3, folder 1.

———. "It's the Concepts!" Unpublished manuscript, n.d. Archives, Department of Philosophy, Oregon State University.

———. "Knowing Who You Are." Unpublished manuscript, n.d. University of New Mexico, Center for Southwest Research, V. Cordova Papers, box 2, folder 2.

———. "A Linguistic Perspective." Unpublished manuscript, n.d. Archives, Department of Philosophy, Oregon State University.

———. "Mankind." Unpublished manuscript, n.d. University of New Mexico, Center for Southwest Research, V. Cordova Papers, unprocessed.

———. "Matrix." Unpublished manuscript, n.d. Archives, Department of Philosophy, Oregon State University.

———. "MOTHER EARTH: The Implications of a Belief." Unpublished manuscript, n.d. Archives, Department of Philosophy, Oregon State University.

———. "Native Americans in the New Millennium." Unpublished manuscript, n.d. Archives, Department of Philosophy, Oregon State University.

———. "Oh father, holy sun . . ." Fragment, n.d. Archives, Department of Philosophy, Oregon State University.

———. "On Being Human." Unpublished manuscript, n.d. Archives, Department of Philosophy, Oregon State University.

———. "The Perspectival Approach." Unpublished manuscript, 1997. Archives, Department of Philosophy, Oregon State University.

———. "The Philosophical Questions." Unpublished manuscript, n.d. Archives, Department of Philosophy, Oregon State University.

———. "The Philosophical Roots of Ecological Crisis." Lecture delivered at the Colorado State University Colloquium sponsored by the Center for Applied Studies in American Ethnicity, n.d. University of New Mexico, Center for Southwest Research, V. Cordova Papers, unprocessed.

———. "Philosophy and the Native American." Unpublished manuscript, n.d. University of New Mexico, Center for Southwest Research, V. Cordova Papers, box 3, folder 4.

———. "Philosophy as Method." Unpublished manuscript, n.d. Archives, Department of Philosophy, Oregon State University.

———. "The Problem." Unpublished manuscript, n.d. University of New Mexico, Center for Southwest Research, V. Cordova Papers, box 3, folder 4.

———. "Rethinking the Human Character: First Steps in Creating a New Environmental Awareness." Unpublished manuscript, n.d. University of New Mexico, Center for Southwest Research, V. Cordova Papers, unprocessed.

———. "Savage Thoughts: Reflections on Post-Columbian America. Coming to America. America. Academics." Unpublished manuscript, 1992. University of New Mexico, Center for Southwest Research, V. Cordova Papers, box 3, folder 2.

———. "Some Conceptual Differences." Unpublished manuscript, n.d. Archives, Department of Philosophy, Oregon State University.

———. "Spirit, Soul, and Self." Unpublished manuscript, n.d. Archives, Department of Philosophy, Oregon State University.

——. "Time, Culture, and Self." Unpublished manuscript, n.d. Archives, Department of Philosophy, Oregon State University.

——. Untitled manuscript, n.d. University of New Mexico, Center for Southwest Research, V. Cordova Papers, box 4, folder 6.

——. "*Usen.*" Unpublished manuscript, n.d. University of New Mexico, Center for Southwest Research, V. Cordova Papers, box 2, folder 2.

——. "Values" and "Place and Identity." Unpublished manuscript, 1997. University of New Mexico, Center for Southwest Research, V. Cordova Papers, unprocessed.

——. "What Is It to Be Human in a Native American World-View?" Unpublished manuscript, n.d. Archives, Department of Philosophy, Oregon State University.

——. "What Is the Role of a Human Being?" Unpublished manuscript, n.d. Archives, Department of Philosophy, Oregon State University.

——. "What Is the World?" Unpublished manuscript, n.d. Archives, Department of Philosophy, Oregon State University.

——. "When the Sacred Is the Mundane." Unpublished manuscript, n.d. Archives, Department of Philosophy, Oregon State University.

——. *Who We Are.* Fort Collins, CO: Center for Applied Studies in American Ethnicity, Colorado State University, 1994.

——. "Why *Native American* Philosophy?" Unpublished manuscript, n.d. Archives, Department of Philosophy, Oregon State University.

## About the Editors

Kathleen Dean Moore is distinguished professor of philosophy at Oregon State University, where she team-teaches the course Native American Philosophies, and teaches environmental ethics, philosophy of nature, and critical thinking. She is the award-winning author of academic books (*Pardons: Justice, Mercy, and the Public Interest* [Oxford UP] and *Reasoning and Writing* [Macmillan]) and books about our cultural and spiritual connections to the natural world (*Riverwalking, Holdfast*, and *The Pine Island Paradox*). Presently, she is coediting a collection of essays about Rachel Carson.

Kurt Peters (Blackfeet and Powhatan) is director of the Native American Collaborative Institute at Oregon State University, where he is associate professor of ethnic studies. His most recent book is *American Indians and the Urban Experience*, a collection edited with Susan Lobo. It was the winner of a Choice Outstanding Academic Title Award from the American Library Association. Other publications are "Indians on the Chicago Landscape" in *Native Chicago*, edited by Terry Straus, and the afterword to *Changing Landscapes: Telling our Stories*, proceedings of the Fourth Annual Coquille Cultural Preservation Conference. In progress are essays for *Oregon Mosaic: A Multiethnic History of the State* and *Altering Nature: How Religious Traditions Assess the New Biotechnologies*, a collaborative volume funded by the Ford Foundation.

Ted Jojola (Pueblo) is regents' professor at the University of New Mexico, where he is a member of the faculty of the Community and Regional Planning Program. The former director of the Native American Studies department, Dr. Jojola now teaches courses such as Planning for Native Lands, Human Settlements, and Cultural Aspects of Community Development. Among his many publications is the forthcoming article "Indigenous Planning: Clans, Intertribal Confederation, and the History of the All Pueblo Planning Council."

Amber Lacy holds the MA degree from the Department of Philosophy at Oregon State University and is currently a candidate for the DVM degree in the College of Veterinary Medicine. She was recently granted a Student-Faculty Research Award for work in the V. F. Cordova archives at the University of New Mexico.

## About the Author

V. F. Cordova (Jicarilla Apache/Hispanic) was raised in Colorado and New Mexico. She earned the PhD in philosophy from the University of New Mexico—as far as we can determine, the first Native American to earn a philosophy PhD. Until her death in 2002, she held faculty positions at the University of Alaska, Colorado State University, Oregon State University, Lakehead University, and most recently, Idaho State University, teaching both Western European philosophy and Native American philosophies. She was cofounder of two journals, *Ayaangwaamizin: The International Journal of Indigenous Philosophy* and the American Philosophical Association *Newsletter on American Indians in Philosophy*. Three articles, "Approaches to Native American Philosophy," "Ethics: The We and the I," and "Ethics: From an Artist's Point of View," are published in *American Indian Thought*, edited by Anne Waters.